The Power to Dream

The Power to Dream

———

INTERVIEWS

with Women in the Creative Arts

JODY HOY

Global City Press
1995

Contents

Preface

This book began to take shape in 1974, but as happens so often with women's projects, it took a long time to complete. In the early seventies I had gotten married, given up a rewarding job, moved to Southern California, gotten pregnant and finished my doctoral dissertation on Jean-Paul Sartre—in that order. Working on Sartre was about as deep into my intellect and as far from my emotions as I could possibly get. After many years in graduate school "being a boy" as Judy Chicago put it, I was thoroughly fed up with my graduate education and feeling alienated from myself. I knew I couldn't go back to the kind of academic work I had been doing, but I didn't know how to go forward or what to do. This was the point at which a friend called and invited me to a lecture by Anaïs Nin.

That evening changed my life in more ways than one. Anaïs, who was sixty-eight at the time, arrived wearing one of those inexpensive, floor length Indian cotton print dresses you order out of a catalogue for $29.98. In her hair she wore a black velvet band with round balls on it (I found out later she had made this out of curtain trim.) She spoke for about an hour, then a phalanx of university professors (male) in the front row barraged her with hostile questions. Anaïs paid no attention to their hostility and responded with insight and charm. She was beautiful, intelligent, articulate, fascinating, and she was unconditionally *present*.

Later, Anaïs spoke informally with members of the audience. As soon as I met her I knew I loved her and wanted to write about her. On the way home I told this to my friend, who encouraged me to contact Anaïs directly. She was completing a dissertation on four women authors of whom Anaïs was one, and she gave me Anaïs's address. "Oh," I said, "I could never do that!" Then I ran home, sat down and wrote a letter describing my idea for a book, mailed it off and tried to forget about it. Little did I know that Anaïs Nin made a point of answering every letter she ever got!

About a week later the phone rang, and a gentle voice with a distinct French accent said, "Hello, this is Anaïs Nin." She expressed interest in the project and invited me to come see her in Los Angeles the following week. I was extremely excited and drove to her house in what can best be described as an altered state, a state which didn't diminish, although it certainly waxed and waned, over the two years or so that I worked with her. I'm sure the joy I felt was partly a contact high from being with such an extraordinary person, but it was also about doing meaningful work, a theme which comes up in the interview with Frances Moore Lappé as well.

Anaïs Nin lived with her husband Rupert Pole in the Echo Lake section of Los Angeles, in a home built by Frank Lloyd Wright, Rupert's stepfather. Tucked into a wooded hillside above a reservoir, the house is simple but spacious. There is a large central living room with a cavernous stone fireplace at one end and a breakfast nook and kitchen behind it. At the other end of the living room are a bedroom, bath and study. The center section of the living room has a wall of sliding-glass doors looking out onto a back yard which is a welter of trees and bushes. In their midst is a swimming pool painted a startling deep aquamarine, one of Anaïs's favorite colors.

That first day we talked for several hours. Anaïs expressed her interest in the project and said, "I will help in any way I can." Then she made lunch—a ham and pickle sandwich on pumpernickel bread, and coffee with brown sugar—and encouraged me to come back in a few weeks.

Thus began an extraordinary period in my life. Every two weeks I would drive to Anaïs's house in Los Angeles. Piccolo, her white poodle, would bark his noisy greeting; Rupert, her husband, would give me a hug; then Anaïs and I would talk for several hours. I would drive home, make copious notes on our conversation, return two weeks later and do it all over again.

I was completely enchanted by Anaïs: by her intelligence, her warmth, her mischievous sense of humor, her ability to be so completely present, and above all by the confluence of literature and psychology which informed her mind. The book I wanted to write was neither scholarly nor sensational. I was already interested in the themes of the creative will and the conflict between the creative will and women's lives, themes relevant to her life, and most women's lives, but not to scholarly tomes. The dicier details of Anaïs's life are now common knowledge, but at the time this was not the case. I felt very protective of her and had no interest in writing about them. Eventually, the project was published as a lengthy article in a journal devoted to Anaïs's work. (See *Anaïs*, vol. 4, 1986.)

One day I asked Anaïs if she would allow me to make a videotape interview. She had just celebrated her seventieth birthday, and I was afraid of losing her. A videotape was closer to life than a book and seemed appropriate. Her answer? "Of course!" Several weeks later I returned with a student crew from the University of California at Irvine and we filmed Anaïs, first in the living room and then in the garden. The resulting interview has been shown on campuses across the country and was used by the University of Maine at Orono as part of its radio series commemorating the first International Women's Day. It is the basis for the interview reprinted here.

The interview with Anaïs led to other interviews and ultimately to this book. It was Rupert Pole, Anaïs's husband, who spoke to me about Beatrice Wood, the extraordinary ceramic artist, now 101 years old, who lives in Ojai. Rupert's father, the well-known British actor, Reginald Pole (architect Frank Lloyd Wright was his stepfather) had been Beatrice Wood's lover. It was also Rupert who initially suggested I contact Laura Huxley, although I met her later through photographer Nancy Ellison.

In most cases, one woman led to another. Phoebe Helman encouraged me to interview Esther Broner, whom I already knew from summers on Deer Isle, and Esther encouraged me to contact Lucy Lippard, with whom I had gone to college. Esther also introduced me to Meridel LeSueur and Marilyn French, as well as to the Global City Press. LoraLee MacPike, with whom I had worked as a consultant for the National Endowment for the Humanities, introduced me to Maxine Hong Kingston. Maxine Hong Kingston's generosity made it possible for me to contact Alice Walker. And Catherine Saltzman, a wonderful student of mine, introduced me to Bella Lewitzky. Other women I contacted on my own.

Why was I interested in these particular women and what was it I wanted to learn from their lives? There was a theme that was being played out on a daily basis in the lives of practically every woman I knew (not to mention my own): how can a woman satisfy the demands of the creative will and still preserve an intimate life? All of the women I interviewed were driven in one direction or another by the fierce imperative of the creative will—whether to art, literature, psychology, or music. And all of them refused to sacrifice the private dimension of their lives; all were unwilling to give up the intimate and sexual rewards of a woman's life. Not all of these women were married, but there was always a sustained, long term relationship, and/or children, a close and abiding link with a significant other which allowed for an emotional life as well as a work life.

These interviews document the joys and difficulties of being a productive human being in the shape of a woman. The women in this book are very different from one another in their personalities, their family constellations, their religious affiliations, their race, their art, and the ways in which they cope with their lives. But their differences are as instructive as their similarities: how they have dealt with the variables provides helpful insights for the rest of us in dealing with our own parallel issues.

Meridel Le Sueur says she doesn't believe in role models, but for many of us there is a desire or a need to be with, share with, learn from, and identify with other women. As our peers and role models do courageous things, the horizons of what is possible for us expands as well.

Although these women have struggled and achieved their victories independently, whenever I think of them their voices merge and soar like the glorious antiphonal voices I once heard singing in the chateau of Tarascon in the south of France. I have interviewed dozens of women, but there are hundreds, thousands, whose voices could swell this chorus. They have made bigger lives possible for the rest of us because voice by voice, step by step, life by life they have demolished that invisible, but oh so solid wall keeping us from what has been allowed to men but forbidden to women: a full life. The creativity of art *and* the generativity of life.

A brief introduction precedes each interview. My intent was to communicate some of the flavor of each of these "femmes fleurs," to borrow a phrase from Esther Broner; these women warriors, as Maxine Hong Kingston might call them.

Doing these interviews has been a source of immense pleasure and deep personal satisfaction. As I mentioned earlier, putting the book together has taken a long time because life constantly intervened. Initially, I was teaching and being a single parent, doing one interview each summer. When my son went off to college I began doing two and sometimes three interviews a year. Then, during a sabbatical semester, I completed five interviews. I have continued to do several each year.

I would like to thank the following people for their generous support:

First and foremost, the wonderful, generous, and loving

women in this book who granted me interviews and allowed me into their lives.

The Board of Trustees of the Saddleback Community College District for the luxury of a sabbatical to work on this book and for trusting that the work was important enough to deserve it. My colleagues Lisa Alvarez, Dale Larson, Margie Luesebrink, Peter Morrison, Elaine Rubenstein, Linda Thomas and Rebecca Welch of the Irvine Valley College English Department, to my mind one of the best English departments anywhere, for their encouragement and support. Teri Ciranna of the Irvine Valley College staff for her invaluable and unstinting work in translating these interviews into readable and handsome documents. Librarians Dave Everett, Fred Forbes, Ellie Kato, Larry Kaufman and Jane Senegal of the Irvine Valley College Library for their help in tracking down information on interviewees. Librarian Jeannette Edinger at the University of Maine library at Orono who located a copy of Marilyn French's *Beyond Power* when I couldn't find it in either New York or California. Also my thanks for trusting a stranger who walked into her library without even a library card. Martin Rosen, for encouraging me with this project, for helping in whatever ways he could and for being always a supportive friend. John Metcalf of Stonington, Maine, for the loan of a computer, which allowed me to work during the summers, and for being thoughtful, generous and available. Helene Rohl for the loan of a word processor during my sabbatical, which allowed me to complete massive amounts of work in a very short time. David Peck, for his constant encouragement when the going got tough. And, last but not least, to Josh, Jill, and Jennifer, les enfants de mon coeur.

The Power to Dream

Anaïs Nin

I met Anaïs Nin at a lecture in 1972. That meeting and its subsequent impact on my life are detailed in the preface of this book. Anaïs Nin was born in Neuilly, France, on February 21, 1903. Her father, Joaquin Nin, was a well-known pianist and composer who abandoned the family when she was a young girl. Her mother took the children to Cuba, and from there to America. On the journey to America in 1914 Anaïs started writing letters to her absent father. These became the beginning of the diaries, which she continued to write up until her death in 1976. A child who wore the cast-off summer clothing of rich Cuban relatives through New York winters, Anaïs later dropped out of high school and supported herself as an artist's model and Spanish dancer. She married Ian Hugo, an American banker, and lived with him in Paris, where she met Henry Miller and studied psychoanalysis with Otto Rank. When World War II broke out, she and her husband returned to New York. There Anaïs practiced analysis briefly, but gave it up in favor of her writing because she couldn't separate herself from her patients' lives.

According to Anaïs, the association of the personal and the intimate is the source of women's strength and humanity. She was herself an alluring example of what it means to be a woman, which is why people not only read the diaries but also flocked to see and hear her. She used her intelligence and her sexuality to create an extraordinary life and to give voice to a feminine vision of the world, all of which she detailed in the diaries.

All her life she had difficulty getting published. She wrote a study of D.H. Lawrence, short stories, essays, a series of novels and two books of erotica. She once told me that *Winter of Artifice* was rejected 176 times and *Spy in the House of Love* was rejected by 100 publishers! The publication of the first volume of her diary, in 1966, and then *Cities of the Interior*, a collection of five of her novels, coincided with the re-emergence of the women's movement in America, and Anaïs was discovered. Finally, she received the recognition for which she had hungered.

After Anaïs's death her second husband, Rupert Pole, who is the executor of her estate, continued to publish the early diaries, including a volume entitled *Incest*, in which Anaïs detailed her incestuous relationship with her seductive and probably schizophrenic father. This astounding admission was even more remarkable in that the experience seems to have liberated her and allowed her to become whole. Anaïs died on January 14, 1977, shortly before her seventy-third birthday. She had two husbands, both at the same time, no children, many lovers, and hundreds of thousands of admirers. Over 20,000 pages of her diary manuscripts are housed in the UCLA library.

Where the Meshing
of the Dream and Reality
Takes Place

An Interview with Anaïs Nin
Los Angeles, California
July 1973

JODY: At what point in your life did you recognize your commitment as a writer?

ANAÏS: Very early, because of a mistaken diagnosis when I was nine years old that I wouldn't walk. I immediately took to writing. After that I began the diary at eleven. Then I wrote stories which I signed, "Member of the French Academy"...so I must have felt the vocation.

JODY: Did you read a great deal as a child?

ANAÏS: Voraciously.

JODY: In the diaries you speak frequently of Marcel Proust's work. Was Proust a significant influence on your writing?

ANAÏS: Very important. He was the first one who showed me how to break down the chronology, which I never liked, and follow the dictates and intuitions of feeling memory. Proust only wrote things when he felt them...it didn't matter when they had happened. Of course, that became very strong in my work.

But also there were other influences. I wanted to write a poetic novel, and for that I chose models like Giraudoux, Pierre Jean Jouve and Djuna Barnes, an American writer who published a beautiful book, *Nightwood*. I thought, "That is what I would like to do in a novel." So she was an influence. Then, later on, it was D. H. Lawrence. Lawrence indicated the way to find a language for emotion, for instinct, for ambivalence, for intuition.

JODY: When you were living in Paris did you ever meet Djuna Barnes?

ANAÏS: No, I only saw her at a cafe. I had written her my first fan letter and she never answered, which is why I answer all the letters I get.

JODY: Do you consider Lawrence in any way a feminine writer?

ANAÏS: In the sense that he was very concerned with feeling and intuition and instinct, which we say a woman is, yes. Also he tried very hard to understand the feelings of women. When he was trying to describe lovemaking he described as much the women's feelings as the men's, which was unusual at the time.

JODY: How would you describe your relationship to surrealism?

ANAÏS: Although I didn't join the surrealist group and didn't adopt the dogma, which was very severe, we all lived and breathed the air of surrealism in the thirties. Everything was surrealistic—all the things we saw, the Cocteau films—the influence was continuous. I used surrealism only when the novel was concerned with superimpositions; I didn't use it all the time. And I didn't believe in the novel anyway, so it is a sort of adapted surrealism. But I realized how strong the influence was as time went on with the emphasis on dreams, which made me write *House of Incest*. And then, you know, as Breton said, we had to rediscover love.

JODY: There is a striking similarity in structure between your continuous novel, *Cities of the Interior*, and Lawrence Durrell's *Alexandria Quartet*. Your novels were published prior to Durrell's—is there any possible influence here?

ANAÏS: It's very hard to say because I don't know if Lawrence Durrell had read me at that time. I do think there are convergences in literature as in science…that people make the same discovery or arrive at the same point at the same time. So I am really unable to say we influenced each other.

JODY: How has your long friendship with Henry Miller influenced your writing?

ANAÏS: I think we influenced one another very much at the beginning, because mine was a sheltered life and his was a life in the streets. He would say, "Write more loudly, and funnier," and I would say, "Well, write less ponderously, and don't develop so much." We had an influence on each other for good, really, at the beginning, and then of course each of us went a different way.

But he pulled me out of the French writer's syndrome, whose life is confined to his home, and into a much wider experience. More openness. And I wanted him not to develop so much, not to say "It was Tuesday afternoon," not to give so many details.

JODY: Do you think of yourself as an American writer?

ANAÏS: No, I think of myself as an international or universal writer. All of us now are beginning to think beyond our own cultures and countries. I can't say I'm really an American writer, but I am identified to the new consciousness, very strongly.

JODY: Many of our major writers have their roots in two cultures. I am thinking of Albert Camus, whose initial upbringing and loyalty were to Algeria, although he belongs to the classic French tradition, and Jean-Paul Sartre, who in *The Words* talked about his Alsatian roots. Then too there is Ionesco, who is Romanian but writes in French, and Thomas Beckett, who is Irish and writes in French and English. And of course Hemingway and Fitzgerald spent extensive periods of time in Paris. Is that cross-cultural identity a significant one for you?

ANAÏS: It is very signficant, very important. We also have Nabokov and other foreign-born writers who have been incorporated into American literature. The difference is

France never said, "foreign-born Camus", and Americans still say "foreign-born Nabakov", and "Paris-born Anaïs". I wish they would forget that: I'm really writing for America and in English. America doesn't seem to absorb its foreign-born writers, and for a long time it kept me on the periphery. But today all of us are reading writers from every country, so I think we ought to stop making these boundaries.

JODY: There is a characteristic flow and internal density in your works. Where does that come from? Is it rooted in that cross-cultural identity?

ANAÏS: I always felt the inner quality came out of the traumatic experience of being uprooted and of losing my father and realizing that I had to build an inner world that would withstand destruction. The child who is uprooted begins to realize that the only thing that is going to last is what he builds within himself. After that comes the realization that this was the center from which we have to build in order to withstand shattering experiences.

JODY: We have a three-year-old who loves to play with the snails who eat the flowers in our garden. It occured to me as I watched the snails that as we grow beyond childhood, and particularly for the writer who leads a nomadic existence, we become like the snails, carrying our symbolic homes on our backs. Everything we care about we internalize, we become. Do you think that is true in your case?

ANAÏS: Very true. That is what I call the spirit house, the building of an inner core which is strong and can be moved about without being destroyed. The snail is a very good image for that.

JODY: Music also saturates your works, which are often reminiscent of symphonic form. Your father and your brother are both musicians and composers. How has music influenced your writing?

ANAÏS: Very strongly. I think I even said as directly as that in the diary that my ideal would be if I could write a page of writing that would be like a page of music. That was really an objective: I felt there must be a language and a way of expressing things that bypasses the intellect and goes straight to the emotions. I wanted to have the same reaction from writing that I have to music.

JODY: In the fourth volume of the diaries you said: "Truth and reality are at the basis of all I write. I can always bring forth proofs of the incident which inspired the character or place. But in order to capture emotion, the reality of how we feel or see the world, I have to go beyond appearance, and then it takes on the quality of a dream. But it is not a dream, it is the way our interior life is lived." How do you move from the interior life, the interior vision, to its exteriorization in literature?

ANAÏS: This was really due to the concern I had for external reality as holding a secret or a metaphor. So that I would never describe the city, or the ragpickers, or a person without really looking for the meaning. Then, of course, everything becomes transparent because you are concerned with the metaphysical meaning. I never described a city for its own sake but immediately had to find what its spiritual qualities and symbolic value were, and that made it seem transparent. Then people would say "dream-like," but I knew that wasn't what it was.

JODY: What about the significance of the dream in your work and the importance of communication between the conscious and the unconscious?

ANAÏS: Unfortunately, we tend to separate everything: we separate body and soul, we separate the dream from our daily life. What I found so fascinating in psychology was the interrelation between them. Once I found that the dream was so interrelated with life, then I wanted to keep those passageways open and move from one to the other, not divide them, as they are really all one. Of course, next was carrying it into the novel, always starting a novel with a dream and having that dream be the theme of the novel that had to be developed, understood at the end and fulfilled if possible. And then to be able to move to the next experience.

JODY: In the diaries you quote Jung and you emphasize the phrase "Proceed from the dream outward..."

ANAÏS: That was a very important phrase, yes, that was really the way I wanted to situate my work. That was the core. But it wasn't Jung I was interested in at the time, it was Otto Rank. He had more interest in the artist and he was directly responsible for my concern with what I call the creative will, which is a transformation of life, the metamorphosis of everything. Rank put a greater emphasis on that than Jung. It is only recently now that I have been able to enjoy Jung, having solved the problem of the creative will, which was Rank's great theme.

JODY: How do you explain the almost universal identification on the part of women readers with the characters in your novels and the persona in the diary?

ANAÏS: People have written me letters and said, "My father was different, my country was different, my background was different, but the feelings are the same." That means that what unites us are our emotions and feelings toward experience. The actual facts were different, but the women felt the same way. So I think that I must have done unwittingly what Ira Progoff described as going so deep inside the personal well that you touch the water which connects all the wells together.

JODY: Are there certain archetypal feelings in every human experience?

ANAÏS: Yes, I think that is where we are alike. Our experience may be different but our feelings are the same—anxiety, fear, timidity. The whole process of growth, reaction, rebellions: those are the same, those are universal. But if we put too much emphasis on the outer differences, say between your father and my father, then we destroy that sameness.

JODY: Would you agree that part of your uniqueness as a writer stems from the fact that you venture into realms which represent specifically women's situation and experience?

ANAÏS: I wasn't aware of that, but my own subjective attitude toward reality, which was that all I really knew was what I could see and feel, suddenly placed me at the experience of woman. I read a great deal but I didn't imitate men writers. I wanted to tell what *I* saw, so it came out that way: it came out that it was a vision as a woman sees the universe.

JODY: A highly personal vision?

ANAÏS: Yes, a highly personal vision, which I admitted to, and as you know, was often criticized as not being objective, not being a total concept of the universe. Now we know that men didn't have it either.

JODY: In volume two you speak of feeling like the third eye, "the cosmic eye of vision." That's a wonderfully expressive image: it suggests that you didn't want to be limited to what was considered a woman's view of the world or to the alternative, writing like a man.

ANAÏS: Yes, I did want to translate man to woman and woman to man. I didn't want to lose contact with the language of man, but I knew that there was a distinction of levels.

JODY: Among your works is there one which, from your own point of view, you consider the best-written?

ANAÏS: What I feel is that I could never rewrite the short stories. I could never add one word to the short stories, *Under a Glass Bell*. I couldn't change anything in *Collages*. I could have improved the novels.

JODY: Do you use a different artistic yardstick or measure for the diaries? Do you use a different process?

ANAÏS: In writing the diary I was trying really to overlook and to forget *all* procedures of writing. I wanted to be very comfortable, to have no sense of perfection, no demands on myself whether I had written it well or not well. I wanted to shed all that…I wanted the writing to be absolutely automatic. And I succeeded in that because I felt it would never be read. It would never have happened, I think, if I had felt it was going to be read.

JODY: The diaries were originally not written to be published?

ANAÏS: No.

JODY: How did they come to be published?

ANAÏS: Occasionally I would have a desire to share a part of the diary…I would write something I was proud of. The natural thing was, "I'm sorry I can't read it to you." And occasionally I did let some people read a part here and a part there.

For example, when Henry Miller was worried about what I was writing about him I let him read his portrait, and that made him feel all right. So, there was a little bit of sharing. But the feeling that I could solve the problem of editing a diary while everybody was alive didn't come until much later, when, as a practiced novelist, I felt that I could handle the problem of editing. Also, I had to handle the psychological problem: was I open enough? I had fear about exposing myself. I had this terrifying dream that I opened my door and was struck by mortal radiation. But then the opposite happened. That was a psychological impediment which might have lasted all of my life. I overcame that, and then I overcame the editing problems, and then I was open.

JODY: Is the diary a resource for the novels and short stories?

ANAÏS: Yes, it's really a notebook. Sometimes what happens is that if I keep writing about a person that interests me, after a while, cumulatively, I feel I have a portrait. We don't think of our friends that way…we see them a little bit here and a little bit there. Suddenly I see a total person, and then I write the story.

JODY: Are you interested in film? What are some of the problems of translating your works into film?

ANAÏS: I love film. I think my work is very suited to film as we had intended film to be, which is to picture the inner life, the fantasy and the dream. It hasn't been used very much for that. So when an effort was made to structure my novels on film as a regular story, it didn't work. Until someone just follows the book and the atmosphere of the book and the kind of free association I do, it will be difficult to do my work on film.

JODY: Are there any films currently which correspond to your idea of filmmaking?

ANAÏS: There was a film recently called *A Safe Place* by Henry Jaglom, and it was my idea of film, in which all the different levels happen simultaneously. It wasn't an easy film to understand, but I loved it and it had a magical quality. I also liked *Women in Love,* which was very faithful to the ambiguities and ambivalences of Lawrence. They didn't make anything too explicit and they didn't go beyond what he meant. It was beautifully done.

JODY: How has being a woman affected your life as a writer? And how has being a writer affected your life as a woman?

ANAÏS: Freudian theory has admitted that the unconscious does exist and is very powerful, and Freud said that woman had remained closer to her unconscious, so I think the right time has come for women's writing. There are other aspects that are more difficult: for instance, most of the major critics have been men who sometimes felt that women's work, what they called "feminine", was nonrational.

JODY: We do have women critics now: are women evolving a new style of criticism?

ANAÏS: Yes, that struck me very much about the women critics I have known this year. For example, Sharon

Spencer accepts the intention of the artist, she doesn't impose a ready-made formula, she doesn't say, "You didn't write a novel like the eighteenth century novel." She tries to find out what the author intended to do and whether he has done that. I think that is a feminine contribution to criticism, not to impose a certain structure.

JODY: Has your exceptional beauty been an asset to your creative work or a hindrance?

ANAÏS: Sometimes it was an asset, when you could charm a critic, but sometimes it really stood in the way. Even I find myself thinking, "Sharon Spencer is so pretty, she can't possibly be so brilliant"—coming from a woman! She looks fragile, incapable of doing this formidable book of criticism. So I think even women have the feeling that beauty means there isn't anything inside. And I never believed in mine, so that was very simple.

JODY: How do you feel when you see your works translated into so many languages?

ANAÏS: In Japanese, of course, I can't even recognize the names of the characters, and I sign the book at the wrong end. It's always very interesting to be translated; you have the feeling somehow that you are beginning to occupy a new country.

JODY: How many languages have your books been translated into thus far?

ANAÏS: I counted once up to twenty-two, but I haven't counted in quite a while.

JODY: In the diaries you speak with great attachment of your home in Louveciennes, outside of Paris. Do you consider your environment an extension of your personality in the same way that clothing constitutes a symbolic extension of a character's personality in your novels?

ANAÏS: Yes, I do, but I also think we have to change our environment as we evolve. I know that we get attached to a certain house, but I also know that the history of Louveciennes ended at a certain time. Looking back on it, it was the right time. Even though it is painful, and you don't know that you are finished with a certain experience, you do know, and something propels you out. Something propelled me out of Louveciennes. I have been propelled out of several homes, when a certain cycle ends and the house becomes dead. They are reflections of where we are at the moment.

JODY: In your writings you express profound belief in the human capacity to grow beyond neurosis. What is the source of your optimism?

ANAÏS: I never thought about the source. I always felt that impulse in myself, the way plants have an impulse to grow. What happens are accidental interferences and blockages and illnesses, like with trees. But I think the impulse is in all of us: it's in children, isn't it, to use their strength and their skills to explore all the possibilities? Human beings all have that impulse, but then that impulse gets damaged.

JODY: Does that damage stop us from growing? Are we capable of growing beyond the damage?

ANAÏS: What I believe is that we can take notice of the damage which most of us suffer somewhere along the line. We can take notice of it and we can overcome the damage. We all have interferences, and we have discouragements, and we have traumatic experiences, those are pretty common. How much they stop us is up to us. I have met young writers who stopped at the first rejection. So it is a question of how much we will struggle to overcome impediments.

JODY: Would you agree that one of the major themes in your writing is the conflict between woman's role as a dependent and loving being and the artist's drive toward transcendence?

ANAÏS: Yes, it is a very great conflict, because the creative will pushes you in one direction and then you have guilt about using your energy or your time, which is supposed to be devoted to your personal life, and how much you can carry on your personal life and preserve it, while at the same time pursuing your work.

It is a problem for woman. It hasn't been a problem for man because the culture incited him to produce, and so he had no guilt; if he wanted to be obsessed with his work he could be, he was blessed for it. But woman was told that her primary concern was her personal life, and she wasn't encouraged to produce; it would be accidental phenomena in her case. So the guilt for not taking care of your personal life is something that man doesn't have, that we are handicapped with.

If an anthropologist takes a trip to write a book, no one thinks about his deserting his family for a year. But Margaret Mead told the story of how much she was criticized for going off for such long periods away from her family.

JODY: Do you believe that as we grow we evolve out of childhood, away from it, or as we grow do we effect a reunion with a primary self, before trauma? In other words, is growth a linear evolution or a circular return?

ANAÏS: The search should take us to a place where we are able to reassemble all those separate pieces of ourselves. And we ought to be able to keep the feeling of childhood. Wallace Fowlie gave as the definition of the poet as one who is able to keep the fresh vision of the child within the mature man. And I believe that—except that during trauma these pieces break off, just as we break away from the parents. Esther Harding tells us that we have to recapture our original image of the parents, before rebellion. So it is really a work of connecting, isn't it?

JODY: A circular process of a return to a primary self?

ANAÏS: Before damage.

JODY: There is a similar circularity in your writing, like an archetypal return to the self, to some inner core.

ANAÏS: Yes, because if our mythological journey was supposed to have been through the labyrinth we still had to come out with all of our selves. We couldn't lose parts of our selves in the labyrinth, which we do when we split. You know, as R.D. Laing says, we are all schizophrenic, which means that we left half of ourselves somewhere.

JODY: You mention in the diaries that you are a Pisces. How has water affected your life?

ANAÏS: I'm very related to water. For instance, I feel very oppressed by mountains and I feel very close to the sea. I like the idea of travelling and moving about, the whole journey on water. Also it has an influence on my wanting my writing to be fluid, not static, and not crystal-like.

JODY: Do you attribute the quality of flow and movement in your writing to the fact that you are a Pisces?

ANAÏS: Well, astrologers do, I can say that. Moricand, you remember Henry Miller wrote about him, and I wrote about him too, described me as a Neptunian for whom the world of illusion was more important than the world of reality, where the meshing of the dream and reality took place. Pisces are supposed to be always concerned with compassion. Also, I felt that I wrote better on a houseboat because I could feel the river flowing underneath, that the continuing flow of water did have an effect on me. Everything about Pisces seems to fit.

JODY: How does it feel, after years of striving, to have achieved recognition as a major literary figure?

ANAÏS: Well, I never imagined that. It's a lovely feeling, because you feel in contact with the world, and you lose your sense of isolation. You have a sense of friendliness... you don't feel that you are discarded, you feel useful. It has many lovely aspects. And you can live out your universal life, you are in contact with the whole world, which is probably the wish of everyone.

JODY: What is the source of your inexhaustible energy?

ANAÏS: I haven't thought about that! I guess it's curiosity, the fact that I still feel things as keenly. I noticed that when I went to Fez again after twenty years I was wondering if I would feel things as keenly, colors and smells, and I do. So I suppose that when you feel alive and something propels you always into new experiences, while you are responding, you have this energy.

JODY: Is youth then an internal and eternal quality?

ANAÏS: Yes, it seems to be a quality of responsiveness, of remaining alive to whatever is happening around you. And while you have that feeling, then you go on exploring, and adding. You don't say, "Oh, I've already lived this before," or "I'm not interested in going to another country…" I have friends who say that they don't really care about exploring new experiences. But I'm always curious. Once I was in an airplane accident, one side of the wing had caught fire and we had six minutes to get to Los Angeles, and all I was doing was thinking of all of the places I hadn't seen yet. So that was my feeling, that it was a shame not to see everything, hear everything, be everywhere.

Esther Broner

Esther Broner is the high priestess in the Tarot deck. I have known Esther for over twenty years and her magic increases rather than diminishes with time. When I first met her we socialized as married women with children in the context of a summer community in Maine. Although people knew she wrote, Esther's identity among that group of artists, musicians and literati (which included pianist Harold Bogin, painter Leonard Baskin and his wife Lisa, Karl Schrag and his wife Elsa, artists Jack Sonenberg and Phoebe Helman, painters David and Sally Lund), seemed to be primarily as Bob's wife.

I remember the day that all changed. Esther had recently completed the manuscript of *Her Mothers* and was to do a reading at the Bogin's house. About 15 people had been invited, including those mentioned above.

The reading was held in a long and narrow sunroom, with chairs placed in rows facing one another the length of the walls. Esther was seated at one end, facing us. For the occasion she wore a long black dress with embroidery at the neck. Esther has beautiful, wild, long, thick black hair which frames her face. She sat in a high—backed wooden chair resembling a throne and began to read in a quiet voice. As the text got hold of her, her voice rose and sang like a religious invocation. The text itself was strong, hard, feminist, radical and shocking. I was in the thrall of the same

flush of recognition and thrill of identification I had felt looking at Judy Chicago's Great Ladies, only in Esther's case I was hearing rather than seeing it.

The excitement of the words and the vision of Esther sitting there like a queen on a throne reciting prophesies had momentarily made me forget everyone else in the room. But because of the long narrow shape of the space we were actually facing one another, and I could see them all. They looked as if they had been spun in a centrifuge. Their backs were pressed against the wall, their faces were pale with shock and their eyes looked glazed or trapped. "Bob's wife" had turned into Esther Broner, writer.

Esther is the recipient of an O'Henry award, a Wonder Woman Award and two NEA Fellowships, and is author of two great novels, *Her Mothers* and *A Weave of Women*. She is coeditor of *The Lost Tradition: Mothers and Daughters in Literature* and author of *The Telling*, a book about the attempt to make community among a real group of women, including Bella Abzug, Gloria Steinem, Grace Paley and Letty Cotton Pogrebin. It includes *The Women's Haggadah*, which is also published separately. Over the last several years Esther has published nine stories, seven of them what she calls "ghost stories" about the death of her mother. These have appeared in *Ms., Frontiers, North American Review, Tikkun, Kalliope,* and *Ascent,* among other publications. Her most recent book is *Mornings and Mourning*, about the death of her father.

Finished but not yet published is *The Alphabet of E.M. Broner*. For the last six years Esther has been working on a novel about different kinds of magic and morality and about the triumph of morality over greed.

Esther has four children and two grandchildren. Her husband, Bob Broner is a painter and printmaker. They live in New York City.

Of Holy Writing
and Priestly Voices

An Interview with E. M. Broner
Deer Isle, Maine
July 1981

JODY: What are your thoughts about the general direction
of women's writing? How does your own evolution parallel that general direction?

ESTHER: I do have some thoughts about the direction of fiction because I read a great deal of women's writing. I've just
finished reading a 1914 romantic novel about the painful
and unbearable love between men and women, a forgotten
work by the journalist Mary Heaton Vorse. My own first
novel dealt with that common enough theme, romance or
rather passion, which reflects a change of conception of
woman and her worth. In *Journal/Nocturnal*, that first novel,
there is a triangle, but it's two men and a woman.

Often in early women's writing there are two women,
and the man chooses. *Journal/Nocturnal* is traditional in
its concerns but untraditional in its style and in its perception of the caught, passive woman. As in the old
romantic novel my main character waits for a man to
carry her away (in this particular novel, to enlighten her).
She does not have sufficient fight within. She is enlight-
ened in turn by her radical husband and her conservative
lover.

Where this book enlarges from the usual romantic tale
is in the woman's being a microcosm of the land, for it is
set during the Vietnam war. Her suffering is that of the

society at large, that of the nation divided. I divide her consciousness on the page; the two columns meet and connect at events, but the perceptions of the recorded events of the domestic woman and the "wild" woman are quite different. In the largest sense this book was connected to the epic, and the woman, like the land lying fallow, was there to be used, planted. She is, so to say, on her back throughout the novel.

A secondary theme is the Demeter-Persephone legend, which runs through my next two novels and is stronger in *Her Mothers* than in *A Weave of Women*. Here the pain is not only that of being rejected by a male lover, it is also the loss the mother feels when she is left by her daughter. This is a developing theme in women's literature, for in every way we have lost our mothers and hence our daughters. We are rediscovering our foremothers, literary and historical, and our biological mothers. We are becoming strengthened by the deeds of our foremothers, and we are learning to forgive our mothers. We hope that our own run-away daughters will forgive our mistakes.

So, the love triangle is replaced by the woman alone, hunting for her role in genealogy, in history, in relationship to herself and to the issue of her womb. In *Her Mothers* the main character does not look for her context in marriage and love as she did in *Journal/Nocturnal*. In both books and in *Weave* I used an elegiac style, almost a kind of Homeric prose, to suggest a search, a holy pilgrimage, an enlargement of woman and her pain, her search, her triumphs when at last they come. In Maxine Hong Kingston's *Woman Warrior*, which I read hungrily after *Weave* went to print, I saw that she too, in her search, in her dealing with family and truth, had to use a heightened prose. I think also of the women who write utopian prose, and that speech which sounds trumpets, which is the cri de coeur.

A Weave of Women deals with a utopian community, but

still an endangered community. It is no longer about woman alone, identified by her relationship to men who take her day and night, nor is it woman on pilgrimage. This is woman strengthened by community: rewarded, nourished, or if she deserves, punished by it. She is not so much identified by community as given dignity through it. I also use heightened prose and prayers to deify gender. The male gender has already deified itself by identifying God as a male metaphor. I felt when I wrote *Weave* that we must address the Mother from whom we descended, whom we replicate. We must return to Her in our own image. We are seeing a renewed spiritual quest among women; somewhere, we are all looking to remake our mythic past.

In *Weave* there are too the terrible sacrifices women make; the Demeter-like character, the earth mother loses her daughter (the child's name, Hava, translates into "life"), and another "daughter" of the group is also killed.

What is the greatest loss we women suffer? It is that to which we give life being thought valueless, being taken from us. This, as well as our own dignity and individuality, being historically and slowly stripped from us, garment by garment, royal robe, crown, scepter, all symbols of power and grandeur removed from our heads, hand, shoulders. We are disrobed and dishonored. I had that in mind when I wrote *Weave of Women*.

JODY: In your review of *China Men* you refer to Hong Kingston's form as "grotesque" or "gothic." Could those same words apply to your own works as well?

ESTHER: Maybe. I thought of Hong Kingston as doing personal epic. I think more of the grotesques as in Winesburg, Ohio. The gothic form worries me in the sense that yes, I wanted these women in a house which they would come and visit, and it is a kind of magical house, not a castle on the moors. But I am also worried about what the gothic does to women. It is because of the gothic's passivity that I carefully prepared my women for battle, until they could go off as guerillas or outlaws. I wanted to write books in which men were not central characters. Not that men aren't central to my life. You and I know that yes, we talk about men in our relationships to the world, but when I gather with women, we say, "What are your desires? What do you want to do with your life? What direction are you going in? What hurts you? What enlarges you?" Men enter as a strain in it, but not as the whole. We are larger than that single thread.

All the plays I write have women as their chief actors. In *Body Parts of Margaret Fuller* there are ten women and no men. Out of a strange series of circumstances, I lived in the old Fred Astaire house while I was teaching women's studies at UCLA. I thought it was a schizophrenic life, but women do live these split lives being part of a dominant culture and making their own subdominant culture. While there I wrote a play which has twelve women telling their tales to this character, Fred Astaire. They are young students, movie stars, and aging pioneers. They ask for refuge in the arms of Fred Astaire, but he can give no one refuge and he can understand no tale told him.

We have to think of some men as being Peter Pans or Fred Astaires, who never address themselves to the larger issues in our lives. They don't say to us, "What hurts you? If this is your pain, then let us address ourselves to that." That is of no interest to them. It's "How can you be good girls and obey your fathers, how can you be obedient wives?" Of course, Fred Astaire's advice is wrong: he's telling his advice to women who are being raped and beaten by their husbands and fathers. Fred Astaire belongs to pop culture, to that mythos of evasion and romance. Women have another mythos, and I think our mythos should be named.

JODY: At last, we are in the realm of mythos and magic! In

your review of Hong Kingston's work, you talked about her search for self through told and untold tales. Does some of the magical quality in your own books come from told and untold family tales?

ESTHER: That's a really lovely question. The first book I wrote, *Summer is a Foreign Land*, is based on family legend. I was told my first tales in my grandmother's kitchen, sitting on her lap and hearing in Yiddish about the family. My grandmother made legends of shopkeepers and heroes of mailmen; she dignified peasants. Our family came from poverty, they lived in the shtetl, the ghetto, the small town. We had to have, for our dignity, magic and legend. I learned then that fiction was fact with magic added to it. It has delighted me and my children that there is legend and magic in our lives, for I, a reader of fairy tales to the family, am also the carrier of a magical journey.

JODY: You said of Hong Kingston that she takes data and makes it mythopoetic. Isn't there a similar quality in your work?

ESTHER: I wrote a play called *The Seasons of the Daughter*, which again deals with the Demeter-Persephone legend. There had been some tragedy in the family. When this tragedy happened, I became obsessed with rape. I thought I had to take that, which involved us all for a year, and enlarge the personal, so I again used the Demeter-Persephone myth as the essential rape. I wrote about four rapes, among them the rape of the biblical daughter, whose father sacrifices her. Last year Leonard Baskin, the artist, showed us his sculptures of the sacrificed daughters. We don't hear enough about that, we always talk about the sacrifice of Isaac. Of course, we sacrifice our boys in the war; but we don't talk about the on-going, eternal, long-time sacrifice of the daughters.

I take both historical and personal data and try to make it something beyond that. In *Fred Astaire*, the movie stars are all women who are used up and cast aside, women who are terrified of losing their youth. Judy Garland, another character I use in *Fred*, is all of us who are overused. Ginger Rogers is the eternal patriot and good girl, all because she is so afraid of being disobedient. If she's disobedient, what will happen to her? Will she be expelled from our hearts and our land? The obedient daughter, the obedient wife, the obedient citizen: we have to go beyond all that. We have to break those fetters.

JODY: Was the hostile review of *Weave* in the *New York Times* written by a man or a woman?

ESTHER: It was by a woman. Men pay women to trash other women. There were a series of reviews by women attacking other women: Pearl Bell's review of a book by Alix Kates Shulman and another of Adrienne Rich's *Of Woman Born* began it. It was because of those reviews that *The Feminist Review* and the New York Feminist Writer's Guild were formed. We felt we had to have a voice.

I spent two days this past week comforting friends. One was Blanche Cook, eminent historian, who wrote *The Declassified Eisenhower*. She went against the mythos of Eisenhower the peacemaker to show how he carefully planned the destabilization and destruction of Guatemala and laid the groundwork for all our current policies in South and Central America. The review was given to John Roach, a cold warrior, who demolished her. The review was not just to demolish her but to terrify anyone who would criticize the political mythos of the fifties, which is returning now.

The second time a friend wept was because of a review by someone I repect and whose name I won't mention. This reviewer thought that if she were not allowed pornography, her sexual freedom would be curtailed. So she did a devastating review of Andrea Dworkin's book, *Man Possessing Woman*, and did not choose to understand the larger implications of pornography. In a sense pornography is the slogan and rape is the action: but the larger issue is that civil libertarians do not understand pornography. A case in point is the civil libertarian romance with the defense of de Sade, who raped and murdered many women.

JODY: Didn't Simone de Beauvoir also defend de Sade?

ESTHER: Yes, and she was wrong. We have to learn when we're wrong and correct it.

JODY: Let's talk about the dichotomy between the images of women in literature and the reality of women's lives. At what point did you become aware of this and address it consciously as an issue in your work?

ESTHER: I think about that wonderful book by Ellen Moers, *Literary Women: The Great Writers* and the huge effect it had on me, coming out of the early seventies, making me realize again how we invented the novel, how we were the great writers. When I was in graduate school you could go all the way through your Ph.D. and never read a woman. All of us who read *Sexual Politics* have become aware of what our image was. You could not help but be uncomfortable always being passive: it was unnatural.

In the 1950s, when we were reading very seriously, there were all those men coming back and writing about the war. All of that fiction is irrelevant to me: I was busy reading Elizabeth Bowen, that elegant, exquisite woman, writing of war, writing of the heart. Who ever read her? Now she's being resuscitated, but who was reading women then? That was the age of the Elizabeths: Elizabeth Bowen, Elizabeth Enright, and what gorgeous stories she was writing! Who paid any attention? Fortunately *The New Yorker* did publish quite a few women when I was trying to teach myself how to write the way Kay Boyle was writing, or Emily Hahn. There were a lot of great women writing in the fifties. I remember reading Willa Cather in graduate school and being told she couldn't deal with men—and you are as large as the authors you choose to deal with—and getting a *B* (a very low grade for graduate school).

I read Sarah Orne Jewitt, with that intense relationship between women, women seeking adventure: those are women that changed me. Afterwards I didn't understand Willa Cather, who had to speak through a man, through the archbishop. What happened to her? She was a lesbian, she made all her intense commitments to women: I never understood what happened to her in the end. Maybe other scholars will. Well, we're reading Virginia Woolf now, how could we not help but open up? None of those women were in the fiction I was reading.

I got very sick of the Telemachus thing in the fifties, everybody was Telemachus: here we all are going on a hunt for our father and there is Penelope staying home. Ah, I bet Penelope was carrying on there, I'll bet she was doing all kinds of things. I had to do *Her Mothers* as a very conscious counter-Telemachus, and I had to search for the past because the men were not active enough in that search. I'm carefully making footsteps, I'm carefully saying: Here we are, we're priestesses, we're gods, we made the exodus. We are defining ouselves and finding a new way of looking.

We learn in Hong Kingston's *China Men* to have compassion for the loss of men, the railroads running over the backs of the Chinese men. I don't want to lose my compassion for men in my passion for women, but you have to carefully name your enemy, and your enemy has a name.

JODY: In *A Room of One's Own* Virginia Woolf said that any work of genius is difficult, but for women there are additional obstacles: hostility, no money, no free time, absence of a tradition of women writers, a different language, different values. What is the solution?

ESTHER: The solution is at hand. We are beginning to get our traditional women writers back, we're reading the writers of the past. We're rereading Virginia Woolf, we're reading Blanche Cook's work on the networking of women or her rediscovery of Crystal Eastman. We're rediscovering our mothers. I co-authored an anthology of essays, *The Lost Tradition*, with Cathy Davidson; it reconsiders the relationship between mothers and daughters.

We are gaining back a literary tradition and we are changing the myths to include ourselves. There's an awful lot of work being done on fairy tales now. We are learning what the fairy tale is about and where we are politically in the fairy tale. We are learning where myth has misused us and kept us in place, for example with Zeus raping every ancient woman god. All the ancient earth-women gods were raped. Well, we are studying rape and we're getting smarter. Now we're learning who our women gods and writers are, who our women scientists are, and we're having great adventures. Grace Steward did a fine critical study on woman and the *Kunstroman*, woman and the novel of "woman as artist." In the novels she discusses the woman fails because she has no muse, no support: so she gives up painting, she gives up writing.

JODY: At what point in your life did you actually start writing?

ESTHER: I'd say fairly seriously—stories only—about age thirty. That was twenty years ago. I did a lot of notetaking because I wasn't sure that anything in my life was noteworthy, except maybe those legends of the past. The early stuff I wrote was precious; I call it "ethnic precious" writing, ethnic lyricism. I don't like any of it, it's foreign to me, a little too sweet. But I think it had that same purpose: namely, I had to enlarge myself or make my life something of note. In the 1950s we went to New York. I was out of work and it was very humiliating, I had a poverty-stricken time, but it was also very exciting. I was drinking beer with Dylan Thomas every Thursday night, and Bob at his atelier was meeting all the great artists, and our friends were beginning new forms of abstract expressionism. If you live in a place that tries hard things you are more apt to also, just as in Jerusalem I learned to make my women characters try hard things.

But to get back to New York in the fifties, I began taking notes on the life around me. I counted how many vegetable stands there were on my street (Twenty-third Street), and butcher shops. I began describing the kinds of meat in the window. I walked along the pier, I'd climb on the barges and talk to people. I wrote every day about that life, and I didn't know what I was writing. Ultimately, I tried to put it into a book called *The Jewish Viking*, which failed. But I did learn to take notes very carefully, as if what I did was important. I'd watch somebody make artificial flowers and that seemed very important. I'd watch somebody eating figs and that was very important. I as observer gained importance. I was trying poetry, and it was bad. In my fiction, the form was amateurish. Then I wrote a story called " A New Nobility" which was in my own voice. That was rejected by thirty-five magazines. Ultimately it was picked up and won second prize in the O' Henry contest.

Then in 1968 I wrote *Journal/Nocturnal*, in which I realized (and I as the daughter of a newspaperman knew this more than anyone) that the events of my life were interrupted as if they were newspaper columns and always continued on page three. I had four children: when you're energetic and ambitious that's a lot; you don't complete anything and you have to hold everything over. So I had that sense of many things happening simultaneously and of contradictory things happening, and I wrote—it was a difficult time for me personally—about a woman who leads a very domestic life and also leads a darker life in which she's exploring those other aspects of her nature. I may have felt somewhat imprisoned in my domestic life, for I was doing graduate work. *Journal/Nocturnal* was perhaps another way of exploring fictional alternatives. That was a good novel. That was where my voice began, when I recognized that my life is interruptive and that I had to keep many things going at the same time. I had to use the form of my life in the form of my writing.

JODY: *Weave* is stunning in its powerful eroticism, its rich sensuality. How do you come to grips with the fact that a woman can be both sexual and intellectual, an idea which flies in the face of one of the more traditional (and destructive) tenets of our society?

ESTHER: *Journal/Nocturnal* is also very erotic. My woman makes love, but she suffers from it; she suffers terribly. *Her Mothers* has erotic episodes all the way through. *Weave* is not so much intellectual and sexual as spiritual and sexual. I think there is an intense sexual base for spirituality.

I'm a very rebellious daughter, my mother always called me that. I'm a lover of bodies: I will tell the pleasure we get from every orifice, I will blow in every orifice, I will have liquid coming from every orifice, and I will say it is holy. It is holy to be sexual, it is holy to have breasts, it is holy to have a cunt. I did an article called "The Dirty Ladies" which I read at the Modern Language Association about four women writers who use exquisite sexual language—Erica Jong, Lynda Schor, Grace Paley and Rhoda Lerman. I said that women have to return language to themselves. Several of them use the word cunt; cunt comes from the Roman goddess Cunigen. One used to say "cunipotent." "Cunning" and "cradle" come from there.

I'm sexual, and I like to be turned on in the best way. I'm also very concerned about our writing about our own eroticism and not accepting male pornography. It is not my eroticism to service a man as the porno films show, in a terrible way, or to be beaten. That is not my eroticism. My eroticism is to be lovingly, lovingly caressed, my soul and myself. My skin is the entrance to my soul: I want my skin touched, I want my soul elevated. If that's terribly foolish, I don't know. There are all kinds of turn-ons: I myself find writing erotically a huge pleasure, and women are doing it more and more. Marilyn French's *Bleeding Heart* had explicit sexual scenes. Marge Piercy's *Vida* had marvellously explicit scenes. Erica Jong's *Fanny* is wonderful. Our biology tells us that women are much more sexual than men; we sustain longer, we reach our peak at an older age. We have to be mentors to young men, if not to young women. Women are biologically sexual. On the other hand, one doesn't feel awfully good about the word "fuck"; it has very peculiar, angry origins. "Fiend" comes from that, "foe" comes from that, "fie" comes from that. It's an embattled word.

JODY: Fee, fie, foe, fum, fuck.

ESTHER: It's just that. Swords crossed.

JODY: This is related to what we were discussing earlier: all the victims, the women in fiction who, after some sort of sexual episode, either commit suicide, or have an accident, or die, or are doomed: women are punished for sexual fulfillment.

ESTHER: All right. So what do we read? I read Isadora Duncan's *My Life*: that's marvelously, explicitly sexual. She tells you what happens in your forties. I mean, my Lord, it was very good to find out that she was absolutely right. You feel wonderful, you just feel at your best in your forties, terribly sexual and glorious. Then I began reading all the radical women, like Emma Goldman's *Living My Life*. We women agitate whatever we do, so we might as well be agitators. That is really why I wrote first mythically and why I'm writing now of women on soapboxes. It seems to finally come down to reality and history. I can capture fantasy, and now I want to go into reality; that's terribly hard for me because I'm not an historian.

JODY: How do you feel about lesbian works? Have you experienced any hostility towards you from lesbian women as a heterosexual writer?

ESTHER: First of all, let me quote your dear friend Anaïs Nin to you: "All love is acceptable which is supportive and which is love." All love has to be experienced. Never would I be put off by lesbian writing, nor is it alien to my nature. How could it be for anyone? We all have loved and had erotic fantasies or actual practices with women— call them schoolgirl crushes, teacher crushes, whatever— we've all had longings. Women are so beautiful, how could they not long for each other? There are those who have gone into that other, difficult country of declaring women their own and this as their border. All that stretches us and changes us is the full shape of ourselves.

There are many kinds of love; we are full of many kinds of love. I chose one kind of love. I could easily write a book about lesbian love and indeed, *Her Mothers* is acclaimed by lesbians as a lesbian book. I felt it's quite lovely that I've touched women in all kinds of ways. We're…I don't know if I want to say…"androgynous." I'm really anti-Jung in that sense. I think we're socially set into our roles, but we can love in many ways.

I don't know what is unnatural. I am lucky in not suffering an exclusion. After all, it is lesbian women who are in the forefront of discovering other women. If there are some who are enraged that I bear sons and am married to a husband, well, that's their loss at this moment. I would say that the women most in the forefront of my political life are women who have chosen the lesbian way of living. They remind me each time I become too traditional, with all the limitations of that.

My sense of change is of women getting stronger. We have been dependent too long, we have to become sure of our myths, sure of our voices. We can no longer have highpitched, giddy voices: we have to be very deep-voiced, loud. Women are trained to be quiet, so if there is a single man in a classroom of women students you hear him all the time, never the women. Years have to elapse before we allow men into that psychic part of our world. We must raise tender men and strong women who will be political warriors as well.

JODY: These are relatively abstract notions as opposed to specific visions. When you write do you have specific visions of change?

ESTHER: We must be activists, for we have no choice as regards nuclear proliferation or ecological damage to the earth. I've always been a socialist, I've always been interested in the distribution of wealth, in humanity in the workplace. What interests me now in the character I'm working with (and whom I pray I will sustain through three books) is this: if we are knocked down so often, if our visions are destroyed so often, how do we sustain ourselves? We have our internal and external enemies—look at our own movement, the women's movement in a larger political sense. Look at the communists attacking other communists and speaking out against them, or the socialists in fear. Well, how does my character sustain herself? How does she keep up her courage through the decades? I have to find that out. She's going to tell me.

JODY: Women today are learning to take control of their own lives. That means educating themselves, feeding themselves, learning to function in the workplace, learning to handle money, having control over their bodies. All of these changes are revolutionary, and all seem to bring about repressive measures.

ESTHER: And there are those who would deprive us of access to legal abortion. In one particular community where a feminist health center is being dismantled, on all kinds of pretexts, the women are learning to abort one another. This shouldn't be necessary, but abortion may have to go underground once again, in which case we will do it ourselves: we will no longer go to some butcher who's going to do it to us. There are women I know too who are birthing each other. Sometimes the mothers are in bed with their childbearing daughters, breathing in rhythm with them.

JODY: Is there a dichotomy between feminism and the way traditional Judaism and Christianity portray women?

ESTHER: Are you asking whether or not there is a split between me as a Jew and a feminist? Or are you asking whether traditional religion has any application to my life as a writer?

JODY: Both.

ESTHER: Every time I am impatient with, outraged and humiliated by the way traditional religion (mine in particular) treats women, I'm reminded again by the world that I can't separate my Judaism from myself, because the world defines me always as a Jew. In my writing I try in various ways to both accept and expand my own mythos. I speak with the tongue of my people's prayer, yet I change the gender. I speak out of a history, but I research it, as I did in *Her Mothers*, to name the biblical women in our past. And I arrogate unto myself power that is not allowed us. In the fall I celebrate a "New Year on the Pier" where I do the Kol Nidre, the ancient sacred prayer preceding Yom Kippur, and no power has allowed me to do this. I do it in the name of woman judges and warriors of my past, and in the name of the need of the women around me.

I, probably more than anyone, am aware of the shame, the humiliation visited upon the Jewish woman by the Jewish patriarchy. Yet I have not rejected Judaism the way Mary Daly, the Catholic writer, has rejected the Catholic church, because the world will still destroy me in the name of Jew. The holocaust is still very recent, therefore I would be a coward to run. After all, I am named for somebody who had to choose, Queen Esther. She said, "Why should I identify myself when I would be destroyed for that identification?" "Because," her cousin replied, "what happens to your people will happen to you." That is a lesson I have learned very well. On the other hand, I can be regal and queenly in my context, but I also have to wear blinders: I can't go to traditional places, or I'll be hurt. I know I make a very small wave; I change things a tiny bit with my left hand. With my right hand I'm writing a book called *The Ceremonial Woman*. I think women have to celebrate together, and it cannot be the usual celebration.

JODY: How much of what you write is inspired by what you read?

ESTHER: I'm not a writer who has to *not* read other writers when she's writing. I feel competitive, you know, in a good way: "You did this great thing, now I've got to do a great thing," but I don't close the door on other voices. With *Weave* I had ancient books with me; I had a lot of Biblical literature. Before I wrote that book I wrote a note to myself: "I want to do holy writing and make a special calendar for women, and I want to speak in a priestly voice." That was my note to myself. I had it pinned up on the wall so I wouldn't deviate. I didn't have to do a lot of reading, although I did do Biblical and Sumerian research. With the one I'm on now, I'm reading all the time, I'm exhausted with reading. I think one day I'll be found dead with newspapers around me.

Her Mothers came out of a play I was doing on Thomas Wentworth Higginson in the nineteenth century. I had this huge romance with Margaret Fuller and nineteenth century women. I put Margaret Fuller in several works, first in a play and then in a novel. So I had a lot of that research with me, everything on Charlotte Fortin, everything on Louisa May Alcott. All those lives of writers and of brave women are lives of instruction. I do look upon the world as instructive, and so I had their works to instruct me, always in their foolishness as well as their courage, their terrible lack of self, that denigrating of self, terrible decisions as well as great courage. We need each other, we have to read and meet each other. Reading other women makes me more powerful.

For my newest book I read all the time. It may be what slows me down so terribly. I'm reading about all the things of which I'm ignorant: the history of trade union women and how the daily newspapers either record or distort their role, the events of the time, and whether women are ignored or included. I learned to read the books and press of one decade, then learned that each decade is dependent upon the decade before. Soon I was reading in the 1920s, then before that—and there we were, organizing IWW; there we were, *Living My Life*, as Emma Goldman wrote, or *My Life*, as Isadora Duncan wrote earlier. We were powerful, we were revolutionary. Only by reading would I have learned that.

JODY: How did you get involved with your current project?

ESTHER: *The Plant* is a trilogy of novels: that's a working title which will change. *The Assassins* and *The Agitators* are books two and three. It's about a woman who survives four decades of political change. How do you survive the fifties, for instance, if you are a political activist? How did I get interested in it? Somewhat through Genora Dollinger. I've always thought that the romance of Detroit, the heroism of that impoverished, decaying city was a story of great battles: the battle of the Ford Overpass Bridge, the battle of Briggs, those battles that organized the plants. Those were heroic days. How do blue-collar people live in an atmosphere that denigrates them, diminishes them and demolishes them? How do they do heroic things? How do they become larger than themselves?

I also got very interested in the oral taping of families. Families would be forced to leave their children with neighbors and would come back seven years later to pick them up. My woman is doing a similar sort of pick-up family thing. She says you have to make a local where you find it, so on the way to unionizing the world, she makes little locals of families. Also, I want to give voice to the women who don't have a voice, which is most women, but particularly Polish and Black women.

I have a romance with politics: I've been injured by it, but I do have a romance with it. There's so much out there to kill us; I want to know what's out there to help us survive. We are so close to extinction. I so often wish I were dead, I often do. It's too hard, I'm exhausted, it's just too hard, it should just be over. Then I think, God, how can I go? I hear the trumpets sound and there's another battle to fight. How do people sustain themselves, how do they survive? Nothing interests me more than that.

JODY: Who are your literary and spiritual mothers, your sisters and daughters?

ESTHER: Almost all the women I read. Every time I read a woman, I'm happy. There is Andrea Dworkin, or Phyllis Chesler, whose new book is about women who have lost custody of their children. These stories are so poignant, so unbearable. There are men's groups who work surreptitiously to kidnap children. I could say my writer-mothers are Jane Austen, Harriet Martineau, Harriet Beecher Stowe, Kitty Sklar, that marvellous historian, and Blanche Cook. I guess political activists are in some way my mentors. I read about late nineteenth- and early twentieth-century Russian women in *Five Sisters Before the Tzar*, who went to Switzerland to get educated, who came back before the revolution and who became anarchists. I also think about Lucy Lippard seeing art in a new way, never afraid, now working on a novel dealing with three generations of women. Or Lily Rivlin, who went to Israel to film her family of 5,000 gathering, and feeling herself the black sheep. What courage to make that pilgrimage.

There is the film-maker Mira Hammermesh, married and with a baby, suddenly dreaming she had to go back to the land that had killed her father in the camps. So she went to Poland, to the great film school there, telling them, "You owe me something." "What?" "I want to be a filmmaker." "Why should you be a filmmaker? What are your credentials? Have you made films?" "No." "Well, don't be silly. From every socialist country they are trying to get into our great film school. Who is your family? Did your father get medals?" "Yes, he got a medal at Treblinka. You owe me this education." She was there two years and became a filmmaker. I could think of a thousand people I admire, people I haven't met, like Pat Darrian of the Carter cabinet. I admire Bella Abzug, a wounded warrior. Ever day I meet women who lift my heart right out of me. Carolyn Kizer, that Tallulah Bankhead of the world, astonishing, wonderful, great star. How can I choose? Oh, that flowerbed of women. If I just looked in my telephone book I could tell you 4,000 people who move me deeply. Grace Paley, Tillie Olsen....

JODY: Can you look at your life and say what were specific and major events that influenced the course of it?

ESTHER: I can't tell you everything, because I'm still a private person. Some of what is in the family is private. I told you that rape is important, entering my life very early, and that I had to shape my life around the importance of that knowledge. That's something that's really in my way in life and in the lives of those I love.

I'm a daughter of the Holocaust too. My father would read us the Black Book of the atrocities against the European Jews during the Holocaust and would weep. He would rub his hands and say, "Do something." I was very young, what could I do? I don't know if I was even ten years old. What can you do? I knew I had to do something. I wrote a lot of things dealing with a kind of ethnic past. I wrote a story called "The Woman Who Lived for Ten," about putting the dead on your back, and I had children because I wanted to replace the dead, and I'm always aware of that. So in some strange psychic way I was tatooed like the prisoners in the camps.

Marrying an artist gave me wings. Studying with Edward Albee taught me how to leave the nest and use the wings. Albee said, "You are larger than your family. You are the one who is alive and who is fact. They are all fiction." I was still nursing one of the kids: it was a great thing to be told that, and to be told that I was going to be a good writer. He said that several times to me. I think he was kinder than I deserved, because what I was doing then was very slight. The great, generous nature of that man: I owe him forever.

JODY: Do you feel a kinship with any particular writers?

ESTHER: Certainly Kingston. *Woman Warrior* came out after my book was at the printer's and I had dedicated it to women warriors. I thought: Isn't it interesting how that happened?

JODY: There is an obvious kinship between your works.

ESTHER: I would be honored if that were so: I do feel it, for my part. Anyone who writes mythically I feel intensely connected to. That personal epic of that glorious book—I think they called it autobiography, they didn't know how to call it a novel; nobody knew quite what to do with it—will teach us all how to live, how to write. I love Hawaii's declaring her "a national treasure." And *China Men* is so full of compassion. She's instructive, I teach her whenever I can, as I do Margaret Atwood. But Kingston, more than anyone, lives beyond the ordinary, in the surreal, in the mythic, in the epic.

JODY: Do you consider yourself a utopian writer?

ESTHER: People teach *Weave* as a utopian book and I've seen it listed as utopian literature. I feel that the world as it is is not sufficient. There is a sort of spirituality with which my religious characters speak of the world to come, but my women had to make the beginnings of the world to come in themselves. I think we have to return to the idea of the past matriarchy too. If people are to be made larger than they are, more powerful than they are, you have to give them control over their land and their law, and their mythic and gender context. I am both out of the tradition and a maker of tradition. Maybe we are the rediscoverers and the revisionists of a tradition, but we're also doing an enormous amount of new work.

For survival, we must become active again, aside from marching on the Pentagon, as Grace Paley does, or joining ecological groups, or putting our bodies up against the fences of the nuclear plants. I am writing factual fiction, instructive fiction that will show women today how other women, from narrow pasts, from insignificant places became part of the epic battle. My woman hero is a hero for us to follow.

We have a long, bloody history of being there, of marching and of being in the forefront. Certainly nobody will forget the Lawrence strike, run by women, though the IWW came in and showed them how to do things. Nobody will forget those pregnant women who decided if they went out the police wouldn't hurt them because they were pregnant. So they headed the march and the police beat them and they lost their pregnancies.

JODY: Is women's morality different from men's as manifested in social custom and culture? I am thinking, for example, of Vered's brother in *Weave* and of how the women heal him, resurrect him. No man would have thought of that—or done it, or written about it. This led me to wonder whether perhaps there is a profound difference in our morality.

ESTHER: There is a difference between women's and men's morality. I've collaborated four or five times for long periods of time with women. I've collaborated twice with men, and our working patterns were different, our morality was different. I had to be a very different kind of person. When I work with women friends, each time we sit down we say, "How are we going to work it out? How are we going to work out the day?" And then, in the course of that we solve a little bit, we say our lives. Women say their lives and then they do their work. Men don't say their lives: I think that's why their books are so relentlessly and uninterestingly autobiographical. They don't know how to talk to each other. Women hear each other's lives. I don't want to totally romanticize women, but it is easy to do so. We think of the continuity of our lives and what we will always be connected to. It seems to me men think of the discontinuity in their lives. After all, they separate from their mothers right away, don't they? We have to separate from our mothers for health, but we also have to connect to another kind of mother for strength.

Meridel Le Sueur says that the narrative style has always been a male style: one man tells his stories and the rest of us listen. I thought it radical that I interrupted a tale, as in *Her Mothers*, or had multiple women's voices, multiple narrators, as in *Weave*. Now with *The Plant* I interrupt the chronology, the narration, to remind the reader in inset, in aside, that this character is but a continuation of the actions of earlier women activists. I will suddenly bring in the Lawrence strike and Gurley Flunn's writing about it while I'm in the midst of writing about a strike thirty years later that my heroine participates in. I'll bring in the daily press to show political bias of that time. I dare to interrupt and interweave—and that's political. There is no chief storyteller of women's history: we made history together.

JODY: What do you get out of being a writer?

ESTHER: A persona. In some ways that's the real self, sometimes the daily self is unreal. I feel I can fly out of the house that way, I can leave countries. That's the ego part of it. The other part is that I can right parts of the world that are untidy. I can make packages, I can understand, I can connect things that seem disconnected, and I can howl in pain in a way that is acceptable. I cannot do that in the real world.

Meridel Le Sueur

It was Esther Broner who introduced me to Meridel Le Sueur. Both Esther and Meridel had been chosen for the Wonder Woman award, a short-lived but wondrously whimsical honor for women who had achieved in their respective fields. Esther is a wizard of description, and she so inspired me with her description of Meridel that I bought le Sueur's *The Girl* and read it at a single sitting.

Meridel le Sueur lives in Minnesota; however, one of her daughters lives in Northern California and I was able to arrange to meet her there. I recall in detail our time together because Meridel's was one of the most difficult interviews I have done.

I arrived to find her outside her daughter's place, wrapped up in a blanket against the cold and sitting in a wooden chair. Next to her was a table on a swivel base, and attached to the swivel base by a long metal chain was a very large, ferocious-looking dog of the Alaskan husky variety who barked frenziedly as I approached. The fact that I normally get along very well with animals didn't seem to impress him.

The first thing Meridel said, casually, was not to worry about the dog, who continued to bark, wrapping his chain around the bottom of the table on which I had placed my tape recorder and tilting the whole thing at a crazy angle, all the while looking at me with blood in his eyes. The second thing she said was, "I don't like interviews. They're patriarchal." I thought, "Oh my God, I've driven seven hours and she's not going to do the interview"! So I asked, "What about questions?" "I don't like them either," she replied. We agreed to just talk, but of course, questions were unavoidable and I ended up getting the interview.

I have enormous respect for Meridel le Sueur. When I interviewed her she was already in her eighties, but she was as young and pure in her radical views as she must have been at twenty-one. She has a vision, and she has integrity, and she has grit. She has seen and lived through things that some of us can only imagine in our worst nightmares, some of which she describes in the interview. And she keeps fighting—not for her, but for the rest of us.

Later that year Meridel came to my home town and did a reading at the local library. I went to hear her, and she was inspiring. There were many young people who came to see her, to talk to her, to be with her—not the way it usually is with a celebrity, but like it is when you're with your grandmother, or some special teacher who changed your life. There was that complicity, that intimacy, that love and connection between them, and it was deeply moving.

I hope it comes through in the interview what a tiger she is and what it was like to be sitting there in the cold with this huge dog growling menacingly, every once in a while tipping over the table, and twisting his chain around my chair, to Meridel's complete indifference. Usually when I do an interview I'm coming from somewhere fairly far away and people will offer me a glass of water or something to eat. Meridel offered me nothing to eat or drink: not a glass of water, not a cookie. At the end of the interview she repeated, "I don't like interviews." But she gave me a terrific one, and she offered me her true self.

One Orange for Christmas

An Interview with Meridel Le Sueur
Graton, California
March 1984

JODY: Was it hard writing and bringing up children?

MERIDEL: We lived in terrible places; we never had a house. They had to live like I did, go where I did, participate. They were in radical parades when they were in baby buggies. I was pushing them down Nicollet Avenue protesting the food budget of the WPA. I had them to live like I did. That's a bourgeois thing: that you have to have something special for your children, or that you're guilty if you go to work.

JODY: Yet kids need to be fed, kids take time.

MERIDEL: It's a pleasure, if you don't feel guilt. I thought having children was fun, and I had to earn a living. I didn't ever think it was so terrible.

JODY: I have a son and I agree. But it takes time, it takes a large part of me.

MERIDEL: But that's the fun of it. You have somebody to give it to. You have a friend living with you. I never thought it was onerous. Radicals today—they get so tired, they get burned out if things don't succeed like they think they should. I get very disturbed at them; I don't think they're going to last till the revolution! My father was a radical attorney and if he didn't go to court every day to fight the enemy he thought the day was wasted. And he never lost a battle, because if you were fighting, you won.

Occasionally he really did win—his radical clients didn't go to jail, or they got thirty years instead of sixty. Even when he was dying (he was eighty-three before he died, during the McCarthy period, with the Smith Act) he was saying, "I don't want to die. Who's going to defend all these people? I want to be there for the fight."

I never had any place to leave my children; I had to work in one room with the diapers hanging. I never thought it was terrible; I didn't have any choice. It seems to me my children have good memories of our poor times. I heard my daughter say a few years ago to a group, "My mother never liked toilet paper." I interrupted and said, "What do you mean, I love toilet paper!" Because for ten cents you could buy a roll of toilet paper, but you could also buy a chop. Besides, Sears Roebuck made their catalogues out of paper for outhouses. They had more delicate paper than they do now. Sears Roebuck was in all the outhouses—free toilet paper, with pictures even! But she seemed to remember that with joy. Then there is the anxiety that children will be successes: if you have a child of your own, you know, you're going to put him in the bourgeois world where he'll be a success, or he's supposed to be. I think it stinks to be a success in the bourgeois world. I don't think anything about saying to a person, "Don't go in that world, you'll die." And they do. It used to be you could get up a little bit, but now you just fall down and lose your happiness or lose your intentions.

It's so terrible to win, I don't have any backwardness in telling anybody, "Don't go in that world." "How not to be a success," I tell people. "That's the worst thing that will happen to you."

Look at all these writers, like Saul Bellow, who paid everything to get the Nobel Prize. They'll write anything to get into that brothel, the Nobel Prize. I loved Saul Bellow. He came from the Chicago ghetto, he could have been a Balzac or a Zola. His first three books are beautiful, human books. Then he began to calculate how to get into the brothel, be successful—he *says* that. So he did, and look at him. He has the most terrible face—even a Chicago prostitute doesn't have a face like that—and he writes the most terrible things, about death and deathly people.

I know a woman who's lived with two great writers. Forty years ago Bellow slept with her, told her she was going to be a great writer. She still lives in that moment. Well, she just did a great thing: she graduated from college. I didn't think she'd ever do it. I said to her when she started, "You'll be sleeping with one of the professors, you'll get so depressed, and he'll tell you you're wonderful…. She didn't. Now her children are raised. It was hard to go back—she'd been on dope and led a kind of loose life. She got all A's, which meant she really studied. I gave her a real kudo. No more Saul Bellows. Imagine living on that for forty years: there's a whole generation of women like that.

What about women getting over their inferiority? I've been waiting for a woman to come and bring me a manuscript and say, "This is wonderful!" Never. They always creep up and say, "Well, I don't think I should give you this, it's no good anyway."

JODY: Is it a sense of inferiority or are they intimidated?

MERIDEL: It isn't me, it's a whole attitude toward their creative life. They don't think they're any good. You know that.

JODY: Yes, a lot of women feel that way.

MERIDEL: *I* feel that way. I never sit down to write that I don't have to say I'm good, that I'm as good as so-and-so, or as good as a man. Even now, it's so deep, it's a terrible thing.

Look at Miss McClintock* who got the Nobel Prize:

*In 1983, Barbara McClintock, then eighty-one, received the Nobel Prize in physiology and medicine for her work on mobile genes in maize. When she had first published her work, thirty years earlier, no one believed her data. Today the cytological technique that she used to identify the maize chromosomes is used routinely.

no one ever listened to her, ever. Most women give up: she just kept on in her laboratory with corn. How many women are buried beside her? Men say they didn't pay any attention to her; it put genetics back ten years. It was the same with DNA, only they killed that woman*. Watson and Crick said in their book that they killed her psychically: they seemed to be bragging about it.

She told them about DNA, that everything that went up came down, which almost any woman could have told them. No, it's going to take a long time to make women feel they can do it.

Young women still attach themselves to poets. Robert Bly has his following of young women who do anything. He has a big meeting in Santa Barbara in July about mothers and sons, and he has one about the matriarchs. I told him when he started to menstruate I'd join his cult. But he still has a following, and older women now follow him also. No, women think they will be relieved of their own creative needs if they serve a man who is creative.

JODY: You say you have those feelings, too, but what about *The Girl*? With her strength of character, wasn't she like a beacon?

MERIDEL: All because of the other women. Only because of the other women. The whole ending is the strength of the communal.

JODY: I see that she is always linked to other women, but like geese flying in formation. She's linked to a phalanx of women, but she seems to be the lead.

MERIDEL: That's a bourgeois concept, even with geese. The wedge is formed communally—there are no leaders.

JODY: Did you intend to draw each of the women in *The*

*In 1952, Rosalind Franklin used x-ray crystallography to show that DNA B-form was packed in a double helix. Her work wasn't taken seriously until James Watson's and Francis Crick's chemical data in 1953 confirmed her data. She died in 1958 at the age of thirty-seven.

Girl as profoundly as you drew her? With Clara and Belle, one has a sense only of presence.

MERIDEL: Individuals are individuals because they are communal. In our society you have individuals who are competitive: they are the great aggressive individuals. Communal structures have leaders, but they are communal leaders. You can't say of a rosebush, "What rose is leading them out?"

There are no leaders in Indian society: we had to make chiefs in order to have them sign something. This is true even today in Indian cultures, economically so battered down. You can't control a communal structure: you have to get the vote of everyone to give away the land. That's why we made the chiefs and got them drunk and pretended they could sign the treaties. But Indians don't have chiefs: it's a very important thing for us to realize. We can't think without a leader or come to conclusions without a leader. Actually, that's the most inferior kind of conclusion to come to. I wanted to show that. I think it's true of women's organizations (even radical women's organizations). Church women I saw were collective against their oppressor, which was the male.

JODY: The history of the Indians in North Star Country is shocking. How did you find all that out?

MERIDEL: At that time you couldn't find out the history. The Indians themselves didn't know it, or didn't speak it. I had to do terrific research in books and also with people. I would have given a lot to be able to rewrite it: there are phrases and things I say I'd give anything to be able to take out, but you can't do it without its costing thousands of dollars. Yet it was considered very radical at the time, and the Indians like it. It does show how we've changed.

JODY: Is it true you are part Indian?

MERIDEL: I think we're all part Indian. My great-grandmother was an Indian, an Iroquois, who unfortunately married a white WASP Protestant who took her to Illinois. They hated her. They never accepted her. Even her daughter never admitted her mother was an Indian. She got very bitter. Sinclair Lewis has a wonderful line: "Every American bears the face of Tecumseh." I think he means that you bear the face of those whom you destroy. You bear the face of those you conquer. The American bears a terrible guilt towards the Indian. We've developed a great guilt over the slavery traffic, and the seizure of Indian lands, which were the basis of American capitalism, the basis of the accumulation of wealth: billions and billions of dollars. People don't know anything about our history because a conqueror can never tell the true history.

JODY: Do you think women's history books are different?

MERIDEL: Well, there *was* no women's history at all. There was no Indian history, no black history, no Chicana history fifteen years ago. When I went to the Minnesota Historical Society, there was no history of women, nothing. Now we have a Women's Tape Library and women's books. So if there was history then, it was something they were writing about men. I found that out with my grandmother when I was ten years old. She hated my writing. She said, "I spent all my life concealing the terrible history of what happened to me and the terrible history of women. Now you are going to tell it!" And I was!

She wouldn't tell you anything, and what happened to her was terrible. She was married into rape, she had five children, she hated their beginning and she hated their birth. She was a brilliant woman, graduated from a Christian university in Illinois. She was also a religious woman. She used to go around Oklahoma in a horse and buggy with a shotgun.

The Women's Christian Temperance Movement had a tremendous organization. They used to have parades, with big hayracks decorated with virginal white, and all those young girls shouting "Tremble, King Alcohol! We shall grow up, and lips that touch liquor shall never touch mine!" We wore little white ribbons. It was a tremendous organization, it was going to save the world. All those frontier towns were terrible towns of violence, violence against women.

JODY: Were you close to your mother and grandmother?

MERIDEL: As close as you could get to a Puritan. My grandmother never kissed anybody over three years old. She wore a corset that went from her sternum to her knees, with steel in it, and I used to put my foot on her back and pull those strings tight. She wore that her entire life. She wore a shift to bathe with. She never saw her body. *Never saw it.* I lived with her during my adolescence, and she didn't know anything about menstruation, she just knew you did it and that you were in danger.

And then, she hated sex. All those men, after they made a success, married the leading virgin of the town—you had to be a virgin—and then they just attacked you. So she hated sex. She didn't know how she got children or how she gave birth. She really didn't know. She said it was so disgusting. She was devoted, she raised her children, fed them.

The interesting thing is that my grandmother raised her children, my mother raised her children, and I raised my children, which says something about the economic base of women. The economic basis for the paternal control of the family ceased in 1900 or before. There's no longer the moneymaker, or the patriarch, or the average father. That's why men drank a lot. Somebody criticized my film, said, "All the men are drunk in your film." I said, "I didn't make it up; they were."

JODY: Tell me about your film.

MERIDEL: About five years ago a group of women in Minneapolis made a film from my notebooks. It's called "My People Are My Home." You can get it from Neala Schleuning, Women's Studies, University of Minnesota, Mankato, Minnesota.

Some libraries have it as well.

JODY: Do a lot of people respond favorably to *The Girl*?

MERIDEL: Yes. It seems to empower women with their own collective relationships. Women have a hard time being together because everything has made them competitive with each other. I just discovered one of the reasons why that is. After the Civil War, which was the bloodiest war we had been in up to that time, two-thirds of Americans were widows. Every household had an old maid. They were the butt of jokes, they did the work and lived with the family all their lives. I never realized that just as the Soviet Union had no men after the war, there were thousands, millions of women who never married.

JODY: Usually one sees women in relationship to men, to other women or to the working world: you rarely see a woman caught up in all the different levels of human fabric the way it happens in *The Girl*.

MERIDEL: Also with the men. There are a lot of feminists who think the men are too sympathetic. I don't make them villains, because they're not. They're destroyed by their own illusions.

JODY: They seemed more real for that reason.

MERIDEL: I think it's important also that women find their own strength, not from the oppressor. I mean, you're not beautiful if a man's not telling you you are? All that Cinderella stuff is still extant. They can't see that they have the power in themselves.

JODY: *The Girl* had that power.

MERIDEL: She got it from the other women. There was that power that didn't depend upon the man. They could even live with the economic pressure together.

JODY: Yes, that was very dramatic in the book.

MERIDEL: Well, I saw that during the Depression. A lot of *The Girl* is made up of the actual speech of women, the actual notes of women. One whole section about her going home at the death of her father is actually a manuscript written by a woman about her father. The people who experience have the real literary words.

JODY: Also, when she said she hated her father, and the way the family began to laugh, it felt real.

MERIDEL: I couldn't have made that up. During the Depression, there was no place for women, there was no way to feed women, there was nothing up until later, with the New Deal. Thousands of women came into Minneapolis. There was also a drought, and there wasn't any food. Literally thousands of farm women and small-town women came into Minneapolis. There were breadlines for the men, but you never saw a woman on the breadline.

JODY: Why was that?

MERIDEL: Well, they were all men, and they would hoot at you. Here's a bunch of men for two blocks; if a woman joins them, or even a bunch of women, it would be a very exposed place for jokes and hoots and propositions and sexual approaches. Women just didn't go on them; even I didn't. They used to gather in the bus stations to keep warm or sit down. They'd be picked up and taken to women's prison and sterilized within twenty-four hours.

We have very good laws in Minnesota now: you can demand a lawyer, you can demand an intelligence test. But those girls didn't know that. My father was a lawyer; we actually went with them so they wouldn't be sterilized. I took the intelligence test: you couldn't pass the intelligence test, it was a class test. You might not know who was president, yet be of superior intelligence: that wouldn't show you couldn't birth a baby, or cook meals.

There were about thirty women: we all got together and went into this empty warehouse with about ten floors. We went to the top floor—you know, it gets cold in Minnesota—and everybody would go out and scavenge for old wood. Well, we took down part of the building and we built a fire in the middle of the floor. And when the fire burned through the middle of the floor, we went down to the next floor. So we moved down. It lasted all winter, till we got to the ground floor. We would scavenge for food in garbage cans. There was nothing to feed you, that only came in 1933 with the New Deal. There was no food, no relief, nothing of any kind. Later came surplus foods; you could get white flour and powdered eggs (if you had any place to cook 'em) and so we'd scavenge whatever we could get.

And then, in the evening, when it was cold and we were miserable and hungry, we'd start telling each other's lives. Some of the farm girls couldn't write very well, so we'd take down their lives. I still have manuscripts from them. I tried to find out where those women went, but there was actually only myself and one other woman who were still alive and not in an asylum.

JODY: An insane asylum?

MERIDEL: Yes. During the Depression that was the only place they had to put women. The city couldn't feed them and the state could, so thousands of women were put into the asylums. Some of them never got out. To get out, until recently, you had to have someone who would take care of you for six months, someone to sponsor you and so on. And their children were taken away from them. I used to go to the asylums years after to see the women who were still there. They'd ask me, where were their children? They never saw them again. How many of them were sterilized and never had protection?

A professor from California, Pompano, I never forgot his name, wrote a book about the solution to unemployment being sterilization. He said it would be nice if you could freeze workers when you came to a period where there were too many workers, and then unfreeze them when you needed them. But since you couldn't do that, the only solution was sterilization. That's coming back now. Half the Indian women of South Dakota have been sterilized, without their knowing it, many of them; and that's only the ones who have been counted. Puerto Ricans are also being sterilized. They've formed an organization now called Women of All Red Nations, a national organization against sterilization of Indians.

JODY: Who is sterilizing them?

MERIDEL: The state. You should get into the Bureau of Indian Affairs' hospitals; that's the only hospitals there are. If you go in there for anything—to have a baby, or a cold—they'll sterilize you. Technically you have to sign something, but some of the women don't speak English, or don't understand. That's genocide. That's what they're doing in El Salvador, too: just doing away with the people. They don't want colonial people, they just want to seize the raw materials. I don't know what they expect to exploit: who's going to do the work?

One of the most amazing things in America is the churches now, not the liberal churches but the Baptist church, taking in refugees from El Salvador. The basements and attics of these churches are full, and that's a criminal offense. There's about thirty to forty thousand white people, reactionary people involved: they just go down to the border and get them.

This is going to change America. Just imagine, Mayans are entering America! Last week, the FBI moved against them for the first time. They arrested a group coming up from the border in Texas and challenged them. But they don't want to get mixed up in these churches, and if they send people back, they send them to certain death. They have to be taken care of like babies, fed and so forth. They are gradually eased into society. Somebody helps them get a job, become citizens. That means taking responsibility. They're bringing up a lot of women and children whose men have been killed. Minneapolis is just full of them. You can understand that the Unitarian church in Los Angeles is full of them; they've always done that. But the Baptist church? And the racist churches? They just can't stomach this brutality. It's a strange world. I just hope I live ten years to see what's going to happen.

JODY: What do you think *is* going to happen?

MERIDEL: What's happening now. We're going to have a free South America to become democracies. It's not in the future; it's right now.

JODY: Will things be better in ten years?

MERIDEL: Things are better right now. It isn't ten years; it's the progress of radical history, of colonial struggles, and it's here now. It's going to be in America. Communication is most revolutionary; it causes identification with others and the raising of consciousness.

JODY: It's a very dramatic time to be alive.

MERIDEL: Most hopeful. A new world, a global world. You never used to be able to say "a global world."

Right here in this valley, Santa Rosa is a little middle-class town which has no industry to speak of. They have a wonderful "Freeze" movement, a Jesse Jackson movement (there are probably five black people in Santa Rosa); they have a Nicaraguan movement, and they're mixed up in the Diablo Canyon movement.

There's a plot to make all this valley a bedroom for San Francisco and destroy this town, cut down the apple orchards and make one tremendous industrial condominium. I don't know if they'll succeed. Not only the poor people, but an aristocratic and middle-class group don't want their lands destroyed. Since I've been here they've kept Rohnert Park, which is next to Sonoma, from becoming industrial. Actually, the university kept it from happening. As I say, there is an uprising of thought in the whole world.

JODY: In Southern California, there is the additional problem of the military-industrial complex.

MERIDEL: I was in San Diego: I never realized what military was. And of course all that industry is war industry. When I lived in Los Angeles it was urban, white middle class. Now the majority of people are not white: that gives me a thrill.

I was there getting a bus a year ago last Christmas and the people who brought me looked into the bus station and told me not to go in. "It's a dangerous place," they said. There was not one white person in the bus station, not one Puritan!

I never got the bus, that night. I just sat amongst these dark people and their families. They've taken out the seats from the bus station now, you can't sit anymore, they don't want people to come in to get warm. I was sitting on the steps. I couldn't stand up anymore and I was afraid to sit on the floor, I was afraid I wouldn't get up. They have cops, they must be six or seven feet tall and armed with I don't what all hanging on them, billy clubs and two kinds of guns. They came up and took ahold of me and said, "You can't sit here." All of a sudden, here were about seven or eight Chicano and Indian young men standing around me who said, "Don't touch her! Let her sit there! She's our grandmother." I didn't know them, you know. And the cops said, "Well, don't sit here too long." I think if they had arrested me, there would have been a riot.

It's wonderful that the majority of people in Los Angeles are dark people. Just the little bit I was driven around, you could see dark people living in the old bourgeois stucco houses. I don't think any radicals ever prophesied that America would be taken over by Asians, by people we have oppressed. Poor old Orwell, he never prophesied half of what was really going to happen.

JODY: In your travels do you visit college campuses?

MERIDEL: I don't solicit them, I just go when I'm asked. I've got to stop that: I've got four books to finish.

JODY: What are you working on now?

MERIDEL: Four books, four symphonies. I call them my letter to the world, I call them "getting in my crop before frost." It's my life's crop I've planted, now I have to harvest it. They're all written, they just need to be harvested. As I say, I'm sort of like a preacher: you know, preachers are always called.

JODY: It's important that you do go, that you be heard.

MERIDEL: Well, sometimes I think it is. When I see young women that you nourish or change I feel that very much.

JODY: Isn't there a need for women to be role models for other women?

MERIDEL: I don't believe that. That's a male patriarchal concept.

JODY: What about your mother and your grandmother, were they role models for you?

MERIDEL: I didn't model myself after them. I have this all the time with the women's movement, especially *Ms.* magazine. The whole idea is you interview women, you interview the successful role model. I consider this male, you know: who wins the football game. I don't think it's part of women's culture.

JODY: I mean that women draw strength from one another and from one another's lives.

MERIDEL: That's true. But you said "a model."

JODY: In *The Girl* her women friends were her models, weren't they?

MERIDEL: No, it was reciprocal, it has to be reciprocal. When I talk to women's studies groups I feel they give back to me as much as I give, and maybe even more. But a model means success. I almost withdrew my interview with *Ms.* I would have done it, but the woman who wrote it needed the money. I don't know what the interview is, as I said to you before, how one woman should interview another to bring out that strength, but not just bring out, "This is a woman who made it. This is a woman who overcame all the opposition. Take after her." I don't agree with that, but I don't know what the alternative is.

JODY: Is that the problem, or is it the definition of success?

MERIDEL: Success only means one thing in bourgeois terminology. I don't consider myself a success. That means you won, that you "made it."

JODY: Well, I consider myself a success: I've got a kid I like, I put bread on the table. I think I'm a real success.

MERIDEL: But you have to make another category because there's such a thing in the bourgeois world, it has a reality.

JODY: So you're saying that *Ms.* uses the bourgeois standard or definition of success?

MERIDEL: Yes. And I think that attitude toward Mother Earth is ridiculous. Do you smoke cigarettes?

JODY: No, do you?

MERIDEL: Yes, I do. I have to have some vices. Smoking and coffee are my only vices. I shouldn't do either one, I mean just physically. One cup of coffee in the morning. I have to have three years without sclerosis setting in, or any of those things that set in when you get older.

JODY: They say healthy eating can make you last a long time.

MERIDEL: Well, I've done that my whole life. My mother was a vegetarian. The Middle West was ruined by hog meat and potatoes and gravy. She helped change that. She lost her first baby because he couldn't eat. He died at about a year old, so she studied food. She got goat's milk, she tried every kind of thing, she studied and experimented. He might have had something organic, I don't know, he really just starved to death. So she studied that up.

I was born after that. I'm sure she had all kinds of theories. Nobody knew about calcium then: I never realized it until I went to Ireland, where it seemed like two-thirds of the children had bow legs from lack of calcium. You hardly ever see a bowlegged child now. Well, my mother was propagandizing for calcium for bow legs. I remember in school we accepted it as a norm that you were bowlegged, and had no idea why. I think we had pellagra too, because by January all the fruit was gone. You never had any fruit; no fruit was ever shipped in. I never saw an orange: one orange for Christmas. All your vegetables you put up yourself were gone by January. We had terrible sore throats and fevers in the spring. I think it was pellagra.

JODY: Did your mother use herbs or regular allopathic medicines?

MERIDEL: Herbs and vegetables, and you went out and got dandelion greens. Vitamins, too, she believed in, and they were very expensive, but none of that pork. Pork, potatoes and gravy was my grandmother's idea and, if you could afford it, a can of peas. Of course, we put up things in the fall, but that didn't last very long. Eating in America has really changed, you can get a vegetable diet almost anywhere. It's amazing how everything in America can change because of communication, like "Where's the beef?" can become national advertising. If you started to say the right things over radio, what could happen?

JODY: May I take your picture?

MERIDEL: Take it without my glasses, I hate my glasses. If you have any other questions, you can always write me.

JODY: I'm sure there will always be more questions to ask you.

MERIDEL: Well, I have a feminine point about questions, too.

JODY: I know that.

MERIDEL: You do?

JODY: Sure: you warned me before we began. You said that questions were patriarchal.

MERIDEL: Questions and answers (laughter).

Phoebe Helman

Phoebe Helman and her husband, artist Jack Sonenberg, lived in New York and spent their summers in Deer Isle, Maine, which is where I met her many years ago. Initially Phoebe intimidated me. In those days she was usually obscured behind a protective cloud of cigarette smoke, from which she would emerge to speak with passion and eloquence about social or intellectual issues of unbelievable complexity.

Over the years I became good friends with this intense and intellectual woman. She had a rare combination of drive and passion and the ability to articulate her vision with a clarity few possess. I remember one summer, before they finally bought their own house, Jack and Phoebe rented a cottage down by the water. At that time Phoebe was making abstract forms out of clear lucite and white polystyrene, sails bending before the wind encased in large, lucite boxes. When I went to visit I was very taken by the sight of these pieces on the table in their living room. Phoebe had captured the curve and bend, the strain and motion of filled sails. All the grace and power of boats running before the wind were in that box: just looking at them lifted your heart and carried you right outside to the shore.

Phoebe died this past summer on July 3, 1994. Several days after the funeral Jack told me a wonderful story about Phoebe as a young woman. When they were both in art school in New York they used to go and draw at the ballet and the opera. Then, one day, they decided to go over to the Barnum and Bailey Circus. After a few weeks of drawing there, the man in charge asked Phoebe if she wanted to be an elephant girl and travel around with the circus. Phoebe was very excited about this until Jack pointed out to her that the women riding the elephants all had scaly thighs from gripping the elephants' sides! I particularly liked the story because one of the things Phoebe, Jack and I did together in Maine was go to the circus, an event which seemed to give her immense pleasure, and which I now understood at a deeper level.

A conversation with Phoebe was a special kind of gift. This interview reveals her keen intelligence, her intense nature and self-deprecating humor, all of which transformed a simple communication into an occasion. For me it is the portrait of a woman who kept the flame alive, no matter what. Both Phoebe and Jack taught at the Pratt Institute of Art. Phoebe and Jack's daughter Maya is a writer, which doesn't seem surprising.

Please, I Was
with Billie Holiday

An Interview with Phoebe Helman
Deer Isle, Maine
July 1984

JODY: What was your childhood like? Did your parents
encourage your art?

PHOEBE: I grew up in the co-ops with a mother who was
a Communist party organizer. It was the first worker-
cooperative in New York City. My mother was organizing
for the Amalgamated Clothing Workers' Union. My
father was a laundry man. My mother came to the United
States in 1905, completely disillusioned with the failure
of the Russian Revolution. My father came later, to avoid
being drafted into the Lithuanian army. Both were very
supportive. I was an only child, but most of us in the co-
ops were only children (which was unusual at the time)
because our parents had a lot of other things to do. It was
a place I didn't like: there was just too much community,
too much fitting in. When my mother saw that I was
interested in art she set up an art class so that not only I,
but other little kids who were interested could study art.
My father took me to a lot of museums. He felt I should
know the city, so on Sundays he would take me to different parts of New York, and part of that was going to
Peggy Guggenheim's and to the Modern when it first
opened. He was very interested in art; actually he had
wanted to be a sculptor, but had to go to work.

JODY: Did you know you would be an artist early on?

PHOEBE: I knew it, yes. When I was five I knew that's what I was going to do. Later on I became interested in set design and worked with sets in the Catskills when I was thirteen. I was seriously interested in it, but there was no way I could get into the union, because set designers were all men. The business of building sets finally came into the work when I became a sculptor.

JODY: Did you begin as a painter or a sculptor?

PHOEBE: I began as a figurative painter. I studied with Raphael Soyer when I was fourteen. Raphael never taught anything. He'd pat you on the back and say, "You're doing very well" which was very nice, except that when I finally went to the Met one day and looked at Degas and said, "Hey, wait a minute, those aren't dancing girls, they're something else," I began to realize what art was about, that it wasn't making pictures, it was something else. I was a kid, I didn't know what the something else was, but I said, "It's not what you're doing. It's something else." It was a vision, an understanding of the world. I knew those dancing girls weren't dancing girls.

JODY: Were there other artists who had a profound effect upon you as a young artist?

PHOEBE: Cezanne was a very strong influence. I came to Skowhegan when I was sixteen and the landscape there was for me a lot like Cezanne. I loved Cezanne, I was trying to expand Cezanne, I was painting *through* Cezanne. To get to know what painting was about with Cezanne was certainly one influence. Picasso was important for trying to understand. Franz Kline was an artist I felt very drawn to. Some of Tony Smith's sculptures—*Cigarette* is a masterpiece, I think. Reuben Nakian's *Rape of Lucretia*. I don't think I would talk about artists, but rather work that I responded to and remember—for example, a couple of pieces of Richard Serra's that just knocked me out. We tend to be more impressed when we're very young: we learn to write, we learn to paint. It's like a little child who learns to talk, who tries to mimic the sounds he hears: it's the same thing. As we get older we slowly begin establishing a vocabulary, hopefully personalized and meaningful, and we respond to the work, but the influences become less because we become more.

JODY: What was it about Cezanne that fascinated you?

PHOEBE: I couldn't understand what those paintings were about, that's what got me. I had to find out. The thing about Cezanne and the South of France was that I could never find out where he stood. With Van Gogh, if I went to Arles or to Saint Remy, I could put my feet exactly where he stood and painted a picture. With Cezanne I could never put my feet where he stood. Yes, there was a silhouette of Mont Saint Victoire, it was unmistakable; but if you begin walking, there's no way to say, "This is where he stood." We take a lot out of the art of the past that we need for the present. My involvement with Cezanne when I was very young was really a spatial and formal one. He wasn't painting landscapes, so what was he painting? Landscape was a vehicle: of course he was painting landscapes, but what was he *really* painting? I thought once I could find out I could understand. Then when I saw the big Cezanne show and the late Cezannes at the Modern, my feeling was he was painting himself, he was painting his own despair. That's what these paintings are all about, Cezanne painting his own despair.

JODY: In what ways are your own sculptures and paintings autobiographical statements?

PHOEBE: Well, they're all about me: they're all about anger, about aggressiveness…whatever I am.

JODY: We are following on Cezanne's despair here?

PHOEBE: One hides behind an abstract vocabulary, one hides behind realist vocabulary too. It's important for the artist to be able to touch on himself or herself. That's a lot of what the work is about, if the artist can do that. We don't do it all the time, but it's a courageous thing to try to do. Then the work has meaning. When I talk about meaning in the work, that's what I'm talking about, finally; regardless of the style, work is autobiographical and the artist *can* touch on himself or herself; otherwise it simply becomes a thing or a picture.

JODY: When you work, either in painting or sculpture, do you work for a dominant feeling or for a dominant image?

PHOEBE: The image has to carry the feeling, and the feeling reinforces the image. When I think up something and I want it to surge, that's feeling, and I have to find the forms to express it. I've been working on a series of pieces that relate visually to my experiences in Rome of piazzas and arches. Then, yes, I'm thinking of the forms, but the forms by themselves aren't enough. Into these forms has got to be embodied the emotional content of the work.

JODY: I'm assuming that you are driven by something to do this work. Is it an idea? Is it an image that expresses itself inside you and you must work with the image? Is it a feeling?

PHOEBE: I don't know how I can unlock them because one is always tearing at the other. I don't know how one deals with feelings without image. Now someone like Artaud tried to deal with theater without words.

JODY: Yes, but even with Artaud there was the idea of terror which he wanted to express.

PHOEBE: I think the primary drive is to work.

JODY: Where does that come from?

PHOEBE: It comes out of a need to stay sane. I find that the kind of exercise my mind gets in the process of working is very important, much more important than going swimming. A cousin of mine, a psychiatrist, whom I'm very close to, is intrigued by art and artists. He did an article for the *Print Collector's Newsletter* in which he talked about why people become artists. He said that artists are people who can't deal with a sense of loss. That continuous drive to work in the studio is the drive to keep replacing what you've already made because once you've completed something, you've lost it. And once you show it you lose it even further, because then you're giving it away, it's not yours anymore. The continuous drive to work in the studio can be rationalized on many levels, like "I have a new idea," but the underlying need is to keep replacing what you've lost by completing it. And you have: you've lost tremendous involvement with something that has meant a great deal. It's like having continuous love affairs, and I guess that's the way you feel when a love affair is over...you know, you go hunting around for another guy. Sometimes it's very intense and you really want to sit back and be depressed and read for a while, and then you go back in again.

JODY: What about the desire to make a statement, the famous "I'm here"?

PHOEBE: That too. That's what I was talking about when I said it keeps me out of the nuthouse. There is the whole question of loss and how difficult it is to deal with. My cousin Eugene, the psychiatrist, feels that artists have particular difficulty with this and cites Keats, who was able to replace senses of loss in the rest of his life by writing poetry; but when the loss became too intense, he couldn't write. It has to be just the right balance.

JODY: Do you think his theory is valid?

PHOEBE: I think it's pretty valid, yes, because long before he wrote it, I suffered a tremendous sense of depression when I completed something. Older artists, well, we learn to discipline ourselves, but young artists will sometimes prolong a piece and then not be able to finish. I asked one of my students, "Are you afraid when you finish it that you'll lose it?"—she had a whole array of unfinished pieces—and she said, "Yes." It wasn't that she wasn't smart enough to finish them. Yes, I think it's valid.

JODY: I just finished reading Alice Walker's latest book of essays. There is one on writing *The Color Purple*. She talks as though her characters come through her; they're not her creation, but they're there and they tell her, "Look, you've got to sell your house and move to San Francisco." She actually has conversations with them. It is as if they were being born and coming through her, emerging with their own ideas and wanting to do what *they* want to do. Does that sort of thing happen to you with drawings and sculpture, i.e. do they come *through* you as opposed to being the product of your intellect?

PHOEBE: At some point a work insists on itself, but I don't feel as though it's coming through me. Maybe writers feel this more because they're dealing with people and with known language. At some point the work has a mind of its own, and I had better give up all of my ideas about it and accept that this is what it's demanding of me. But I usually think of it as setting up a dialogue, that it's got to tell me what to do and then I do it. Then I say, "No, you're all wrong" or "Maybe you're right, if this gets shifted over a little bit," so there's a continuous dialogue that starts at some point.

When I begin working on a piece of sculpture or a drawing, I'm starting with nothing. I start with a blank piece of paper or a lot of air space and I put something down. As I work, the decisions and the choices close in. They become less and less random as the thing begins identifying itself. At first I can make a mark on a piece of paper anywhere, it doesn't matter. But as the thing moves along in time toward becoming, finally I'm down to "I'ts got to be the absolute right choice; otherwise, I'm going to blow it." Then if I try to take anything away and it's no good, and if I try to add anything and it's no good, then I know it's complete. That's really the working process: it happens in painting, it happens in sculpture, it happens in drawing. That's the process by which I work. That's what happens with prints: I just can't print another plate, it won't be right. At first it's like a big, raucous noise, and then it gets honed down and honed down until it's something that's finely tuned.

JODY: You said earlier that drawing has always been a way of thinking for you. What about sculpture?

PHOEBE: It's all a way of thinking. Sculpture is just much slower, the gratification isn't immediate. In drawing it's immediate misery, immediate gratification. In one day I can be finished with a drawing, so it's a quick way of gratifying myself but also of throwing out ideas. The drawings are never drawings about sculpture; they exist in their own time and space. A drawing is as complete a work for me as a piece of sculpture. It's never a drawing for something else, but it's a very quick way of thinking. With sculpture or painting, or even with these flat sculptures I'm doing it's a much slower process. It's not that sculpture isn't about thinking; it's just that it's a much slower process.

JODY: I recall one critic's statement that your paintings deal with examining imaginary, contradictory planes. How does painting fit into all of this?

PHOEBE: I am trying to deal with different spaces, I don't think they are contradictory planes. A lot of the things that happen in the paintings happen in the sculpture too. I try to deal with a kind of multiple scale and multiple place so that you don't quite know where you are. Either you're being pulled in or pushed out. I guess the word fragmentation encompasses the whole thing.

JODY: You said once that where Cubist painting fragmented the image, American painting fragments the space. Does that apply to your own work?

PHOEBE: Fragmentation is a very strong element, and the different places, different spaces all deal with the fragmenting of time. You see, I think the Cubists were still interested in the picture plane, coming out of Cezanne. What's happened is that the fragmentation goes beyond, moves beyond the picture plane into the space itself. It's really hard to remember what you meant when you said something a long time ago. And then, all of these ideas we have are simply impetuses that start us working. Very often the work has nothing to do even with the impetus that starts us: it's almost an intellectual stand that I have to take in order to work. And if the work finally has anything to do with that intellectual stand, I don't know. I suppose it's the way a landscape painter might be moved by a landscape—yet what the landscape painter paints finally isn't the landscape that he or she is looking at—it becomes that magical place on the canvas.

JODY: If there is a vocabulary for your art then, is it an abstract vocabulary? What kind of language would you use to describe it?

PHOEBE: There is an abstract vocabulary which grows and changes as a result of having to let go of certain elements in order to add new elements. The work changes slowly, of course, but there's always this letting go of elements and a real sense of loss at letting something go at the same time that there is a sense of excitement at finding something new.

JODY: I remember when you were doing the lucite pieces in boxes which evoked sailboats before the wind. They were relatively small, but they had a monumental quality to them...very physical, if I can say that, but also pictorial at the same time.

PHOEBE: The paintings were on many different canvases and had a kind of referral to altarpieces. I realized when I was in Italy last summer that I found myself really responding to the altarpieces, to Ducio's *Maestra*, partially because they're sculptural pieces. My paintings are also the paintings of a sculptor because I'm interested in the physicality of things. That's sculptural, not painterly in the same way that I think of Picasso as a sculptor and Matisse as a painter. I've been working on what I call flat sculptures, and there I've become very interested in surface. I spend a lot of time building up the surface so I can get that kind of tactility.

JODY: At what point does painting become sculpture or sculpture painting?

PHOEBE: Thanks to Cubism that has been completely confused. Because a thing is on paper doesn't mean it's a drawing. That's what Cubism really did: it confused all the categories. It is whatever you call it. So if I'm calling these paper things sculpture, they're sculpture.

JODY: Do you agree with one critic's statement that your paintings are non-logical, horizontal, spatial experiences?

PHOEBE: Well, they are non-logical. I was talking to one of Esther and Bob Broner's boys up here in Deer Isle years ago. I kept talking about wanting the work to be illogical and I don't remember whether it was Jeremy or Adam said, "No, no, you don't mean illogical, you mean *non-logical*." The idea of non-logic is something that interests me, that a piece can finally make its own meaning. Yes, meaning is very, very important.

JODY: Are you saying that meaning has nothing to do with logic?

PHOEBE: It doesn't have to. It can, but it doesn't have to. By non-logical I was talking about things that don't exist in their own spaces but *make* their own spaces. Her (the critic's) statement is pretty accurate, because I was involved in the paintings and all those panels and making each space a different space. When I began painting them I hadn't painted for a long time. I'd backed away from sculpture at that point because I felt as though I had used up my own vocabulary, as though I knew it too well. It was almost as if no matter what I began building, I couldn't surprise myself anymore. I couldn't put myself in the position of saying, "Wait a minute, this is the way it should happen," which is like an awakening. So I moved to painting, and I moved to drawing.

I was doing a lot of different things in order to find a

way to go back to sculpture that would allow me an opening again, allow me a place to move. I went into the studio and stretched these canvases, which were going to be one painting, and I looked at them. I'd been talking to my students about object or surface and I sat in front of these canvases and said, "Is it an object or is it a surface?" After three weeks of going into the studio and sitting there I finally said, "You know, you can't decide this. You better start painting and find out." I discovered it was both an object *and* a surface, but it was also a sort of journey through time. Time is something that keeps moving into the work, whether it's sculpture or whether it's the prints, in the passage of time from the back page to the front page. The painting is maybe more linear in time in one's having to walk by it to see the whole thing, not being able to encapsulate it visually at one time. The large sculpture is certainly about that, having to walk around it.

JODY: How big is a big piece of sculpture and how little is a little piece?

PHOEBE: You mean in the three-dimensional sculpture?

JODY: Yes.

PHOEBE: A big piece is thirty-five feet long, fourteen feet high and twenty-two feet wide. A little piece is maybe eight feet square and three feet high.

JODY: Why do you work so big?

PHOEBE: I can't bring it down any smaller in scale because the forms won't function any smaller. Smaller for me becomes too toylike. I don't make models for sculpture: whatever it is I'm making, I plunge right in and build. For me to make a model and then begin marking it up doesn't make sense. There's only one artist I know who can do that, and that's Ronnie Bladen; he has an uncanny sense of scale. For other artists the work loses a sense of scale. I'm never really working small, I'm working the size it is. At one point I was playing with the idea of making small sculpture because I wanted the emotional experience of looking at it to say, "Ah, this is very big, but it's only three feet high." I'm not as interested in that now. Rome has gotten into the work…piazzas and spaces opening and tightening. Arches seem to be coming into the work. I don't know what they're about yet; I've only been working with these ideas for about a year.

JODY: What materials are the larger pieces made of and how much do they weigh?

PHOEBE: They weigh a lot, but actually they're very light for their size because I use a wooden inner structure that I build, and then the faces—I think of the faces almost the way an architect thinks of a curtain—are something called laminite, which is an epoxy. I can swing those four-by-eight foot sheets around myself, which I can't do with plywood. I usually say they're painted wood because then I don't have to explain what laminite is, I just say wood and that's the end of it.

JODY: How far can you take sculpture off the floor without making it into painting?

PHOEBE: The desire to make something float can be very strong in a sculptor…you know, how do you finally do the impossible? You can get that clear fishing line and hang it from the ceiling, but that's not the answer. In working with paper I can make things float. I've been working with a piece of sculpture here, and I think maybe I've gotten some of that into the sculpture as a result of an extreme jump in scale. But I won't know until the piece is finished.

JODY: How long does it normally take you to complete a piece?

PHOEBE: The big sculptures, three to four months at least. Small ones…well, I have one that is close to completion. I've been here three weeks. Whatever has to be done can be done in two days with a carpenter—putting a surface on it. And then I want to put color on it, which might help things float. So it just might have to be all summer, depending on how much trouble I run into. I'm very determined when I start something. In the physical sculpture, the things that are really three-dimensional, I usually don't make a change, I insist on building on what already exists. Partially it's laziness, because I don't want to start taking something apart after I've put all that work into putting it together, and partially it becomes the way in which the sculpture develops. The paper, because it's stapled to the wall to start with, I shift around a lot but it's always—in both paper sculpture and the three-dimensional sculpture—it's always working it until somehow or other I can get a hold of what it is I want out of it. And sometimes it's a formal idea that starts, "The thing has to move this way, not that way," but embodied in that is the meaning of the piece. I suppose I think intellectually, and it happens with the paper things, an idea "This cluster has to really be an umber," and then it begins making sense spatially, and it begins making sense emotionally.

JODY: Do you work on a sculpture and a painting at the same time, or a sculpture and a drawing?

PHOEBE: There are times when I can work on sculptures and drawings at the same time. It varies. Sometimes I get sucked into something and I become completely stubborn and don't want to do anything else. When I started the prints I was also painting, and I remember doing drawings that were very organic for a show in Spain. I thought I was becoming completely schizophrenic, the drawings became completely organic and the prints so rooted in sculptural vocabulary. So who are you? I finally said: "It doesn't matter. It just doesn't matter who I am."

JODY: What impact did going to Europe have on you as an artist?

PHOEBE: I was very comfortable in Italy, not so comfortable in France. I was in the South of France, and the first time I was there I got this feeling that all those artists were on my back, all those ghosts were sitting right on my shoulders—Cezanne, Matisse, Picasso—all of them that had worked in southern France. When I went to Paris I was much more comfortable because I've been trained in the French intellectual tradition. But I was disappointed because there wasn't that energy that I imagined existed in the 1920s. Paris felt like a very, very beautiful but middle-class, middle-aged lady. I wouldn't go to Italy because I was terrified of the Renaissance. How could I compete with that? Finally I went, and I was completely taken aback by the beauty of the country although it's not as beautiful as France, by a kind of magic Italy has for me that no other place has. That encapsulation in time in Florence was almost a little too precious, a little too much like a museum piece, whereas the layering of time that exists in Rome interests me a great deal because it interests me in my work. I had the same response to the altarpieces: I respond to the art moving from the Byzantine, from the Middle Ages into the Renaissance. I found myself drawn to the more primitive work, again because of the fragmentation of space. The command of real space doesn't matter.

JODY: And here in the United States? How does being in Maine affect your work?

PHOEBE: I took the sailing ships and made them urban, that's exactly what I did. I took them also and made them mine. When we were in Ed Hodgin's house on the water I could sit and watch them a lot and got to know each one because of the way it moved. Their movement came at a time when I had used up the wall. I didn't know what to do with the wall anymore: I had painted rectangles on the wall, I had broken the rectangles on the wall, I had brought the wall into the paintings. Plus it was something a lot of artists were thinking about…you know, what do you do with the wall? It wasn't the feeling that painting is dead: it was, "So what do you finally do with the rectangle, and what do you do with the wall?" If you break the rectangle, you have the rectangle with the wall—and then what do you do? Seeing those ships came at an important point for me in my work. When I took them back to New York, they really became urban landscapes. That's something I'm still involved with. I'm really a city artist: even when I come up here, I'm a city artist.

JODY: That mythic quality of the sailing ships—is that the part you take back to the city? What is it about the city that has that same quality, and that you put into your work?

PHOEBE: Probably energy, the energy that drives the wind. The energy that drives the boats is very similar to the energy that drives the city. One of the things I like a lot about New York is the continuous surging energy, and the fact that we put things up and we pull them down. In no place in the world do they put things up and twenty years later pull them down. What a phenomenal job it is to put up this building, pull it down, and build another building in its place—not better, not worse, just another building. Do I like these buildings? Most of them no, but it's a kind of continuous affirmation of living, not being locked into time, which is something I love when I go to Europe but is probably why I couldn't exist as an artist there.

JODY: I just saw your big piece in the museum. It's like a mythic wood: one really wants to go into that museum piece. Does that come from what we're talking about now, about entering temporary spaces, knowing they don't last?

PHOEBE: There's one piece I built and couldn't think of a name for it, it felt to me like a gate. I wanted to call it *The Nuremberg Gate*, but that was too specific, and the work was too abstract. I finally came up with *Checkpoint*, which is an exit and an entrance, but also one that's difficult to maneuver. The whole idea of letting people in and then stopping them interests me.

JODY: Why stop them? Does that come from theater and
your work with set design or does it come from something within yourself?

PHOEBE: Something within myself. It's a problem, getting
psychoanalytical about it, maybe not letting people too
close. There's the whole idea also of control, controlling
the situation. Art is manipulative, all art—good art, bad
art. When it's bad it's badly manipulative and when it's
good it's manipulative in a strong way. For me the end of
the work is showing the work: it's important for me to
show the work. We all make a lot of work that never gets
shown, but for me, as I become more mature as an artist,
that contact with whoever sees it is like a symphony that
is finally played. It doesn't exist until it's heard, my work
doesn't really exist until it's seen. I mean, it exists for me
on one level, but on another level it needs that contact.

JODY: Would you *not* work if it weren't going to be seen?

PHOEBE: No, no. I worked for years without the work
being seen, but the work being seen is really the end of
the work. That's when I have finally given it away completely and I don't have it anymore. I've given it to whoever is seeing it: it isn't mine anymore.

JODY: You told me that you consciously work against
pleasing or ingratiating. Could you explain that?

PHOEBE: My dealer came into my studio one day and said,
"You know, Phoebe, these sculptures are terrific. You
know it and I know it, but maybe you should put a little
color in, then people would like them more." And I said,
"Max, go away, I don't care what people like." Not that I
don't want a kind of contact with people. I had an interesting contact with someone around one of the pieces I
built. I was in the Hudson River Museum installing a
piece and had two people working with me. One of the
guards came by and the first thing he said to me was,
"You're installing your husband's piece?" And I said, "Get
out of here, would I be doing a thing like that? No, this

is mine." He said "Oh" and he went away. (This was the piece I call *Checkpoint.*) He came back maybe two days later when the piece was almost completed and installed. He stood and looked at it and looked at it and he said, "Pearl Harbor, it reminds me of Pearl Harbor. You're old enough to remember Pearl Harbor?" I said, "Yes, I'm old enough to remember Pearl Harbor." And that pleased me, because he got the meaning of that piece.

JODY: Are there people in your own life who have influenced you?

PHOEBE: My mother and father both, for very different reasons. The Soyers, because they were the first artists I met. They showed me a way of life that was different from the way of life I was used to. I studied with a man named Paul Burlin who was influential, both for good and bad: for good because it strengthened me, and for bad because it was so hard for me to get over his influence. Friendships have been important to me, not so much in my work but in sustaining me as a human being.

JODY: Why do you have a photo of Billie Holiday in your studio?

PHOEBE: I was a big Billie Holiday fan when I was a kid. When I was fifteen and sixteen, I would follow her around fifty-second Street. A friend of mine and I would find out where she was jamming after the clubs closed; I wouldn't get home until four in the morning. My mother would be hysterical, she'd say, "Where were you!" And I'd say, "Please, I was with Billie Holiday." I have every recording she ever made, all on 78s.

JODY: What was it about her that fascinated you so?

PHOEBE: It was that amazing voice, and the blues. I was interested in jazz, and that was jazztime in New York. It was just that amazing, amazing voice—and her physical presence.

JODY: Was she as beautiful as in the photos?

PHOEBE: More. She was very beautiful when she was

young. When I saw her the last time in concert at Carnegie Hall it was a disaster, but she was more beautiful. And she did things—like one night we were at the Five Spot and she walked in with a tall, young, blond man on either side, dragging a white mink coat through the rubble of peanuts and cigarette butts, and got on the stage and began to sing and cry at the same time. Everything stopped. Nobody ordered drinks, the waiters didn't move, the whole place just froze. To be able to do that to a place like the Five Spot…amazing lady. Jack and I call her "Lady Day."

JODY: This is a complicated question, my last question. It has to do with the way we treat ourselves—Billie Holiday, Phoebe Helman, all of us—the degree to which we are capable of accepting ourselves. Perhaps it goes back to our mothers, to our learning how to provide that nourishing, supportive love for ourselves, to ourselves—in a sense becoming our own mothers. To what degree have you as an artist become your own mother?

PHOEBE: I don't think I've ever become my own mother. That's too hard, that's really too hard. It took me years to become my own person, let alone my own mother. I'm also not sure I know what you mean.

JODY: I mean the unqualified and loving acceptance of oneself.

PHOEBE: Never. That's the perfect mother, and who ever had that? And are we that good to ourselves? No, we're not, or I'm not. I'm hypercritical all the time. God forbid I should lose the hypercritical eye. I need it.

Beatrice Wood

It was Rupert Pole, Anaïs Nin's husband, who suggested I interview Beatrice Wood. His father, Reginald Pole, a well-known English actor, had been Beatrice's lover. She was a close friend of philosopher Krishnamurti and lives in Ojai, a small town inland of Santa Barbara, where she first came to hear Krishnamurti speak. Beatrice, who is well-known in India and has spent a great deal of time there, dresses in exquisite saris and heavy silver jewelry. She affects a gentle and pixie-like quality and is an accomplished flirt, but she is also a powerful force of nature.

Now 101 years old, Beatrice's routine has been to get up at six in the morning, work for four hours, have breakfast, talk with visitors, go to the studio, have lunch and a nap, talk with more people and then go back into the studio to work until late at night. Her sculptures are at once primitive and sophisticated; they overflow with wit, humor and social commentary. Her beautiful ceramic plates are highly prized and equally highly priced. Beatrice attributes her longevity and good health to her vegetarianism, although if you ask her, she replies that she owes her vitality to young men and chocolate. On two occasions I was invited to stay for lunch. Each time, lunch was a simple but delicious variation on soup and a sandwich, served from plates and goblets made by Beatrice herself.

Beatrice Wood, Anaïs Nin and Laura Huxley, whose

interview appears later in this volume, were born into a very different world from today. Each adopted a feminine style or persona allowing her to do and say things which would have been unacceptable and/or rejected out of hand if presented in a more assertive or direct manner. Rather than being put off by this contradiction between style and content, I see it as a reflection of history, of the time into which these women were born. Their style allowed them to remain inwardly true to themselves and enjoy their womanness and their relationships with men, something which often seems difficult if not impossible today.

Just Laughing at Life, That's All

An Interview with Beatrice Wood
Ojai, California
October 1986

JODY: Did you want to be an artist early on?

BEATRICE: Yes, but I remember I wanted to be an artist mostly because artists' lives were different from my very conventional one. I rebelled against the conventionality of my life. I had to curtsey when I met older people; I couldn't talk to them unless they talked to me first. I was brought up to be a good little girl, with hand-embroidered lace on my underwear.

When I was nine I didn't know what the world was like, but I knew at some point in time I would have to break free. So I was attracted to art...but I think most children like to make art.

When I was sixteen, I was in Giverny. My mother had sent me to paint in France, accompanied by an "old woman" chaperone (she was thirty and I was sixteen). This woman and I had a fight and I moved to Giverny, which was just a small town. Monet, the great painter, lived there. I went to the inn and the proprietor said, "We have no room." I had canvas with me, and I had a very slim figure, and looked pathetic, I'm sure, so he said,"Well, all that's left is an attic, you'd have to climb a ladder."

That was heaven to me, so I took this large attic and I

painted three canvases a day, all chromos.* Of course, when my mother heard I had run away, she came to Giverny. I can still see her, very elegant, a beautiful figure in a black taffeta dress with real embroidery at her throat, and a hat with a huge feather, and high heels, climbing that ladder.

She came into my palace, which was covered with canvases on the floor, my hopes for the future. I was so proud of my industry. She stood in the middle of the floor, and there was a silence and she said, "How can you live with such cobwebs! I'm taking you back to Paris."

JODY: You said that when you were young you chose to live without material things.

BEATRICE: I do remember that I was in great revolt against the way my family lived. We were very comfortably off; we were not millionaires, but we had trips to Europe, a Pierce Arrow, private schools, a governess, that kind of thing. My mother's friends seemed to me utterly boring, and I was a great snob. Any businessman was below contempt because he was a materialist. I was a monster, you see; it was a reaction. So when I left home, for many years I had terrible difficulty with money. At one time I got down to three dollars. I took various odd jobs. I was very innocent of what life was—much more ignorant, let's say, than most people. I thought that everybody had ten thousand dollars and that cream came out of another udder of a cow. But in me was this slight flame: I was willing to go through any suffering to touch life and to be free. I am blessed that I had it, because many poor little rich girls are not happy but won't break through and pay the price. I've paid the price and feel I know now what life's about.

JODY: If I may quote from your autobiography, you said: "Life is dual, there is matter and spirit and one cannot

---

*chromolithographs: pictures printed in colors from a series of lithographic stones or plates.

function completely without the other. For creativity, the spirit side to work, the matter side must be strong enough to hold the spirit side. If the form has cracks the spirit leaks."

BEATRICE: People don't realize that matter has to be perfect. Henry Moore's statues are marvelously finished, marvelously conceived. Brancusi told me he worked two years on some of his beautiful brass and marble things. We only touch freedom when the matter is in order.

JODY: How would you describe your ceramic figures? Are you striving for that same perfection of matter in your statues as in your vases?

BEATRICE: I get an idea and I get great joy from making them. They are very difficult for me to make because I have no technique. I refuse to study in a school because I want to keep them directly from the heart, very primitive and very much my own. People are divided: some love them and some only like my vases. Roche* and Duchamp† would have loved them. So much of art is superficial and clever. They are not clever, you see: I don't want the sculptures to be clever. I'm always working on them. I work so many days doing vases, which I love to throw: it's very intoxicating, really wonderful to be on the wheel and see this thing grow. Then, when I've given my dealer so many bowls, I go off and just make some idea that I want, and have a wonderful time.

JODY: Does each of your figures have a message, or is each piece an end in itself?

BEATRICE: It's just laughing at life, that's all. I look at my work as what the Indians call "dharma," my own discipline. Pottery is a great discipline. You can't be vague when you make pottery, you have to be meticulous, your fingers have to be alive and feeling. It's great discipline, I love it.

*Henri-Pierre Roche, French writer and author of the novel on which Truffaut's film *Jules and Jim* was based.

†Marcel Duchamp, French philosopher and painter.

JODY: In your book you speak of the hand-made object as having a particular vibration or energy. What is the source of that vibration or energy?

BEATRICE: There is an entirely different vibration between a beautiful bowl that is made by hand and one that is perfect and made by a machine. Our world has become sterile because so many things are machine-made. It's a wonderful thing to have a painting, or a piece of pottery, or something that man has created with his own hands. There's a lot of difference between a reproduction and an original painting. When I was in Spain I was in the Prado Museum and unexpectedly came into a room and saw a Velasquez, one that has been reproduced ad nauseam. It was so beautiful in the original, it had such a force, such an energy that it was a revelation.

JODY: Could the energy you are describing be what attracts us to certain objects? I am thinking of Henry Moore's sculptures, for example, which though totally abstract, make people want to climb on them or touch them.

BEATRICE: Yes, they're very much alive.

JODY: What makes them so alive? How does an artist succeed in endowing his or her work with that life energy?

BEATRICE: Here I think you have to go into physics. There is an invisible world around us that we know hardly anything about. It is so with pottery. As your eye gets trained, some pieces sing and have warmth, and other pieces are cold. All life is energy: after energy comes thought, and after thought comes action. Then, possibly, comes choice. Choice, which is with us all the time, guides the direction of our life. We're not aware of it: we think if we go and do something silly it won't matter. But it takes us off course, and we find out it's a waste of time. We have choice all the time. If I had children I would try and make them aware that we have to experiment, we have to make mistakes, but there must always be this bell inside of us which we should encourage to ring when it's something our soul does not really want.

JODY: Eastern thought seems to have influenced the way you think, how you work, the way you live.

BEATRICE: I don't know about my work, but it has tremendously influenced my life. Maybe that's why I can go through celibacy without feeling frustrated, because I am so taken up with the idea of the still mind, of not reacting, of being impersonal. This is really the great struggle of my life, rather than the struggle to be well-known in pottery. They say the purpose of philosophy is to save man from suffering: I have suffered so much in life that it gives me an understanding that helps me to endure. It's important to know hardship because that awakens our energy and we become alive, we surmount. This is a generalization, because there are always exceptions, but the very rich person who has inherited money doesn't know what suffering is. I feel this applies to my friend Reagan, who for me has no humanity. If he would go and sleep on the street for a week he would see what it's like.

JODY: Recently you were described in *The Los Angeles Times* magazine article as a "rebel." Is that true?

BEATRICE: Just yesterday l remarked that the early part of my life was so different from what my life is now, it seems almost like the lives of two people. And yet when I look at my handwriting done sixty or seventy years ago, it hasn't changed. In a way I'm still in rebellion. For instance, I think the world is crazy, upside-down. The genius of the human race, what man has accomplished, is extraordinary, yet we have bypassed the most basic things. We pay millions of dollars to an athlete for his muscles, but not enough to a teacher to send his children to school. We have scientists working on destruction, to kill people they've never seen or met. It doesn't make sense: if man can use his talent to make Star Wars, to make huge nuclear weapons, he can certainly use those same computers to eliminate starvation, to abolish poverty, to make a better world.

JODY: What about your answer in the *Times* article to the question: "Do you have a philosophy of life?" You replied: "Now," because everything is in the present; "Shit", because nothing matters; and "I do not know."

BEATRICE: Yes. That, in the most economical way, is my philosophy of life.

JODY: You have had a very long and full life. Longevity seems to be a factor in women artists' success, as it takes women longer to achieve recognition. Or *have* they achieved recognition?

BEATRICE: It's hard for women. Women don't have the same kind of aggressiveness as men. On television I see all these government men at the table, and no women. There should be women trying to make peace.

JODY: Have you experienced a conflict in your life between your feminine self and your creative, artistic self?

BEATRICE: When I was in India a clairvoyant psychic said to me: "You have the objectiveness, the mind of a man. If you had been a man you would have been a government minister, but your nature is of a woman." I don't know that it's a conflict; I'm just aware they are like two different things. I love my work, but what I miss most in life is not having a man in bed with me.

I've had a very strange life: the two men I married I never slept with, and the two men I slept with I never married. I would have loved to have been married to Reginald Pole* or Roche, or Duchamp, but they weren't marrying men. Several times people have cast my horoscope and they all say, "You can't have happiness in the house of marriage." But I would drop my work for someone to keep my feet warm at night. People don't believe me. Of course, I'm so old now—I'm ninety-five: what charming young man is going to sleep with an old woman? So that's out. I was in love with an Indian

*famous Shakespearean actor, also the father of Rupert Pole, Anaïs Nin's husband.

twenty-five years ago, very much in love with him and he, I think, was in love with me. But he would not see the relationship through because it would have hurt his parents. He was not traditional, but his family was. India is like that, you know. In some traditional families they will break the dishes after a foreigner has eaten at the table. That's the last romance I've had in my life.

I've lusted after a lot of beautiful young men who come here, but they don't know it. My nicest story is about a young English pilot of twenty-four or twenty-five. He was charming and we had such fun together. As he was leaving I said, "Ah, if only I'd been five years younger!" And he replied with a smile, "If only I'd been five years older!" I admit as a woman I miss very much having a man who loves me near. On the other hand, I'm not frustrated. Sexual energy is so transformed into interest in life, into flirting with young men, into creating, into curiosity, into openness to the world, that there's no frustration. I'm not going to give up, even with the undertaker: I shall certainly kiss him goodbye.

JODY: Where do your attitudes about sensuality come from?

BEATRICE: From the time I was fourteen at Shipley School, a Quaker boarding school, I read Jane Austen, Oscar Wilde, Whistler, everything you could think of. When I was in Paris at eighteen I could read French perfectly, although I can't anymore, so my mind was titillated with what life was about. Yet when I was twenty and my dear schoolmate Elizabeth Reynolds Hapgood was to be engaged and said: "Tell me what marriage is about," I said, "Elizabeth, I can't, I've never experienced sex. But if you read Forel, a great scientist who wrote a book on sexology, it will open your mind." How I came cross this book I don't know, but at nineteen I knew all the perversions that existed. I had read all of Freud so I had no curiosity left. But there were the issues of my own prudery and the fairy tales I was brought up on. I still cling, I'm sure, to the idea that there's a wonderful man on a white horse ready to ride off with me. I'm still caught in it, you see?

JODY: Did the fact that the first two men whom you loved were French influence you in any way?

BEATRICE: Absolutely, though it shattered me when Roche said he had slept witha hundred women. I was so innocent, I thought you could only have sex from the energy of being in love. Duchamp had a tremendous impact on my thinking. I was in France during the first World War and I was partly educated in France. A great deal of my reading had been French authors. When I returned to America after the war I was very unhappy, and I had a French accent; it took me years to get over it. Now I love America, I don't feel European at all. I feel very Californian now: very open, very kinky.

JODY: What brought you to Ojai?

BEATRICE: That's very simple. I had heard there was a young Indian, Krishnamurti, who was a great thinker, speaking in Ojai. Reginald had broken off with me, I was at loose ends and very unhappy, and I said, "Well, maybe I should go and listen." Also, my friends the Arnsbergs had moved here. So I took one hundred dollars, my last extra money, and moved to California, and came to Ojai to hear Krishnamurti, and fell in love with the valley. I wanted to move here, but it was twenty years before I was able to do so.

JODY: How much of leading an exciting life is being in the right place at the right time?

BEATRICE: I never felt my life was exciting. I've never felt I've been in the right place, never.

JODY: Yet your life seems very exciting when you tell it.

BEATRICE: I feel now my life is exciting because I have the freedom to do what I want and I have enough money to get through the year instead of the next two or three hours. Dr. Annie Besant, a great thinker, said that every man has choice but not everybody takes advantage of opportunities. Perhaps as I grew older I had the capacity to take advantage of opportunities.

To give you an example, twenty years ago, Kamaladevi, a very famous Indian woman in government, came into my exhibition room and said: "This is the most beautiful pottery I've ever seen. Would you like to come to India?" Immediately I said: "Yes." "Well," she said, "I'll make it happen," and walked out. I never gave it another thought. Months later I got a letter from the State Department saying they were sending me to India at the request of the Indian government. I went without hesitation.

JODY: Perhaps the answer lies in your ability to say "yes" so spontaneously. Or is there more to it than that?

BEATRICE: Yes. One should say "no" most of the time. When I was thirty-eight I had to deliver my pottery to one of the big stores (I was selling to Bullocks Wilshire, Neiman Marcus and others). This manager said, "Where's your invoice?" And I said, "What's an invoice?" She said it was a list. I replied: "Madame, I don't make lists. I'm an artist, not a typist." Then she said, "Sit down. How do you expect to get paid?" That was a great revelation in my life. Something exploded within me: I realized that when we have relationships with the world we have to be correct and have invoices. That is something like being in the right place, facing reality. It knocked me off my loop of being slothful and absent-minded. Ever since, I've tried to be very correct, but only in business: I'm not interested in being correct in any other way.

JODY: I know you don't eat meat. Have you always been a vegetarian?

BEATRICE: I became a vegetarian when I was seventeen, in Paris. I don't know what I read that made me become one. I don't like proselytizing, but I think it's a very good thing to be. First of all, animals are killed in terror and their meat is poisoned. I love little animals and have great respect for everything that lives. Then, from personal experiences, the body has a resilience as a vegetarian that it does not have when one eats meat. Over forty-five years ago doctors thought I had this neck injury because I didn't eat meat. So for one year I ate meat, with great conflict. Then one day I read, "Man is the protector of his younger brothers, the animals." This meant so much to me, and I was no better, that I stopped eating meat the next day. In a short while I was aware my body felt lighter. I can't prove it, but I think there is a different quality, a different vibration to vegetarians.

JODY: When do you work?

BEATRICE: Usually mornings I go into my office and take care of correspondence. I'm apt, if I can, now that I'm so old, to take a nap in the middle of the day. Then I come to around two-thirty, but there are always visitors, so I do a little bit of work through visitors and then a great deal of work from five till ten-thirty or eleven at night. I do most of my work at night and I go out hardly at all socially.

JODY: That's a long day. How do you manage? Do you take vitamins?

BEATRICE: Yes I do. I'm also taking something wonderful called "Willard Water" which is helping me because my neck injury takes a lot of my energy. But I'm feeling much better. I've been talking since early morning, there have been people here all day, there was a man here for at least two hours looking at drawings, and I still have energy. My program for tonight is to listen to "60 Minutes," hoping that nothing will be interesting, and then get back to my desk and write letters. Then tomorrow I go back and begin glazing, and then for two days I have to give up everything in glaze and try to get some new things ready because I have a deadline. I have one tremendous gift, no two: the love of study and the fact that I'm naturally organized: not commercially minded, but very organized.

JODY: If you had to choose three adjectives to describe yourself, which would they be?

BEATRICE: Silly, argumentative, miserly, generous. I don't know at all. I wouldn't know how to describe myself.

JODY: For you I would choose intelligent, lively, loving.

BEATRICE: Yes, I am relatively intelligent compared to many people, and I am lively, and I am curious: I would say curious. Yes, that I am, curious and a hard worker. Yes, those things.

JODY: I had the privilege of interviewing Meridel Le Sueur, the Minnesota writer, not long ago. She spoke of her current work as her "message to the world." If I asked you what is your message to the world, Beatrice, what would you say?

BEATRICE: I have one message: be honest, regardless of everything. Be absolutely as honest as possible, as free of the cunning of the mind as possible. Then, whatever happens your life will be built on rock and not crumble. This is my only religion. I've really tried to be honest. And one can be honest without hurting others.

JODY: What is the source of your obvious joy and openness to life?

BEATRICE: Well, I wasn't joyous as a child; I was too unhappy. But I've been joyous most of the time since I moved to Ojai. I think I've always had a sense of humor, an ability to see both sides to a question. Suffering cracks an individual, and when they come up to survive, they can only laugh.

JODY: Anaïs Nin called it a quality of responsiveness. When you talk about saying "yes" to choices, "yes" to life, there is a responsiveness which must be part of that, don't you think?

BEATRICE: It is an openness, a going out to life. She is quite right, that is exactly it.

Diane Wakoski

Born in Whittier, California to Polish-American parents, Diane grew up in Orange County and returns there frequently to do poetry readings. She studied music and poetry at UC Berkeley and published her first collection in 1962. The first time I heard her poetry was in a good-sized auditorium in Laguna Beach. As Diane read she was transformed from a rather plain woman into a passionate flame point: that's the best way to describe what I saw. Shortly after this reading I met Diane at Anaïs Nin's house and subsequently read the loving tribute she wrote to Anaïs, which prompted me to contact her.

Diane's poetry is a unique blend of fire and ice. Her poems have been described in *American Women Writers* as "a record of her imaginative confrontations with the relationships between beauty and pain, love and rejection, identity and roles, power and submission, greed and generosity, sacrifice and reward, and loyalty and betrayal." She has been married three times, to S. Shepard Sherbell in 1965, to Michael Watterlond in 1973 and to her current husband, Robert J. Turney in 1982.

The last time I saw Diane she had lost weight and looked ten years younger. Sometimes women who marry late give ourselves permission to be happy, or perhaps we succeed in finding ways to eliminate the self-defeating behaviors which have stood between us and the happiness we sought. My guess is that would accurately describe Diane's life. She is a prolific poet and has published many, many collections of poetry. Her most recent books are *Emerald Isle*, *Medea the Sorceress* and *Jason the Sailor*. She lives in Michigan and is resident poet at Michigan State. Her husband Robert is a photographer and travels with her on her poetry reading tours.

Birds of Paradise as
Common Flowers

An Interview with Diane Wakoski
Laguna Beach, California
February 1988

JODY: You once said you wanted "to live the most intense, full and real and aware and perceived life possible. And of course that is the source of my sanity and whatever sanity there is and the source of my madness and whatever madness there is." Would you change or add to that today?

DIANE: As you get older, one of the things you learn to do is make compromises for survival. The young have a legitimate complaint against the old in that we are not living in that fullness and intensity, or we have chosen to substitute something else for it. I worry so when I see college kids thinking more about how to manage and control their lives than doing what they believe in, something passionate and intense within. I worry about twenty-year-olds living middle-aged lives. In middle age I am more willing to make those compromises. I still sometimes burn my bridges behind me and make foolish judgments, but if I were today the young person I was then, I probably wouldn't have the happy marriage I have. All happy marriages have prices on them—giving up certain kinds of things you once thought you couldn't live without. I probably wouldn't have the *very nice job* I have because I wouldn't be willing to spend my life as a school teacher. Or I wouldn't want to live in the Midwest, or all those things. They are all grist for my mill right now, as things to think about and talk about.

I'm glad I've reached the stage where I think and feel slightly differently, but I don't repudiate anything I've said. I've just entered a different stage of my life.

JODY: Do you recall saying you would like the reader to have that sense after reading a poem that one has when waking up from a dream so vivid you can't get rid of it? I think I'm asking what boundaries and control have to do with your poetry.

DIANE: The metaphor I like to use for successful poetry is very ordinary: the poem has to create a bridge between the mind of the reader and the mind of the poet. In the landscape of our imaginations, as in a dream, you have very intimate and charged experiences which mean absolutely nothing to anybody else. They are completely locked in there, unless you can do something with them. I see the craft of poetry as doing something very physical, like building a literal bridge between my mind and your mind. If you build that bridge technically, and well, I come over as the reader across that bridge into your, the poet's, mind and imagination; I can feel comfortable and walk around in there and experience it. That's a well-written poem. But for a poet's work to be really successful, something happens over in the poet's imagination that allows you to leave and walk back over the bridge and go back into your own imagination, and feel as if you've made a successful journey, and that you understand that world as well as yours. It's that wonderful feeling of recognition.

Sometimes the excellence of a poet's craft can almost force that to happen—poets like Galway Kinnell or William Stafford or Denise Levertov. These are poets who bring you over into that world of the imagination, and then you walk back and feel like their mind is not that different from yours. There is a sense of identification and a familiarity. I suspect that, for beginning writers, one of the real problems is not being really sure they want to bring anybody into that world of the imagination. They want you to say "this is wonderful," but do they really want you in there? Yet, if you do it really well, the reader walks back over the bridge in his own imagination and doesn't invade your space at all. It's a perfect connection; in fact, now you have two spaces instead of one, you have the reader's mind as well as your own.

JODY: What is the connection between poetry and music? Is music associated with beautiful sounds, permitted sounds in a universe of silence? Is poetry then a kind of personal assertion?

DIANE: Music will always be the first art for me. I'd be happy to be born into my next life, should I have one, as a musician. I believe that there's a possibility for universal response to music which is not a possibility for language, for a number of reasons. Certainly not the language of poetry—partly because poetry is an educated art, not a primitive art. This idea of popular poetry where masses of people listen to it, to me it just seems like bullshit, frankly, or if not bullshit, that we're turning poetry into propaganda or something that I personally don't want it to be. But music is different. The way in which poetry participates in music obviously is that it is sound, so there is some little aspect of poetry that always dips into that wonderful reservoir of possibilities. Frankly, I can't have any respect for a poet who isn't trying to find some of that music for his work: that's where my priorities are.

JODY: All of modern French poetry has been influenced by Verlaine's statement, "La musique avant toute chose." All poetry which has come after is committed to the sound, the music being as important, if not more so, than the other poetic elements.

DIANE: In 1989 people still like to say that American language is very ugly, or not musical or all free verse. It irritates me that people still don't understand William Carlos Williams' incredibly interesting metrical experiments, that here is someone trying to work with the metrical aspect of music and use it as the American language is spoken rather than to make it sound like Dylan Thomas, or W.H. Auden, or someone else who has a beautiful music, but not an American one. I don't think I've ever been accused of being unmusical after someone hears me give a poetry reading, but my poetry is often accused—maybe not in that term "unmusical," but of something very like that—when people read it on the page. I've come to accept that this is one of the problems of trying to make poetry that is both oral and for the eye. The oral is more important for me, although I'm always trying to balance the two.

JODY: How did you become interested in chanting your poems?

DIANE: I suspect it was my association with Jerome Rothenberg and his ongoing interest in primitive poetry. It's also related to the fact that I was trained to be a musician and I've always searched for the musical element in poetry, having abandoned traditional prosody and the strict metrics of that, and looked for melody as a form of music rather than rhythm, if you can separate the two. Chant for me was a kind of excuse for a melodic structure of the voice which makes poetic sense out of those prosy lines. When your voice moves around in what you could roughly describe as a melodic way, that creates a totally different kind of music from the sonnet, which is musical rhythmically.

JODY: There is something special in the readings where you chant: it reminds me of Christo wrapping the Pont Neuf in Paris—you never see the Pont Neuf the same way again. It's almost as if you hear poetry in a different way after listening to the chanting.

DIANE: Most people don't know how to listen to free verse as poetry. If you use chant as a kind of gate or doorway into listening, it just as firmly as the sonnet establishes that this is the same language you and I are talking, but it is used in a stylized way. Then you can read or listen to more prosaic lines and hear them. This is where your metaphor is exactly right: you will never see the Pont Neuf in the same way again.

JODY: In judging a poetry competition you talked about the search for a big vision to illuminate "terrible reality." What terrible reality did you mean?

DIANE: I think for most people the terrible reality is that love and sex don't usually go together, that beauty and harmony and all those things we want are not easily achieved, and that they often have to be compromised and even sacrificed. Or the terrible reality is that we are animals, and that what makes civilization so magnificent is that we have imposed this sane, rational, good reality on what is basically a very rapacious, ugly, terrible condition. One of the terrible realities is that we have to die. One of the terrible realities is that you have to live within the context of the culture in which you are born, with age and its limitations, and that even with the incredible mobility we in twentieth-century America have, you usually can't escape culture. And that basically whatever your talents are, they have to be sacrificed to making the best out of that situation. I admire the poet who, whatever world he comes from, is willing to face that bigger vision of life. I don't care if you live a bourgeois life or not, you still are capable of facing that terrible vision. Sometimes it's harder to uncover or it's less desirable to uncover it or it seems gratuitous, or people try to uncover it in foolish ways: but I think it's still there.

JODY: This is somewhat related to my previous question about terrible or painful realities: when we talk there always seems to be pain around the subject of your father, who was never there. What about the children who were never there, the children you had and gave up for adoption? What were the circumstances of your life at the time? Why did you make that decision, and how do you feel about it now?

DIANE: I know that I grew up idealizing my father, and in retrospect it's possible that is largely because he wasn't there. On the other hand I grew up with that desire for him to be there and to win him over, to please him. I always had some kind of secret thought that my mother drove him away. I think that part of my dislike of my mother or my rejection of my mother had to do with the feeling that I didn't want to be like her because maybe that was what would drive my father away or drive any man away. I grew up with this inordinate need to please my father, to get him back and to find a man whom I would please and who would not desert me like my father did. Of course, built into all that are the patterns driving people away.

Or maybe, as other people suggest, I select, or I did when I was young, men who had some kind of adventurous spirit or quality that would make them by definition seem to be going away. Of course, my interpretation would be that they would be leaving me, not just that they were adventurers, and I would be only part of their adventures that they would go on from.

At any rate, in both my sister and myself it created a pattern of desire for a very constant, loving, present husband. In my sister's case—she's a more fearful person than I am, although it's hard to think of anyone more fearful than myself—she found her husband when she was eighteen, married him, and completely circumscribed her life so that it would be steady and unthreatening, as it still is.

I guess I was still searching for the romantic adventurer who was my father and wanting to put the impossible thing together of having him also be a steady, loving husband. I could never at an early age make that compromise of accepting that if you found someone steady and loving and present who wouldn't adventure himself away, that you might have to give up (as I saw it) the love, sex and romance that surrounded men that you wanted to be with. I still see perhaps all of us carrying these impossible combinations of personality that we see as an ideal mate.

JODY: So how does that lead to having children and then giving them up?

DIANE: Probably the most understanding thing I can say about that is that I didn't want to be my mother. I didn't ever want to be my mother, the person who said her whole life had no meaning except for her children...and she wasn't someone who particularly made herself or her children happy. I guess that was one of my earliest feelings as a little child: "I don't want to be a mother if that means I have to be like my mother."

When I was eighteen years old there was no alternative: if you had sex you had babies, and I didn't have enough control in my life not to have sex. Of course, there was no abortion...I assume now that I would have had an abortion, but how do I know that? You don't know those things until you make those choices. But that was not even an option for me: abortions were illegal, and I didn't have money or know how to even think about how to go beyond that. So it seems like the only choice I had was to do what I did.

I've always felt noble about this, although that's perhaps just denial and self-deception. I was sure that, given all the rules of adoption, at least any child I had that was given up would get excellent parents, the kind of parents that I would have wished I had. I suppose that's another part of my psychology: I grew up as a child not imagining how I could be my mother's daughter but fantasizing, wishing that I was a changeling and imagining how wonderful my life would be if someone else had adopted me.

I realize now, to my chagrin, that most adopted children think that it's a disgrace or that it means something terrible. I saw it as the most wonderful thing that a child born to a poor person could have, adoption into a comfortable middle-class family of intelligent parents. That's what I knew and that's what I understood and that's what

I tried to accomplish.

JODY: Have you ever tried to contact your children, or they you?

DIANE: No. Now that it's possible for these records to be unsealed...of course, I'm somebody who reads Greek tragedy and is totally involved in what Freud calls the family romance, so I've always been positive that somehow these children would come back into my life, and always been a little fearful that it would be some kind of a tragedy. It's always been a kind of fictional aspect of my life that that could occur. I would never create it because that would have to happen on the initiative of fate intervening; it would never be my call. I feel that what I did was in a way destined, and therefore if there is any further complication of the story, it would have to be part of destiny or someone else's choice.

JODY: What about the loneliness in your life which you refer to, a kind of larger, dogged loneliness?

DIANE: I think that's because I've always had a secret life, and a secret life by definition is something you can't share with other people. One of the things that drew me so powerfully to poetry after that event when I was eighteen was that it was a way of talking to people that wasn't documentary. It was a way of telling my secrets in a form that was literary...by some people's terms disguised, by mine just turned into the real stories, not document or fact, which to me is boring and tedious and troublesome.

I guess my life has been full of secrets or things that seemed if not shameful, things that couldn't be told or talked about in a way that anyone would ever understand. I've always had these stories and wanted to tell them, but the fact that I've created that as a whole way of living my life means by definition that I can't just sit around and talk about them to people. I don't believe in psychotherapy and in only one short period of my life did I ever have a very desperate, needy time of talking to people. I didn't find in that instance that there was any kind of intelligent listening the way there is intelligent reading of your work.

Recently I've gotten so unhappy with school it's occurred to me, since everybody says I'm depressed—I don't believe in depression, I think that I'm just suffering from what we're all suffering from who live in this particular world and have intellectual idealism and see what is happening to it—it has occurred to me that it would be fun to have a Jungian therapist in order to try to see the patterns in all this, and to find out why this particular crisis in the university seems to be bringing me so close to the edge of constant despair when in some ways it doesn't affect me at all. I mean, I can ignore my job if I want to: it's by everybody's standards a great job, and yet it constantly brings me to the edge of despair. So I suppose that interests me, what kind of archetypal patterns I have set up here that puts this external thing in my life so close to the edge of that other kind of pain, anguish or loneliness and despair that came out of my teenage sexuality and domestic failure.

JODY: You spoke of defining the content or the territory of your poems, as opposed to the content of your life. What did you discover?

DIANE: One of the things I discovered was that I am a creature who has always been looking for a balance between my mind and my body, my emotions and my rational vision of the world. Poetry, like everything else, was another balancing attempt. I don't think when I was a young poet I had any idea of what I was looking for. I don't think I understood why I loved those Wallace Stevens poems. I could have given you reasons for it, but I don't think I really understood the way I do now. I instantly saw that excruciatingly beautiful balance of mind and emotions, which was what I had always longed for. The truth is something that almost sounds like a cliché, that poetry has to be reinvented by each person who writes it. No matter how well you know the traditions and you know what you love, you don't really know how you can use those things: you have to invent the art of poetry for yourself.

When I was in high school, I most wanted to write poetry like Shakespeare's sonnets, that expressed how deep my emotion, my feelings of love were, mostly sexual love. Of course I didn't realize that I wasn't a lyric poet and that the sonnet is a lyric form, so I had to struggle. I'm glad I did, because it taught me a lot. But I had to learn that I wasn't a lyric poet, even though the main thing in the world that seemed to move me, stimulate me, structure me, were these powerful, sexual and romantic and personal feelings of love. I had no way of talking about this. One of the first successful poems I wrote was a poem called "Justice is Reason Enough," where I had to invent a passionate enough history for myself in order to feel justified to write a narrative poem. It was the only way I could really handle talking about how profound my feelings were. That was an entree into what I was to discover.

I'm not a narrative poet in the sense of telling stories, but I'm a poet of the personal narrative. I'm always talking about my life and alluding to my life story or my mythic version of it. Again, I had to just keep writing my way through different models of what I saw and what I liked into what was eventually going to be me. Maybe what I'm doing now looks very traditional, or looks like it came from obvious models, but there was no way I knew how to find that thing. For many people one of the greatest pleasures of writing poetry is that it is constantly an act of discovery. I suppose that's one of the things that makes poets so narcissistic; we get so involved in what we are doing that we just assume that everyone else is fascinated by it. But it's partly because you read a poem and think, "God, did I write that?" and "Where did that come from?" and "Isn't that fascinating?"

JODY: You always have something magical, like a naked girl riding a zebra, or clocks on your elbows. Where does the magic come from?

DIANE: Probably from two sources, one obviously being my Southern California landscape. I always want the exotic, and I think that's imprinting. When you grow up with birds of paradise as common flowers, you are always going to have that. Also, I was a little girl who grew up with fairy tales. Because I lived in a very physically poor and shabby world, and an intellectually poor world of people without much imagination or a life of the imagination, it was overwhelmingly exciting to me to read about castles and jewels and wonderful adventures, and of course romance, and being surrounded by beauty and pleasure and comfort. In that sense I was imprinted by those books, always wanting and perhaps always feeling that the only way you had those things was through something magic. A major theme in fairy tales was the poor, simple youth or the wretched Cinderella sweeping up the ashes who, through the fairy godmother and the magic wishes, makes the world good, and the magic door is opened to beauty and splendor. For me it became an article of faith. Whether or not you can actually transform your real life here in Orange County, California, is another story, but through the doors of the world of poetry, through books, you always have access to those magic things. They're in your mind; it's the way you think about things.

JODY: You refer to yourself in "Variations on a Theme" as a visual poet. What does that mean for you personally?

DIANE: I love the color of things, I like the shape of things. I'm very involved with light, and therefore the reflections and perspectives that you get from things. Consequently, it's almost impossible to find a poem of mine that doesn't have a physical object in it that isn't described visually, either in a painterly way through form and color, or in a photographic way through my sense of light and perspective. When I sit and write, whatever I'm looking at physically is usually what I start with. I start with my eye, and my eye leads me inward to another landscape.

JODY: You described yourself as a "twentieth-century materialist" in your obsession with technical detail. Could you expand on that a little?

DIANE: Probably one of the most useful things I can teach a writing student is to be meticulous about his use of metaphor. Don't compare something to your shirt if it's not going to be soft, and made of cloth, or in some way lend itself to the idea. Don't compare things to plants or birds that you've never seen and make them physical impossibilities. Don't use the physical universe until you know it. I don't care if you know it from a book, books are perfectly legitimate ways of knowing things. I am obsessed with the fact that the only thing we can ever know about the metaphysical world is in what ways it parallels or corresponds to the physical world. One of my problems with accepting death is that there is nothing in the physical world to compare it with. The closest thing we come to is the clichéd comparison of sleep. That's a nice comparison if you like to sleep, and it's one I think about a lot, but it doesn't seem like a very satisfactory comparison. That's really what I meant when I said that I am obsessed with how things work.

If I have one regret in my life, it's that my education was not good enough in the sciences, that I don't have an equal knowledge of the scientific, technological world as I do of the world of the humanities. I'd love to see people be dual chemistry and English majors, get both sides of the world. I predict that there is going to be a whole generation of people (if we're lucky enough to create that kind of genuine liberal arts education) where people study the sciences along with the humanities, of poets who understand as much about nuclear physics as they do about poetry and are able to use the postmodernist, post-Newtonian world to make wonderful observations about what life means, what death is about, about how we achieve love and fail at it in our lives. Today's poets, and I consider myself one of them, are terribly lacking because there is no way we can know that. Most of the popular writers from the sciences are so busy trying to be poets that they don't give this access. In universities now they give a bonehead physics class called "Physics for Poets." It's for people who are dummies. If you consider poets dummies, why should you listen to them? We're supposed to be the shamans, we're supposed to be the people who understand so much about the physical world that maybe we can understand a little bit about magic and death and the things beyond. I don't think my poetry students, for the most part, have any better science education than I have. We have to create a whole new age of education, put the arts and sciences back together.

JODY: What do you mean when you call yourself a mythologist?

DIANE: In spite of the fact that I'm a physical realist, I don't think the physical life is worth anything unless you also have the life of the imagination. Again, it's that desire to put the animal and the spiritual nature together. No matter how good your physical life is, if you don't have a spiritual life, it's empty, and no matter how rich your spiritual life is, if you don't have good health and certain basic conditions, you soon lose your spiritual life because you die, or you have to spend so much time attending to the pain and the physical reality that you can't have a spiritual life. So I see making myth as putting those two together and coming up with the magic that makes us bigger than life, that gives our lives some kind of excitement. The scientists can be in control technologically of the physical world, but what does it mean to be able make as much wealth as possible if you don't know how to use it? Or when all the pleasures come from designing beautiful furniture, or writing books, or making music, or the beautiful way food is presented or appreciated? You have to balance those things.

JODY: You once said: "A woman writing today should speak as an artist rather than as a woman." Do you still feel that way?

DIANE: I'd take the "should" out. As an artist you speak about things that are meaningful in terms of creation. As soon as you start speaking of your experiences as a woman, men are not permitted to identify, even when they want to. An artist is someone who procreates, and in that sense is not gender specific. An artist is someone who is on the fringe of society, who is not necessarily one of the money-earners, not one of the power figures. So, culturally you are speaking of experiences that women often speak of but are still not gender specific. When you speak as an artist, both men and women can identify with loss of power. It's another reason why I'm not a feminist.

JODY: You also said that poetry is about beauty and that "it rescues us, if only through our fantasy lives, from what is mundane and dull." Do you believe people still have active fantasy lives? Or has the poet become the guardian of that gate, the perpetuator of the fantasies of the people?

DIANE: That is one of the functions of poetry, but it's a function of many things. I do think young people have as much fantasy life as people have ever had, but it takes different forms and comes from different sources. Because there isn't a lot of what we see as "poetry" in their lives doesn't mean they don't have very active fantasy lives. In fact, the kind of culture we've created is under attack by all of us who are intellectuals or who work in any kind of educational system. It's a very passive kind of life, which comes from watching television, from walking around with a Walkman on all the time so you have something fed into you. We see that as a substitute for a fantasy life, but in fact what it is is the nurturance of people who live almost entirely in a fantasy world. The stereotype of the nerd who disappears into the computer is someone who lives almost totally in his imagination, in his mind and his fantasy. In some ways I envy young people because they seem so much more autonomous, less needy of love relationships. They have become dependent on different things, and those things are what provide their fantasy lives. You can't tell me that somebody sitting and listening to his records, whether they are heavy metal rock or whatever, for seven hours isn't having a fantasy life. That person isn't vegetating; he is moving into his fantasy. What all of us care about is how people translate that fantasy into building civilization.

JODY: And human connection?

DIANE: One of the reasons that poets are left out of Plato's Republic is that they are idlers, liars, and people who have fantasy lives instead of doing things that make government or community. Well, we now know that you have to have a fantasy life in order to be able to go out and do something. This is what a liberal education is all about, that you have the dream, the fantasy, the knowledge that you then put to work "doing" things. We think they don't have any fantasy life because they seem to be living totally in a fantasy world with no sense of how you bring it into connection. Certainly the dropouts of the sixties became very successful businessmen in the sixties and seventies and mothers and fathers of yuppies and people who seem to have a total "do" ethic instead of a "dropout" and "think and love" ethic. These people who seem to be doing nothing right now, it doesn't mean they're not getting ready to do things. I know in my own case that what fantasy is about is making up for the things you can't physically have in your life. My desire to have everything—love, money, comfort, security—and the fact that I hadn't had these things made me have a very active fantasy life. But now that I've reached a stage in my life where I have a lot of those things, one of the great surprises is that I have just as much a need for a fantasy life. I have a smaller gap of the unfulfilled in my life, yet my need for a fantasy to fill that up is just as great.

JODY: I remember your saying that reading poetry is like having a lover. Not everybody is suitable for everybody else and it doesn't mean you are a bad lover because one person doesn't want to go to bed with you, you just have to find the right person. Who are your poetic lovers, the people to whom you respond passionately?

DIANE: I started wanting to write poetry when I was young so that I could write poems that expressed my sense of the beautiful world. I'm not sure that I had any identification with particular poets, or even specific poems. By the time I was in high school I knew that I wanted to write poems that expressed my feelings about love, sex and romance, so I really identified with Shakespeare's sonnets. Shakespeare's sonnets are still models for me of great love poems, although I'm not a lyric poet.

JODY: Yet your poetry is lyrical and often daringly, dazzlingly sexual. Is that intentional?

DIANE: Oh yes. The next poet I really identified with (although like Shakespeare, I eventually didn't come to model myself on him) was Wallace Stevens. I still love Wallace Stevens' poetry as much as anything in the world; I realize no one else perceives my poems that way, but the worldly imagination is as important to me as it was to Stevens. The poems I particularly identify with are early Stevens, "The Snowman," "Peter Quince at the Clavier," "Sunday Morning." I see them as extremely sensuous, erotic poems, even though they are poems of idea and imagination. I would more than anything in the world love to be able to put the mind and the body together. I don't have faith that I can do that in my human life, but maybe, once in a while, that can happen in my poems.

Someone suggested to me, I think it was poet Bob Peters, that my continuing to long for the perfect physical lover in my poems seemed so contradictory, in that I obviously have a nice personal life, and my fear of death seems so exaggerated and absurd. Maybe it all fits in together with my idea of the perfect lover as some beautiful young man sitting and reading my poems and lusting for that person who is Diane, who may be dead, or ninety-five years old, or non-existent. We're back again to the fact that I think you have to experience a real life to even understand what imagination is. Maybe that is putting the mind and the body together, maybe that's where they really come together. You have to have had real experiences in order to imagine other experiences. Stevens will always be that model for me. Then I discovered Lorca's poetry in translation. If ever there was sensuous language...I have tried to model my poems—that's where I think "Blue Monday" comes from—on Lorca and the desire for that erotic, sensuous surface of language, the color and music of that language. Then I discovered Yeats and the interaction of idea and this surface of rich textured, physically beautiful language. Those were my college influences, in the formative days of my poetry. Then I discovered Gertrude Stein and another sense of poetic sensuousness in that repetition of language. I think what I've always been looking for is a way to put ideas together with the physical sensation of the tactile and the visual brilliance and shimmery exoticness of language. That's what I keep trying for.

JODY: What is the function of loneliness in your writing?

DIANE: You can never say what you would or wouldn't have done, but I see loneliness as what forced me to write and continues to make me write. I'm not sure if I'm confusing loneliness with being alone; when I was young they were synonymous. As I've gotten older and I'm not so fearful of being alone, I realize that some of what I mistook for loneliness was simply being so inside myself or alone that it terrified me, and I couldn't relax. Now I can use that state to either just simply relax and do nothing except think, or I can use it to take me to my typewriter and write. I feel like maybe I never have to be lonely again, because being lonely is misidentifying what being alone is all about.

JODY: Is writing poetry in a way an attempt to break through, to establish contact?

DIANE: I always thought it came from loneliness and feeling so isolated that I would disappear if I didn't reach out and make that connection. It had to be really forceful and shocking in that I had to reach out and grab, almost in desperation. That certainly may give my early poetry a sense of urgency that is artistically probably a good thing. But I've discovered, living on the other side of the coin, a feeling that I'm not going to die if I don't reach out. It's only when you're alone that you are really in touch with all the things you are thinking and feeling.

To get back to our earlier dialogue, is the teenager who sits with his earphones for seven hours listening to heavy metal rock and not saying a single word to anyone not having a fantasy life or not carrying on civilization? I simply can't believe that at some point it won't become necessary for him to reach out in some way. I think this is a serious question for educators: are we giving them the tools to reach out with? Is this what teenage suicide is about? They don't have any tools at all for reaching out? We had very traditional ones: we talk and we write. When do I write letters? When I don't have anyone I really want to talk to. Now I've discovered I'd rather write letters than do the actual talking, but they are the same thing.

JODY: Isn't that what this generation's music is about?

DIANE: One of the things fantasy and science fiction always imagines is a kind of communication that has nothing to do with language. Maybe we are developing it. What we have to worry about is not losing language. It does seem to be a serious evolutionary problem.

JODY: I was struck by something you said about Beethoven: "When I'm listening to Beethoven, Beethoven is alive for me, and more important than he ever was as his slobbish self in Vienna getting kicked out of one rooming house after another for his bad habits. In some way I think of his art as transcending life, because it makes him viable in forms without the flesh." What does that say about your relationship to your own poetry? Maybe a more appropriate question is, How do you wish to be remembered?

DIANE: I wish to be remembered as the Diane in my poems much more than the Diane in my real life. I wish to be perceived as a poet who really was strange, a poet of the mind and the body together. I can't say how happy it makes me that you perceived my poetry that way from the very beginning, as that is the way I would like to be perceived. I would also like to be perceived as one of the pioneers making this a possibility in the American tradition, putting the mind and tight elegance of Emily Dickinson's poetry together with the passion and big spirit of Walt Whitman. You see, we still haven't married those two things in American poetry. It's fascinating that we choose as the father of our poetry Whitman, who represents female traits, gushiness, sentimentality, effulgence, overflowing of emotion and as our mother Emily, a tight, masculine, metaphysical writer, very intellectual. This is not to say that one isn't intellectual and the other isn't emotional, but the man Walt Whitman has the feminine surface and the woman Emily Dickinson has the masculine surface. Maybe it's time for us to start marrying them finally so that we don't have to have two separate kinds of poetry. I'd like to be remembered as somebody who was trying to do that and occasionally succeeding.

Maxine Hong Kingston

I was introduced to Maxine Hong Kingston by Loralee MacPike, a mutual friend. When I met Maxine on a trip to Hawaii, I invited her to lunch at the Waimea Tea House in Honolulu. At 5'½" I towered over her! Maxine must be around 4'8". She looks fragile and delicate like the flowers that surrounded her that day, but she is immensely strong and wise. She brings to mind the Native American saying, "Women hold up half the sky." When I met her she had long, lustrous, black hair with a single, broad streak of gray in it. By the time we did the interview several years later, her hair was just as beautiful, but almost completely gray.

Maxine and her actor husband Earl had moved from Hawaii to the mainland, where I interviewed her in a rented home in Southern California. Maxine's combination of clarity, humor, whimsy, intelligence and passion were most exciting. She has an exquisite mind. Subsequently I heard her speak at UC Irvine, UC Santa Cruz, and eventually on my own campus, where she was 1990 Commencement speaker. She is so petite that a special box had to be built for her to stand on so the students could see her over the podium!

Some of my more conservative Orange County colleagues probably regretted that students could see and hear her, as she began by saying this was her first commencement address, and then went on to tell them that when she graduated from UC Berkeley she hadn't been able to find a job.

Eventually she got a job doing drudge work in an office, from which she escaped by writing novels in the rest room. Personally, I loved her candor.

In public, Maxine speaks with the same small voice she describes as belonging to the main character in *The Woman Warrior*: yet the voice says things of amazing eloquence, power and passion. There is a parallel between the small woman with her enormous power and the small voice with its powerful message. In person Maxine is gentle, warm and full of pixy humor. Maxine the writer is ferocious, sensual, inventive, funny and shocking—a literary trickster, to borrow one of her own images.

Currently she lives in California with her husband Earl. Their son is a musician and lives in Hawaii. Maxine is the author of *The Woman Warrior*, *China Men*, *Tripmaster Monkey: His Fake Book* and other works. Not long ago Maxine lost the entire manuscript of her latest novel in the fire that ravaged the Berkeley hills—as well as both backup disks—a dastardly blow of fate, even for a woman warrior.

To Be Able
to See the Tao

An Interview with Maxine Hong Kingston
Los Angeles, California
June 1986

JODY: I read somewhere that *The Woman Warrior* was not your choice of a title. Is that true, and if so, what was the original title?

MAXINE: Yes, that's true, my original title was *Gold Mountain Stories*. The publishers didn't like a title that sounds like a collection of short stories; they never like to publish collections of short stories. I wasn't that happy with either of those titles, I think that calling that book *The Woman Warrior* emphasizes "warrior." I'm not really telling the story of war, I want to be a pacifist. So I keep hoping we will all take the woman warrior in another sense, that there are other ways to fight wars than with swords.

JODY: I took it to mean someone of courage and strength. Isn't No Name Aunt a warrior in her silence, in the fact that she never revealed the name of the man who got her pregnant, and that she took the baby with her—given the choices she had? Fa Mu Lan and Brave Orchid are warriors in that sense too, and Moon Orchid is a kind of failed warrior, isn't she? I saw Moon Orchid as on a journey which she cannot complete. Then too, there is the character who is yourself as a child. Why did you choose to write about these particular women?

MAXINE: I think there are more. There is the woman who is captured at the end and taken into the desert, and she comes back with the songs. Then there's the woman who appears briefly and dies during the Japanese bombing.

JODY: The crazy woman?

MAXINE: Yes. The people said, "Oh, she looks like a spy, she must be a spy for the Japanese," and they stoned her to death. And somewhere there's a pair of sisters who are wives of a warrior. When I was writing about these women I didn't think of them as warriors, I saw some of them as people who didn't know how to fight, or who were outdated. Also, they were living at a time when their abilities were not useful. My feminine women I killed off. Even Moon Orchid, who knows how to dress right. She's feminine in this sense.

JODY: In the sense of role?

MAXINE: Yes, literally role. We've had three workshops for a play or a movie of *The Woman Warrior*. During the casting there were no end of women who can do Moon Orchid, or any of the failed women. But it's really hard to find anybody to do Brave Orchid. I think this shows that in 1986 the feminine, bound-foot, dainty type is with us. But where is the peasant woman with the big feet who is fierce and strong and of the earth, and yet beautiful? There aren't any, there isn't anyone out there. It's very sad what's happening to us now. Why aren't there actresses to choose from to play the powerful woman?

JODY: The story of No Name Aunt is a terrible introduction to menstruation: talk about a curse!

MAXINE: Isn't that awful?

JODY: You labelled it "a story to grow up with." You said that whenever your mother wanted to warn you about life she would tell you one of these stories. How did you receive such stories? Did they frighten you a lot? Did you experience them as truth? Did you identify with them? How could anybody grow up normal, being told stories like that? They are so powerful, they touch every woman's fear. What was your response as a young person, hearing a story like that?

MAXINE: Joyce Chopra told me when she read that story it reminded her that some Jewish mothers, when the daughter starts to menstruate, slap her face. And I thought, my God, I would feel the same way as if I had had my face slapped. Now, picture a hard slap...I don't picture a ritualistic little tap. I was so mad at my mother for telling me a cruel tale for the joy of the telling. I told her it wasn't a true story, yet part of me was really interested in hearing the story. I don't know that I'm all that normal; I also have that joy of telling. My mother and I are both artists. My fascination in the story is saving it: I've been given this thing that I'm going to write down...a gift. It's merely a story. I've thought: there never was such a woman. But as I got older I saw that the stories seemed to check out, they're probably true. I bet that story is true.

I used to spend a lot of years being very angry. I think that anger was a basic emotion for me for about twenty years—I thought anger was just the way you feel. Maybe when I was writing "No Name Woman" I got more complex and began to see this woman as a romantic figure, a person who was capable of going outside her culture sexually, as very daring, vengeful. Then also there was a battle against silence in that story: my mother told me not to tell anybody. There was an artistic battle of what can be told and written and what is unwritable.

JODY: Meridel le Sueur, the Minnesota writer, interviewed her grandmother, who said, "I've lived all my life trying to suppress these stories of what happened to me, and now you're going to write them." And she did, and they were sexual stories too: how her grandmother had been married off into rape and had children when she was very young and didn't know what sex was or where babies came from. Meridel wrote it all down.

MAXINE: I think maybe I'm not crazy because I wrote the unspeakable out. I spent a lot of years trying to break the silence and may have failed. I was about thirty-five when

I wrote *The Woman Warrior*—that's sort of old for a first publication. I have met women who have told me that they had great stories but decided not to write them. I can picture myself in those women's places very easily. A way I could write it was to write very convoluted stories that set up the possibility that nothing happened at all. I often say, "Well, maybe it didn't happen." I suggested there was maybe love, or that she wasn't responsible, it was just rape, which is a saving story too: "Wait, I didn't have anything to do with it, it was forced on me." This complicated way of writing allows me to write.

JODY: What about exclusion as a theme, exclusion from Western culture as an Asian, exclusion from Chinese culture as a woman: is this part of the impetus to write? What permits you to do the big deeds, write the big books? Where does the creative drive come from, and is exclusion a part of that?

MAXINE: Exclusion plays right into the hands of the American writer. There have been amazing coincidences of exclusion, so that I become a person who is able to look at everything from an interesting perspective. The alienated, individualistic writer or hero or heroine is a tradition in American literature. I take that stance very easily: I don't worry whether my voice is "our" voice. Even though I have a peculiar voice I'm able to speak to everyone from my stance of exile, as outsider, and then I can make my way in. I like the way Anaïs Nin often talked about being a spy; one can be invisible and spy on everybody.

In America, typically writers are isolated geographically from one another: Arthur Miller in New York, Hemingway in Florida, Faulkner in Mississippi, Steinbeck in Central California, Gary Snyder in the California mountains and Kerouac on the road...and so forth. There are all these voices calling out to one another across a vast continent. Writers, though, in this country keep trying to have a community. I've always envied Ginsburg his getting beatniks together, and Ken Kesey who bussed the Merry Pranksters, and Anaïs Nin with Henry Miller and Lawrence Durrell. But when I look at those groups more realistically, community seems like their dream only.

If you looked at how many times people actually met, they didn't see each other that often. The community was a dream they wrote about, that they imagined. I would like a community, not just for writers, but for everyone. I would love to be able to speak about my tribe doing this or that. I'd like to say "we women," but community has yet to be invented.

JODY: Is there perhaps a different kind of community, a community of writers going back in time who move through you and provide a different kind of support?

MAXINE: Yes, I do feel that. There are writers both living and dead—we don't have to physically live in the same commune, we are doing something together. On the other hand, I also feel the isolation: I am doing something all by myself that nobody else is doing, and maybe nobody will ever read it—and it's all right.

JODY: To what degree have you had to work alone? I mean this in an ontological, not a literal sense. You described your husband as your most sensitive reader; you said he feeds you (that's your own image), that he has fed you in that sense. But what about the actual work of being a writer and having to do it all alone?

MAXINE: I remember saying that my husband read my work at the end. This means that there were five, six years by myself, and he reads after the work has been perfected.

JODY: Isn't that aloneness characteristic of all artists? There is also such an isolated quality in Americans which is not true of Europeans, and which is balanced by a dream or a communal fantasy in our culture, as you've said.

MAXINE: That's right, and isolation's not true of Asians either. Artists always take to extremes what everybody else is doing. I don't think it's just the American writer; I think Americans are alone. There's the ideal of the individual, and also we are physically very apart. I saw it clearly when we were in Asia, how life can be a party all the time: all you had to do was go out in the streets, these narrow streets, and everybody else was sitting in the street eating. Any time you feel like it you can go outside and have company. Also in the house—you have so many people living in small quarters. They don't seem to think they're small rooms, it's just being with your people. I felt so sad because I realized my parents left that village, and tribal life, to come to a country where they were, they are, so alone. But they aren't the only ones who are alone; everybody in America is lonely. We have to make these appointments in our books way ahead of time and drive for miles to get together. There isn't a community, there isn't just walking out in the street and being with your people. When you walk out in the street you're out there with strangers. So when writers speak with the alienated single voice, they are speaking for other single voices all across this country. What we have to do is make the communities, and that's really far off now. People join the army in order to be in a community and they have this wonderful, high experience of going to war together.

JODY: Do you believe in the possibility of social and spiritual change? And are your books written with that in mind?

MAXINE: I am not exactly sure how the spirit and the world are connected, but there have been times when I have believed somehow that we create the world by our way of seeing and knowing. Literature has some way of changing atmosphere and changing mind—and then mind creates the world. However, there are also times when there is chaos in the world that is so powerful, and the world's weapons have gotten so strong...What are we going to do about the bomb? I don't know what the people with right politics and gentle weapons such as words

can do. I remember during the Vietnam war Allen Ginsburg declared an end to the war on PBS, and he did it
poetically. Do you remember when they tried to levitate
the Pentagon? I asked him about that and he said they
hadn't done it right. He said they used the wrong sylla-
bles, they were doing "om," but "om" goes around and in
again. They should have said "ah," and then it would have
levitated. Even if we're going to lose we're still going to
have to use the words. We still have to keep saying "om"
and "ah" and all those other words, because as soon as we
pick up a gun, we lose. So, we're already on the right path
to keep writing, and ahing, and oming...

JODY: In your books you move from the biological family
to the extended family to the cultural family to the
mythological family, and all those are connected. Are you
speaking for a larger family at the same time as you are
speaking for yourself?

MAXINE: Yes, and as I have the dream of a larger family, I
also criticize the small family, because there's an idea
abroad in the world that Chinese really have these terrific
families and that's why we do so well. But when I portray
the family I show the terrible problems, fights, wars
within the family—even mother and daughter who love
each other so much and yet have wars that tear them
apart—and families fighting families. And then the
fathers go across the ocean, not just because they want a
better life, but because they can't stand their families.
And what do they look for? They look for another family.
One of the talents that's needed today is the talent to
make a community. Everywhere you go, like school,
"How am I going to find my friends? How am I going to
find a community?" If that talent isn't in us, then there's
loneliness forever. Also, there may be something just
wrong with nuclear families. Maybe we shouldn't have
them, because maybe they stop us from finding our larger
human family.

JODY: That sounds like my son's struggle in high school to find *his* community.

MAXINE: Those awful, sick communities in high school, that's one of the worst places! That's why kids have gangs, because there's all that romance about the brotherhood. I feel grateful that my son's friends didn't become a gang.

JODY: Why did you leave Hawaii?

MAXINE: Earl is an actor and he wanted to do some auditioning here.

JODY: Was that hard?

MAXINE: To leave Hawaii? Yes, because that means leaving our son. He's decided he's really a Hawaiian now. I know he became a Hawaiian because Hawaiians have a sense of the community and the tribe, which has become his, along with the music and the mythology.

JODY: I sense that you'll go back.

MAXINE: We're going back this summer.

JODY: Several times in *China Men* you describe your father's arrival in America, and each time the story is different. It made me think of film, the way film can tell a story and change it over and over again in a way which is very hard to do in literature. I had never read anything like that before.

MAXINE: No, I think of film as a plot. My flexibility with versions came from talkstory, the way I actually heard my mother and their friends telling about how they came to America and what happened. Each time they told a story, they told it differently. The stories change according to personalities, occasions and listeners.

JODY: There is a circularity in the books and also in the recreation of myths, which you reenter and change.

MAXINE: Yes, that is what I was doing. I have to assert myself as a storyteller too, so I also claim a right to change myths, to have *my* versions. It's a powerful assertion, because all of the storytellers I listened to are older people, and as a listener I was a child, or a woman, or somebody who hadn't lived adventures. And a writer does not come from a talkstory tradition, but from a literary tradition. To write in a culture where most readers do not have a background of Chinese or even of Chinese mythology, or even of Chinese-American history, I felt I had to educate the reader at the same time that I was playing around with these stories. I got really mad at critics who said, "She really messed these stories, this wasn't the way they're supposed to be told, this isn't the traditional story." And all along I was asserting the right *not* to tell a traditional story. I'm not an anthropologist or a historian: I wanted the right to play around with the stories.

JODY: In the article *China Men, Song of Solomon and Ceremony*, Paula Rabinowitz commented on the importance of the mythos, legends and stories that surrounded your early years, and the recreation of the elements of dream and folklore, repetition, fantasy and circularity in your works. Could you comment on that?

MAXINE: Yes, it looks like Leslie Silko and Toni Morrison are doing what I'm doing too. When we've talked about our backgrounds in myth and storytelling, it sounds like we grew up in very similar ways. Toni was trying to figure out where we belong, and she kept using that term "magical realism"; she thought we were in that tradition.

JODY: For whom do you write and to what part of them: the mind, the heart, the spirit?

MAXINE: I write for everyone, and I mean even people in the future. When I thought I couldn't get the books published I was going to leave xeroxes all over the place and then people in the future would read them. So I was writing for all the people now and all the people in the future. And I was writing for Western people and Asian people, I had that sense of a world-wide and present and future timeless audience. I wanted to be able to take people's preconceptions and break them apart. This means going so deep inside people that I would just shatter them, then take them higher.

In the mythical sense I wanted to take them to a point where they would experience enlightenment and they could do it by reading my words. That was why I wrote the visions of light, and what the grandfather saw on opium. I wanted people not to take drugs, but to take what I wrote and be able to see the Tao. Emotionally, I wanted to give the reader the anger that I had been feeling for a long time, and also disgust—physical gross-out—and up to higher emotions. I wanted the reader to feel being separated from people they loved; one would be in China and one would be in America. I wanted them to feel the physical loneliness of that, and then the joy of coming together. So, I would give these emotions and also that other thing which I don't think is an emotion but a spiritual high. I don't know what you call that.

JODY: What do you think about revenge?

MAXINE: I come from a culture where revenge is important. So many of the stories and operas I grew up on have that theme of revenge. I think revenge has something to do with justice in our lifetime rather than justice in another reincarnation. But in American culture revenge is really questioned. Christianity says no revenge. The vengeance I will permit *myself* has to come in a new form. I wrote in *The Woman Warrior* that the Chinese idiom for "revenge" can also mean "reporting to five families." If you can find the words for an injustice and put it in some artistic shape, and let everyone know, then revenge has taken place. It has something to do with broadcasting the reputation of one that you want revenge against. Revenge cannot take the form of an eye for an eye, not like that.

JODY: Is Chinese morality different from white Western morality? And if so, in what ways?

MAXINE: Morality is morality: whether we practice it or not, that's something else. But human beings have basically the same morality everywhere, through all time.

Maxine Hong Kingston

JODY: In your books white people are confronted with the way Chinese see themselves and also see whites. In *China Men* readers feel the experience of discrimination and exclusion. Has your writing perhaps made a change in the way people see one another?

MAXINE: There is a change that has been happening in the last ten or twelve years. I don't know how much credit to take, but it's the same credit that writers take for changing atmospheres, which is very little, and very humbly. Everything has been happening at once: there have been women's studies and ethnic studies and my books have been coming out, and also lots of new people are coming to this country from all over. The reviews for *China Men* were much more understanding, much less racially stereotypical than for *The Woman Warrior*. Not so many reviewers saying, "sweet and sour" and "inscrutable."

JODY: There are constant references to white experiences, familiar parts of white culture, which you dress up in Chinese clothing, like the story of Robinson Crusoe. Do readers recognize what you are doing?

MAXINE: Yes, they sometimes recognize it. But I get the same flak about the Robinson Crusoe story from critics that I get about Chinese mythic stories. The editors wanted to shorten it because they said everybody knows what's going to happen. I don't think everybody knows, because what I'm saying is, "Now look, I've done the same thing to Chinese traditional stories as I'm doing to this one. This is one we're all familiar with, so let me tell it in my own voice and see what's going on." I'd heard the Robinson Crusoe story first as a Chinese talkstory. The Defoe novel had become Lo Bun Sun. When I retold it, for some reason, Friday's father became a major figure. *China Men* is a story about a search for my father, or all of us searching for our fathers—and Friday found his father. There's wonderful, loving, physical touching between the two of them. To show these two black men having been apart and coming together is a healing thing for all of us, to look at the Defoe story not as man on an isolated island but man finding man, hugging him and touching him.

JODY: What about craziness, wackiness, female behavior outside the parameters of what is considered normal and appropriate? I'm thinking about the boy who keeps coming to the laundry and the things you did, like effecting a limp and picking your nose. What about craziness as a response to sexual or cultural oppression?

MAXINE: I don't think I ever use the word "crazy" about my mother. I tell enough of her story from her own point of view and with enough understanding so I think we all see her as a powerful, positive woman. But if you just look at her from a kind of side view, she is very eccentric. But Moon Orchid is crazy, the lady in the swamp is crazy, Crazy Mary is crazy. The narrator's struggle was to follow the way of the powerful, wild, strong, eccentric women and not go crazy.

JODY: Does that quality in your mother give you permission to have it too? Aren't we talking about the issue of competence and power, i.e., how can one be a beautiful, intelligent woman and also a creative artist?

MAXINE: The price for not knowing how to be a beautiful woman is enormous; it's a terrible price: no husband, no children, not being able to play in sexual games that are fun. Have you read Susan Brownmiller's *Femininity*? How do you choose your dresses and eye makeup? What happens to a woman who wears fuck-me shoes and skirts? I've fought hard not to be eccentric like my mother. I am nevertheless most eccentric.

JODY: In her article on you, Rabinowitz made a comment I found particularly interesting. She said, "Women are traditionally bearers of meaning". For me that is a good way to distinguish among the various women in *The Woman Warrior*. Some are bearers of meaning...

MAXINE: Very nice: and some are creators of the world.

JODY: In *China Men* men are viewed through the eyes of a
female narrator. Were you conscious of that at the time as
a major reversal?

MAXINE: I thought that was such a coup. I had always
been much more interested in writing about women.
When I started *China Men*, I had doubts about whether I
had enough sympathy for men, whether I had enough
sense of masculine adventurousness, whether I had
enough appreciation of physical labor. I saw men as people who were adventurous and worked with their bodies.
So while I was writing I did things like use a ballpeen
hammer and an axe, because I wanted to feel those body
muscles. As she enters the Land of Men my feminine narrator becomes less obtrusive, but at the same time, she's
not killed or anything. She becomes a most understanding person, a very large person, she can understand men
and encompass them and create their lives. I'm glad Gar-
rett Hongo said, "This is a man's book." I'm very proud
of being able to write the men's story, and I feel very
happy when men come up to me and say they want that
book autographed. It's surprising, but when I'm auto-
graphing books men buy *China Men* and women buy *The
Woman Warrior*. And I think, "Why don't they buy the
other book?"

JODY: Women respond very personally to *The Woman Warrior*, they feel an intimate connection with it, don't they?

MAXINE: Oh yes, they do, they tell me it's their diary. But
when I love a writer, I want to read everything else she
wrote. I want my readers to feel that way too, because I
want them to watch that woman grow up in *China Men*. I
believe that in order to truly grow up, women must love
men. That has to be the next stage of feminism: I can't
think that feminism just breaks off at the point where we
get to join the Marines.

JODY: What is the relationship of your life to your art?

MAXINE: I think I can't set boundaries. I am very much

the same person as the person who is in my books, that same sensibility, but I become older and new stuff happens to me. The books are a way to tell exactly who I am, that I am some being that is in this universe and my life and seeing are immense. There is also that part of me which is living a daily life: I have to eat and clean and in most of my life apparently nothing happens. That part is not in the books because it would be boring. How do you do that? To be very truthful to what a human being is I would have to talk about getting up and combing my hair and brushing my teeth and then repeat that 365 times and that would be truly life. I'm on the last two pages of reading *Moments of Being*. This book is made up of pieces just found in the British Museum. It's incoherent, because Virginia Woolf would start off telling the story of her life and then get sidetracked and put the manuscript away. Then she would start again the story of her life, but different in style and tone. She really teaches me a lot: you have to write about what's happening to you today as you write about what's happened in the past. And what's happening right now affects what happens in the past; the whole thing keeps changing all the time. I used to be less disciplined, so that everything I wrote kept swimming in what was happening right now, I could not stick with one idea. That's my first book, which isn't published. Everything flowed from my today diary—life into the novel, and I could never separate them.

JODY: You kept a diary?

MAXINE: It wasn't exactly a diary. I was trying to write a novel, but my life, like going to Safeway, would get mixed up in my book. Those boundaries between life and my work were not sharp. As I've gotten older they've gotten sharper and sharper, and that's these other two books, where I could keep myself as a narrator separated from myself as a writer. Chronological order is very new and difficult. I don't think I answered your question at all.

JODY: Yes you did. Actually, it's the same problem Anaïs talked about with the diary.

MAXINE: God, is she an inspiration for me. I really found those books a guide to life, and life as a writer. It was wonderful what she said about creating your life, that your life has to be creative, and your writing has to be creative. Will there be a book some day with the sections of the diary that have not been published?

JODY: Yes. Rupert Pole, her widower, is editing them now.

MAXINE: Well, he had taken out all that stuff about himself.

JODY: No, that wasn't Rupert. Anaïs had two husbands: the first was an American banker, Ian Hugo, who was considerably older than herself and whom she married when she was quite young. They lived in Europe but returned to America when World War II broke out. In New York she continued the psychoanalytic training she had begun in Europe with Otto Rank. Somewhere along the line, she met Rupert.

MAXINE: How long was she married to Hugo?

JODY: Hugo died only recently: ironically, he outlived her. Initially, he had refused permission to be included in the diaries, which is why at the end of volume one there is that unexplained stillbirth. Eventually she met Rupert and came to California with him, but she never divorced Hugo. She made extended trips to New York to be with Hugo, so she led a double life. Hugo knew about Rupert, and Rupert knew about Hugo, and each knew the other knew, but they conspired not to let Anaïs know they knew because they both loved her. Isn't that the ultimate form of love? Shortly before she died she married Rupert—which technically made her a bigamist.

MAXINE: It's wonderful she was able to live like that. Most people would break one of their hearts.

JODY: What if she had told the truth?

MAXINE: That would be asking too much. She paid a price

as a writer, having to hide part of the diary during her lifetime.

JODY: Have you read Joseph Campbell's *The Hero's Journey?* Were you aware of Campbell's theories when you wrote *The Woman Warrior?*

MAXINE: I haven't read it, but I know his idea of the journey and the quest.

JODY: The journey or the quest is often to exotic lands. From the white American perspective, it is reversed in *China Men*: America is the gold mountain, the faraway place, the exotic land: very much what we were just talking about.

MAXINE: No, but I do feel we are on that quest, and he talks about the path, how the hero dares, and the hero may also get lost en route. I pictured the hero as the artist, the artist going on explorations, and how it is very possible to lose your way and not make it to the end of the book.

JODY: No Name Aunt and Moon Orchid....

MAXINE: Very similar.

JODY: What of women making the journey alone? Historically, women have not been allowed to go on the journey alone—or not at all. It's a recurrent theme in Esther Broner's work, and Margaret Atwood's work, and Alice Walker's work.

MAXINE: Now women are *forced* into the journey alone. I've often felt that men seem to be playful and adventurous and loose; they tell jokes really well, they're fun. Women are not fun, women are not loose and playful. Why is that? Is it because women are oppressed and not allowed to play? Part of men's going out on the journey seems to be in their sense of curiosity. Women always seem so worried, as though if you let a woman free she wouldn't like going on the journey. But they have to go on arduous journeys because they have to make a living, families break down. The women in my books do not readily set off on journeys: the men left them, so they have to carry on by themselves. But they are not going anywhere; their adventures are within the village. They stay at home and something happens to them anyway, and they are forced to make the journey.

JODY: Well, it's a gift isn't it, in a strange way?

MAXINE: Yes, and then it becomes—you're given—a quest. So these women's quests aren't like the men's.

JODY: How large a role did your mother and father play in your choice of a career as a writer? You became a writer and a teacher like your father, who was a teacher and a scholar. Your mother was a teller of tales and you became a literary teller of tales. She was a healer, and a writer is a kind of healer. What are your thoughts about that?

MAXINE: Well, I can see those coincidences. I don't know how direct their influence is on my writing. I have a lot of brothers and sisters, and we compare how we see life. "Is that the way it went?" We compare our strange childhoods. Certainly they have the same mother and father, and yet none of them has that mania to put it all down into words. They inherited the same stories, and yet some of them will say they never heard those stories before. Sometimes I think writing has nothing to do with the way one was raised, or genes. Characters come and say, "Tell my story." They only come to some people. Certainly, having parents that found books and writing and storytelling important—whatever I had I guess they nurtured by example. My mother couldn't help it, stories just kept coming out of her—not to give something to me, but because it was something in her.

JODY: Your son has chosen to be a musician. He is the son of a writer and an actor—doesn't that imply certain shared values?

MAXINE: It was amazing, when we went to my mother's village in China there was one good building—it's a village with a lot of huts, but there was one building which stood out. It had tiles, it was special, it was large, and it had a sign on it. I took a picture and brought it back and my mother said it was the music building. That was where they went to play their music and put on shows and concerts for each other. For the first time I realized that she came from people that were musical. Music was the whole focus of that village. So now I realize my son may have inherited his music.

JODY: What "size" is your mother these days?

MAXINE: You know, just when I think things are normal, that we're just like everybody else, then she will do something immense and enormous. Recently I said, "Remember you told me the story of the ghost sitting on your chest?"—I was showing her pictures I had taken of her school in China—and I said, "So that really happened?" And she said, "Of course, and not only that, but the ghost had a foot sticking out." And I thought, "My God, she's still adding." I had just written it all down that there was this hairy thing, but I didn't write down that it had a foot. She's the size that she can say, "There's more, you haven't written it all down yet."

JODY: When you tell a story like the one about the newsboy ghost, where the kids follow him in the street and he goes to a house for directions and they're eaten by gypsy ghosts, what is your intention in blurring the line between reality and fantasy?

MAXINE: Well, I think all children think like that. And in our culture the mythic is real. There are people who are people, and there are people that are ghosts doing real things, like selling newspapers and bringing milk and driving taxicabs. So I am describing an actual cultural phenomenon. These books have the artistic problem of how to write the true biographies of real people who have very imaginative minds. And there is always the exciting possibility that I will break through into another world that's about to happen.

JODY: Where did the idea of calling white people demons and ghosts come from? Is it personal or cultural?

MAXINE: Oh, it's cultural.

JODY: How did you find your voice?

MAXINE: I told myself, "Even if it's stupid, write it down." There was a point when I thought that what I wrote was incoherent, that other people would not be able to read what I wrote. The writers who do experimental poetry and those strange books where the language goes far out like *Finnegan's Wake*—that helped a lot, because I thought that if there are readers who are going to try to decipher them, then I could write in my way and maybe it would be all right. Just before *The Woman Warrior* I published a scholarly piece in the *English Journal.* It was a strict essay, with footnotes and everything. That was to reassure myself that I could write in sentence form, that I had the ability to communicate intellectually. That kept me going.

JODY: How long did it take you to find that voice? How long did it take you to get from that first, unpublished book to *The Woman Warrior* and *China Men*, where the voice is consistent?

MAXINE: I think I was always searching for that voice: I guess I started when I was about eight and I published *The Woman Warrior* when I was about thirty-five or thirty-six, so I was trying for twenty-five years.

JODY: You talk about knowing you were a writer as a child. Did you also read a lot as a child, and what kind of books did you read?

MAXINE: I read all the things that children read, but Jade Snow Wong's *The Fifth Chinese Daughter* was important to me. It was published during World War II and for the first time I saw a Chinese-American character, and it was told from the point of view of a young girl. For the first time I could see a person somewhat like myself in literature. I had been trying to write about people who were blonde, or a beautiful redhead on her horse, because those were the people who were in the books. So I was lucky that at a young age I could see a Chinese American. In Louisa May Alcott one of her characters marries a...I guess she calls him a Chinaman, with a long pigtail. He was so funny, he was so weird and different. I was reading along, identifying with the March sisters, when I came across this funny-looking little Chinaman. It popped out of the book. I'd been pushed into my place. I was him, I wasn't those March girls. That kind of reading made me create my new place in literature.

JODY: Was it the foreign-ness and failure in the muteness of the mute girl which made you attack her? Did you blame your own foreign-ness and muteness on your cut tongue?

MAXINE: I was fighting her for her muteness, yes, but not her foreign-ness. I now realize she was much like me, although she had pink cheeks and pretty pastel clothes. I think I didn't like her because she was too much like what I could turn into. I wanted to be a tomboy and bad, and I wanted to be a person who could talk and fight. I wanted to change. It surprises me that I never saw that until I wrote it down. Supposedly my mother cut my tongue to make me a better talker and linguist. I guess it worked.

JODY: You spoke of being mute, of your black paintings, of the duck voice: and yet in your books, there is this huge voice, writing to be heard. How did you get from one to the other?

MAXINE: I was a teacher for ten or twelve years, I taught high school, mostly. That is the hardest job on earth. If you can be a teacher and last for a few years, you can do anything. That's what did it. When I began teaching I still had my duck voice, and by the time I was through I could do anything. There's nothing I couldn't do. Sometimes I wondered, "God, why did I spend so many years teaching?" But perhaps that was my working out of the voice. A teacher can speak to everyone, a teacher can control mobs. You can break up fights, you can teach a rock to read. Anything you say has to reach an idiot child and a genius at the same time, it has to mean something to both those people plus the other thirty in the class. Maybe that carries over into the writing, where I feel that I'm writing for everyone.

JODY: In an essay on *The Color Purple*, Alice Walker said that her characters came through her, they literally spoke through her. When she was writing the book they pushed her around, told her what to do—they even told her to sell her house and move across the country. You said recently that you have no control over the first draft and you added, "I feel I am chosen by the stories. They come to me without my trying for them. There are things that haunt me, that I keep seeing and won't go away." Then you gave the example of the white triangle and how the story of your father's coming to America came from that image. Do you always think in images? And is it the image which brings forth the story, or does the story come first?

MAXINE: No, the images come first. It's almost as if the images are mute: they're visual and the people are visual, rooms are visual. I do hear people say things, and I hear music, but the visions aren't in words. The words I have to strive for and find and somehow connect with the image so that the reader can have the image. There was a time when I was a painter and I thought that was what I was meant to do. That, of course, comes from the fact that I see the images first, so why not directly paint them and then have people go look directly at the paintings? Why go through all of this with the words? I even took art classes in college and I painted a lot for about a year and a half. Then I realized I had already put in fifteen years of apprenticeship as a writer, and if I put in another fifteen years as a painter I might be in the same place, so I gave up the painting.

JODY: Do you still paint?

MAXINE: No. I'm writing the big books and I don't have time; but I really like to draw, it's so direct, because I see the picture. So why not be more direct?

JODY: Do you see any relationship between the people in your head whom you talked to as a child and the fact of becoming a writer?

MAXINE: Yes, I think it must be the same gift, it's the same state of mind but the people are different. I think it's so weird that they should be different people. I don't know where those other people went. I don't feel like writing about the childhood people, but there were a whole lot of them and they were just as real as the ones I write about, or you or me. I do remember times when those people began to disappear, and how alarmed I was.

JODY: And they never reappeared?

MAXINE: No. If I could understand that...It would be nice to talk to a psychiatrist to see what happened.

JODY: They did introduce you to a process, again, they gave you a gift: maybe that's why they were there.

MAXINE: I learned how I could manipulate them and how I could *not* manipulate them. I think they were there because they were my friends. And I had my own world.

JODY: How much of *The Woman Warrior* is also a fascination with foremothers?

MAXINE: Oh yes, but it comes from them, not only from me. Those women who are so marvelous, so magic, so overwhelming took my life and my abilities and said, "Write about us." It's not as if I had any choice: I didn't go looking for them.

JODY: How about the men in *China Men*?

MAXINE: They were people I could appreciate when I became a more subtle seer. They are people I searched for and found.

JODY: Did you make up details like the aunt's marriage with the rooster?

MAXINE: No, no. I never make up anything: they're all gifts.

JODY: What is the lesson you would like people to learn from your books?

MAXINE: I want people to realize how large and marvelous the universe is and what a shame to blow it up.

JODY: You repeated just the other day that to tell lives truly one must tell people's imaginative lives.

MAXINE: Yes.

JODY: Is this one of the major sources of your unique vision and of the energy behind your work?

MAXINE: There's more to people than their going to Safeway. Although it looks like they go to Safeway and they bring food home and cook it and eat it, there is a universe of adventure going on in each one.

JODY: You said that our society doesn't feed artists, that each artist must find his or her own path. Can you look back at your life and identify any of the significant markers or events along your own path to becoming a writer?

MAXINE: Yes, there are many events. I told you about painting. There was a man who came to the laundry when I was a little kid—this was about the time I was reading Jade Snow Wong—and he could draw anything. He said, "You don't have to have money to be an artist. All you need is pencil and paper, that's all you need." Then he proved it by being able to draw anything. Then, I told you about being able to write a scholarly piece so I knew I could think. At U.C. Irvine I talked about being able to make a living while writing constantly and flowingly. Reading Virginia Woolf's *Orlando* was an event...it's all right to make your man turn into a woman, it's all right to have a century of time flow by here and a moment of time flow by there. She showed me various freedoms I could take in writing.

JODY: The L.A. *Times* did an article on the occasion of your return to Stockton, California, to be honored by the Stockton Arts Commission. How did you feel?

MAXINE: Actually, I felt lots of dread because I was going to run into all those people I wrote about, I was going to have to face them. And my grammar school and high school teachers and Chinese school teachers were going to be there; it was going to be like a high school reunion, all these people. I dreaded it a lot, but it turned out O.K. It was also a power thing to give me an event like that; there were various political enemies who wanted to confront one another. People with their own feuds showed up. It was the wild west, it was a Stockton event, and Stockton is where stories comes from. So the people from my books were there, plus people I didn't have time to write about. They were all there.

JODY: What are you working on now?

MAXINE: I'm working on a novel, and this one is very different. I'm making up everything now. With the other books you could pick out almost any image and it's either cultural or it actually happened. But in the new book I'm inventing everything, so it feels very free in a way, and in another way very difficult, because I don't have boundaries, I could just keep inventing this world forever. At one point it was a thousand pages and I was very alarmed that I would never finish. But I have found its boundaries, so I'm almost finished now. It's set in 1963 and it's about a young, hip, Chinese-American man who has the spirit of the trickster monkey. He has to solve all kinds of problems about who he is, and how he will make a living, and how he will be an artist, and how he will be a Chinese-American, and what's he going to do about domesticity (that was a big issue at the time). And it's about theater, and actors, and it's dedicated to Earl, who is an actor.

JODY: When will it be finished?

MAXINE: I think it will be finished this year.

JODY: Your books are a lot about people's inhumanity to
one another, so I wondered where you find comfort and
balance?

MAXINE: I ask that of myself a lot: where are the sources of
life so that you can renew yourself? I find help in nature.
We should always remember to plop ourselves under the
trees because every time I've ever done that I feel the earth
giving me energy and the sky giving me perspective, and
I come as close as I ever do to satori. Then I realize that
life in the city cuts me up into pieces. I know that, and
yet I don't leave it. All I have to do is go out into nature
and it gives me strength to come back and work on. And
I read—there are writers who give you life whether or not
they write well, it's very odd. I feel that way about Anaïs
Nin, who sometimes I don't think writes well. I re-read
Orlando whenever I feel stuck, and I read poetry.

JODY: Is there beauty as well as sorrow in the human experience?

MAXINE: Oh yes, it's all connected, sorrow and beauty. I
think somewhere in my book I described the bombs that
fell on Hiroshima and Nagasaki and how beautiful they
were. After the little girl draws in black she starts drawing the bombs (because the bombs fell when I was about
five). She can't help but draw the explosion—beautiful,
boiling, red and orange clouds, yellow and white. The
light of the bomb is like the light of enlightenment, it
would annihilate your problems, it would be reaching a
purity. We want to bomb each other because we don't
know that it's actually not the same as the beauty of
enlightenment.

Frances Moore Lappé

Frances Moore Lappé was one of the few women I approached without an intermediary. By this time I had evolved a system for contacting prospective interviewees whom I didn't know personally. I would write a letter, describe the book, request an interview, and include copies of previous interviews to give an idea of what was involved. This is what happened with Frankie Lappé.

By the time I went to San Francisco to do the interview I had reread *Diet for a Small Planet*, that classic in its own time, and read her new book, *Rediscovering America's Values*, plus the numerous publications put out by her Center for Food and Development Policy. However, since I didn't have the advantage of a contact person to provide me personal background details, I knew only what I had been able to glean from my reading. This left the human dimension a complete mystery. Also, most of the interviews in this book were done in women's homes, which always provides personal clues. This one was done at the Center for Food and Development Policy in San Francisco.

Frankie Lappé was in her late forties and didn't look it. She is tall, slim, beautiful, very cool and extremely business-like. That day her "cool" was heightened by a cream-colored silk blouse and matching skirt. A huge beige computer dwarfed the desk in front of her and looked like something out of the movie *Brazil*.

We got right down to business. Some of the topics were obviously ones she addresses frequently, and she replied patiently as we moved through what must have been for her an all too familiar script. But deep into the interview, when I asked her how she had managed to do it all and what her source of strength was she said, "It was my children," and suddenly burst into tears. At that moment she became very human. Although she quickly caught herself and went on, it was the moment I liked the best.

Frances Moore Lappé is as different from artist Judy Chicago as anyone could be. But of all the women in the book, these two deal on a daily basis with the most difficult material of all, i.e., human suffering. They just protect themselves in different ways. When I called to tell Frankie that her interview had been accepted for publication, her secretary told me that she had remarried recently. It's nice to know she will have companionship and comfort on the difficult and heroic path she has chosen.

We All Need a Public Life

An Interview with Frances Moore Lappé
San Francisco, California
December 1989

JODY: How did you become involved with economic and political issues? What was going on in your life?

FRANCES: I grew up in a conservative environment but with parents who were way ahead of their time. They were people who acted on their principles in the larger world, and their church was very much a center of discussion about the social issues of the day. Growing up in that environment, I just always assumed part of my life would be engaged in trying to make the world better in some way.

My initial focus on food was a combination of the era I was living in and my own intuition. Food is so personal, yet universal, it is absolutely basic and measurable. If people don't have enough food you know it, whereas with other things, like housing, you can debate forever what is a minimum human need. With food it's pretty well understood that human beings need certain nutrients in order to thrive. My intuition was that food was the handle, and out of that came *Diet for a Small Planet.*

I set out to learn how close we were to the earth's limits and discovered that the reality was abundance! We are part of a protein disposal system in the United States which takes tremendous abundance in terms of grain and turns it into livestock that returns a tiny fraction to us on our plates. I began seeing hunger as a product of human choices. I thought that if I could just explain to people that hunger was needless, that there was plenty of food, and that the problem had to do with economic structures that we take for granted, that would empower people to make changes.

Now I am convinced that food is not an adequate focus for figuring out what we need to do in the United States. In the Third World, food and land ownership define the structure of wealth and access to life-sustaining resources in a way that food doesn't here, because so few of us live from the land directly.

Since the eighties my focus has come back home. It's the question of belief systems that I'm trying to get at more and more directly, that's really what my current work is about. Americans believe we have democracy here because we have a constitutional government, a two-party system and a market economy. Therefore, whatever shakes out from that is all right, is the best we can hope for. That belief system allows us to tolerate homelessness and hunger because it is "just the workings of the market," that's just the best we can do. *Our belief system allows us to condone suffering.*

JODY: Is your work at the Institute for Food Development Policy considered controversial?

FRANCES: When Joe Collins and I started the Institute in the mid-seventies, it was very much the dominant view that hunger and poverty were a problem of too little resources and too many people, and often ignorant people (the backwardness of the Third World, so to speak). We have really redefined the question to asking: "What are the obstacles in people's path that prevent them from having access to the basic food, land, water that they need to feed themselves? This is now a commonly accepted view. What is not accepted are the logical consequences of that view, the changes it implies in U.S. foreign policy—that is still very controversial. But the fundamental message that the problem is one of human beings, of our relationship to each other, and not the scarcity of the earth is very widely accepted. Clearly we've upset a lot of people because our perspective is very much a challenge to the conventional way in which foreign aid has been carried out.

JODY: Isn't the challenge finding ways to change people's ideas, change the way they see the problem?

FRANCES: Yes, that's it. But now my goal is not just changing people's ideas about an issue, like why is there hunger, but changing their ideas about their own *capacities* for change, and changing their beliefs about what democracy is and what engagement in public life is and what it means to be part of social change.

Until we can create a practice of public life that rewards people and develops our humanity as we go along, then I don't think there is much hope on particular issues. In the eighties we were told that it is *private* life that develops us as human beings. Well, many moral capacities and talents can only be developed in *public* life.

JODY: Is it peculiar to Americans that we do not have, that we do not seek out a public life?

FRANCES: It takes a particular form here, and maybe it's more exaggerated because of the myth of individualism which doesn't leave much room for the development of the notion of a rewarding public life. We have the republican notion of civic virtue, where you squelch your private interest to serve the public. That is pretty romantic and really doesn't fit most people's experience. Most people come into public life (as they should) because they are concerned about something of real interest to them. It's not a question of some self-sacrificing, detached notion of civic virtue.

Narrow individualism, the market model of human relations (which I consider the dominant one) is that public life, to the degree that it exists at all, can be reduced to market exchanges. Candidates are increasingly sold as commodities, and citizens are seen more and more as market segments rather than as human beings with multiple interests and concerns. The market myth as the dominant metaphor for human relationships is to me the biggest obstacle, and that is what I try to bring out in *Rediscovering America's Values.*

JODY: You have made the statement: "We all need a public life." Does that come as a surprise to many Americans?

FRANCES: Yes, and this is the theme of all our work. No less important than the end of changing policy on a particular issue is the means itself of developing human capacities in public life. We have not attended to that, which is why we have burn-out and why we have such a marginalization of people and organizations engaged in public life.

JODY: How have you balanced your own private life and your public commitment? Has it been difficult?

FRANCES: I feel in many ways that I reflect the problem as much as anyone else. There are millions of different ways to answer your question, but the first thing I think of is my children. My children have been the ballast in my life because I got divorced when my daughter was two-and-a-half and my son five. I pretty much made a decision then that I could not be a public person, follow my mission (which I knew I had to do), be a mother (which I knew I had to do), and be a spouse. I felt of those three I could maybe handle two, but not three. The only one I could imagine giving up was the marriage, and so I did.

So basically my experience has been almost entirely as a single mother, except for those early years. My private life has really been my children, more than anything else and I have wonderful children, so I feel incredibly lucky. They have given me a tremendous base of security and support.

So I made that decision. I guess there are women who say you can do it all, you can follow your mission and have a rewarding marriage and bring up your children. I couldn't. I certainly don't put up my own solution as a model: I feel like I am so focused on my mission in the world that it just has not left much time for relationships, whether friendships or partnerships.

JODY: You have said that whether or not people are hungry is the primary test of a just and effective social and economic system. Yet many thousands of Americans go hungry every day in this wealthy country which we love and see as the greatest democracy on earth. What is wrong here?

FRANCES: God, that's a huge one! How do we come to the understanding that institutions—the market economy or constitutional government or the multi-party system—are simply devices, tools that in and of themselves do not guarantee the protection of life and the opportunities for participation and growth and development?

In our culture we learn in school and absorb by osmosis that we're so lucky to be born into a democracy with its constitutional protections that we just have to tend to our own careers and families, and that's enough. Unless we come to a different understanding of our responsibility as citizens, as a society we will be violating our deepest religious and ethical beliefs and stunting human development, leading to premature death. We have today an infant mortality rate that's among the worst in the industrial world, and the gap between the longevity of blacks and whites is widening again. Citizenship is an *active* concept: it's not just a matter of not causing any trouble and letting our institutions be: we have to constantly be remolding them to reflect our values.

This involves a profound rethinking and re-educating ourselves from the youngest ages onward. But it's not a punitive sort of thing, like eating your brussels sprouts so you can have ice cream for dessert! Active participation is necessary to mental health: it's necessary to life gratification, and recognition, and visibility in the world. *Human beings need to feel useful.*

Taking responsibility can be frightening, can be threatening. But on the other hand, the increasing depression that people experience, the mental distress of all sorts is related to feeling detached from public life, to people's feeling they're supposed to find all their meaning in private life which they don't. So they feel angry, without knowing how to express it, and frustrated that the larger world is completely outside of their control. These two aspects of our lives ultimately can't be separated. We really don't have the conceptual and the practical tools or the training for how to be effective public people. We don't have a model for a public life that complements private life. We have to start from scratch and construct it ourselves.

JODY: Turning to some of your other public concerns, you have said that our current foreign aid is nothing less than a betrayal of the national interest. But most Americans have a hard time accepting that because they have a hard time thinking in those terms. How do you get people to think about these questions without feeling unpatriotic?

FRANCES: It's not a question of being unpatriotic, but of really understanding patriotism. Patriotism is love of one's country, love of one's people. What is really in our interest, and whose interest do we share throughout the world? We need a more informed and realistic point of view. We need to understand that the people who look most like us may not really have common interests with us at all, that the very poorest people may be our counterparts, and that our own national interest might be much better served if these people were able to advance, if there could be genuine land reform and an educational health care system. Then they wouldn't be forced to underbid our workers here, which is why plants are moving to the Third World, and they would be customers for what *we* can produce here. There would not be this influx of refugees, of people who don't want to be leaving their own country, who are forced to come here and are miserable to be so displaced and uncomfortable in a foreign culture.

JODY: According to *Rediscovering America's Values* the next step for Americans is to enlarge our understanding of freedom to include economic citizenship and that by so doing we are only claiming our American birthright. How do you see this as our birthright?

FRANCES: Benjamin Franklin and Thomas Jefferson had a very clear grasp of the relationship between the dispersion of economic power and political participation. On this point I often quote from a letter Jefferson wrote in 1785. He had been walking on a country road in France talking to a poor woman, a single mother who was trying to raise her children alone. He wrote home saying that because the concentration of wealth produces such misery for the bulk of mankind (and, of course, wealth at that time was land) that "legislators cannot invent too many devices for subdividing property."

He had a very clear understanding that the wide dispersion of property was the way people were guaranteed a base of security from which to operate as full, independent thinkers—and if the wide dispersion of land was assured then the economic base of democracy was covered. Of course, only white men were considered full people then! But hopefully we will not be so distracted by the narrowness of that definition that we miss the point, which is that you can't be a full participant in shaping your society's future if you are economically desperate. Unfortunately, there was nothing built into our conception of our form of government to insure the dispersion of economic power, and that was a big mistake. As a result, by the twentieth century, we have ten per cent of the people controlling almost ninety per cent of the financial wealth.

It's so obvious that wealth will play out in the political arena. If you have such an imbalance in wealth you also have an imbalance in political power. In my book I quote

Justice Louis Brandeis, who said: "You can have wealth in a few hands or you can have democracy, but you can't have both." It's such a simple insight that one is appalled it's not obvious to everyone. The concentration of corporate control (measured in terms of what percentage of assets are controlled by what percentage of firms) has just about doubled in my adult life. That's an incredibly rapid transformation and narrowing of decision-making in our society. The shift away from competition based on price to competition based on product proliferation and advertising is also a major change.

Enormous corporate power protected against democratic accountability by the guise of private ownership is very recent, at most maybe a hundred years old, and in human history that's a blink of an eye. This structure came from somewhere, it will go somewhere: there is no such thing as a static economic form. Change is happening ; the question is whether it will serve our values or continue to violate our innate sensibilities toward each other and reduce human relations more and more simply to market exchanges.

JODY: Author Marilyn French said that if this current trend is not stopped we may be moving toward becoming the largest totalitarian state in the history of the world. Do you agree?

FRANCES: We are one of the few societies in the world that has any history of democratic institutions, no matter how undeveloped or unused or rigid they have become, or how taken-for-granted or distorted by wealth and by media manipulation. How many countries in the world have any democratic institutions in place to be developed and transformed? In that sense we have to consider ourselves fortunate: in many countries these structures and assumptions do not exist at all.

While there is a great deal of disaffection from the official political system, at the same time, over the last thirty years there has been an absolute burst of unofficial citizen organizing, of citizens taking issues into our own hands. The question is, how do we use this to transform the political process itself? We cannot have a free society unless we *all* are shouldering a greater responsibility and helping to solve community problems.

JODY: What lies ahead for you personally?

FRANCES: Right now I'm in an intensive learning phase and have been since last year. What do the ideas I've been writing about mean in terms of how people do things differently? How do community national non—profits go about involving people? What are the messages, the practices, the opportunities for people to feel that they are really developing their capacities as human beings by being involved in public life? How does any issue serve as an occasion to build democracy? It's riskier than anything I've ever done. Before, I could measure my progress in terms of pages written that day or research done, or things I could explain to somebody on the pesticide problem, or the foreign aid problem or the U.S. agriculture problem. With what I'm doing now, there are no clear measures of success.

I guess all my life I felt at every stage there is no turning back. Once you have new questions, once you have challenged yourself in a certain way, you can't go back to where you were ten years ago: you can't even go back to where you were a year ago. Once you set out on this path, on a quest to constantly go deeper, then that's what your life *is*, no matter how scary or unnerving. So, for better or worse, that's where I am.

Judy Chicago

I met Judy Chicago for the first time in the mid-seventies. I was living in Irvine, California, and struggling through the breakup of my marriage. Although I was already working with Anaïs Nin, my consciousness was far from raised. Judy Chicago's eruption into my life changed all that.

Judy had been invited to give a lecture at the UC Irvine School of Fine Arts. I went to hear her speak and, arriving early, sat down in the second or third row of the large auditorium. She showed up wearing a very tight pair of French blue jeans and cowboy boots. Her brown curly hair flew around her head as she proceeded to flay verbally the UCI Art department members for staying away from her lecture. Then she introduced her series called *The Great Ladies,* honoring Queen Christina of Sweden, Marie Antoinette, Catherine the Great and Queen Victoria. These were followed by *The Reincarnation Tryptych:* Madame de Stael, Georges Sand and Virginia Woolf.

These paintings are very large, and Judy had projected them on an enormous, floor-to-ceiling screen. They were in varying colors, but each one pulsated with rhythm, energy and life. It isn't accurate to say "the moment I saw them," because I wasn't "seeing" them so much as "experiencing" them—but I instantaneously recognized them for what they are, i.e., representations of the pulsating rhythm of female orgasm.

At this point I knew nothing about Judy's battle against phallocentric art nor about her concept of female-centered art, an idea that underpins all of these paintings, *The Dinner Party,* and *The Birth Project.* But I felt a profound shock of recognition. Next, I felt extremely embarrassed and wanted to sink under my chair. Then came an extraordinary thrill and sense of daring at looking at those huge images up there, ten feet tall, for everyone to see. A major and permanent shift in my consciousness took place at that moment.

That evening there was a potluck supper in Judy's honor. I had the opportunity to speak with her, and we even discussed my possible involvement with the Women's Building in Los Angeles. At that point I needed an income-producing job, so it never happened; but I continued to see her shows, first *The Dinner Party* in San Francisco and then *The Birth Project* in Los Angeles, then *Power Play,* which I saw in book form, and *The Holocaust Project,* which I was privileged to see parts of in her studio in Santa Fe as well as at UCLA.

The Dinner Party, which opened in San Francisco in March of 1979, incorporates sculpture, ceramics, needlepoint and china painting—all focused on the theme of women's history. Lucy Lippard said of *The Dinner Party:* "It is a symbol of female power, both as an esthetic celebration and as a standard bearer in the class struggle based on the division between women and men." Lippard's statement is applicable to all of Judy Chicago's work, with the possible exception of *The Holocaust Project,* which focuses on the division between power and powerlessness.

Some male critics have attempted to trivialize Judy Chicago's work by calling it "political." Others have attempted to trivialize it by calling it "emotional." What is so important in her work and what interests Chicago herself is the power of art to change consciousness. She, more than anyone else, has pointed out where the work must be done: "What has prevented women from being really great artists is the fact that we have been unable so far to transform our circumstances into our subject matter [to] use them to reveal the whole nature of the human condition."

The Birth Project took five years to complete and involved over one hundred women and some men making approximately one hundred needleworks of art, all designed by Judy Chicago. These were broken down into eighty separate exhibitions that attempt to make up for the virtual nonexistence of images of birth. They also present birth as a metaphor for creation. The show in Los Angeles was an intense experience. I always have the same emotional reaction to Judy's work: complete identification, extreme pride and an overwhelming desire to weep.

With *Power Play* Judy returned to working alone. This show was an examination of the consequences of power on men. Her most recent work on the Holocaust examines how the Holocaust grew out of Western civilization and is about power and powerlessness acted out in the most extreme forms possible.

In her interview Bella Lewitzky said that she valued commitment, passion, the capacity to rebound from adversities and the power to dream. I can't think of a more fitting description of Judy Chicago. Chicago was born in the city from which she took her last name. Founder of Womanhouse, the Women's Building and the Feminist Studio Workshop, over a period of twenty years or so, she worked collectively. It is in part this community of spirit she created that gives her work such overwhelming impact in conjunction with her vision, her courage and her perseverance. She has been married three times. Her first husband, Jerry Gerowitz, was killed in a car accident in 1963. She and her second husband, sculptor Lloyd Hamrol, divorced in 1979. Currently married to photographer Donald Woodman, she lives in Albuquerque, New Mexico.

Being in
the Presence of Truth

An Interview with Judy Chicago
Sante Fe, New Mexico
June 1989

JODY: How does it feel to be recognized as the foremost feminist artist in America today?

JUDY: You know, my life is very simple: I exercise and I work in my studio and I spend time with my friends and my cats and my husband. What's important to me is how my work makes a contribution to transformation and evolution. I don't know what all that other stuff means about being "the foremost feminist artist in America."

JODY: Yet you have had a tremendous impact on changing the ways in which our culture perceives and relates to and deals with women. What about the ideas you have challenged, the barriers you have broken?

JUDY: I don't really know what the effect of my work has been, partly because I've been very focused on my life as an artist, and partly because to a great extent the art world continues to refuse to acknowledge my influence. In the last two years I can begin to see that obviously my work has had an effect, but it's been so largely outside of the art world that for a long time it was invisible to me. After all, what is important to me is to have my work validated as art.

JODY: All of your professional life you have spoken out with great courage about your own experiences as an artist. Is there a point at which one becomes totally comfortable with self-assertion in opposing to the prevailing consciousness? Or are you ever still fearful?

JUDY: That's an interesting question. I certainly get scared. I feel scared now about *The Holocaust Project* because I'm bringing a different point of view to that subject than has ever been brought before, and it's going to break my heart if eveybody hates it. In this project I've spent years, and Donald and I have done it pretty well by ourselves. Seven *years just painting my heart out without a lot of support is* scary. I do feel comfortable, however, with being who I am: If I get anxious I say to myself, "Well, you just have to trust yourself."

But I want to deal with some of the things that were in your question that you didn't ask. When I was very young I wanted to be famous, I knew I was going to be famous, and it was very important to me to be famous. I was comfortable as soon as I *was* famous. I was more comfortable when I was famous than I was before, because I always knew I was going to be famous so I wanted to get there and get it over with.

What does being famous mean to me? It has to do with having access to, being able to get my work out into the world. That's its most valuable component. But I feel that a lot of people who have become famous have become really jerky. I made a decision a long time ago to try never to let that happen, and to always try and remember that being famous didn't change how hard it was to go into the studio every day or how hard it was to face the void, or how hard it was to run.

That is really where I try and live my life, in the depth of the experience of creating. The outside stuff and my relationship to it mostly is to push it away and to not let it intrude on my sense of what is important—which is, I suppose, becoming more truthful, ever more truthful. Now I guess people have gotten a little more used to me than they used to be. At first people were shocked, which

is why they beat me up the way they did. I've noticed that
there has been a change in the response and I like that
because I don't like being beaten up, I like being appreciated. I think that's probably what you were originally asking. I like the feeling of having my work appreciated—
that's very important to me.

JODY: In the book on *The Dinner Party* you spoke about
working with women and said the most important thing
you gave to those women was to tell the truth.

JUDY: Yes, that was very important, but I think that's
important not just with women but generally—to tell the
truth and to come out of myth and to come out of mys-
tique and to come out of disguise, because that con-
tributes to disconnection and to not knowing where
you're at. I reread recently some of *Through the Flower* not
long ago and it was very truthful. I don't think I feel so
differently now, but I've evolved from that place in that
my concerns are different and what I think about is different and how I see myself and the world is different.

JODY: What is the source of your own personal strength?
Where does it come from in your life?

JUDY: It's been interesting exploring what it means to be
Jewish because I never thought very much about that
when I was younger. Now I see that being Jewish, the
ethical framework of Jewish culture, has shaped me very
much. I was not brought up in any kind of religious background, but I come from twenty-three generations of rab-
bis up to my father. My father rebelled and, as I say,
became a Marxist and a labor organizer instead of a rabbi.
Also, in that second-generation way, my family was very
assimilated, and I grew up knowing very little about Jewish history and very little about the Holocaust, which is
very peculiar, given how political my parents were, especially my father.

But what I did get, very strongly, even though I didn't
get any religious Jewish training, was a secular Jewish

ethical framework and the idea that the world can be changed.

In a certain way it's the same as when I was investigating the nature of female identity and how the female experience could show us or teach us or lead us to an expanded view of what it means to be human.

Jews survived for thousands of years without force, that's one of the things that very much interests me. Not having a state is, I'm sure, connected to an absence of force. Until you have a state you don't have to defend yourselves in that way, which is what is happening to Israel now, of course. What bound Jews together internationally was not only the religious framework, because not all Jews were religious, it was really an ethical framework. It's those ethics that shaped me, very much.

Also, I did not experience what a lot of Jewish women say they experienced, which was second class status. I never experienced that. On the contrary, I was the first-born, I was my father's favorite, and he never treated me in any way or suggested to me in any way that I couldn't be a full person. I think that is probably where my sense of self came from: from my family, from my first years, which were very stable; the combination of being loved and affirmed and asked to perform intellectually. It was expected of me to perform intellectually: my father expected it, he wanted it and I think that was conscious in my family's raising of me.

Something else happened which also had a huge effect on me, and that was my father's death. I was thirteen years old and I had to make a choice between believing my own experience or believing what the world told me. I think that was the single most shaping thing of my young life. It is unusual for a young child to have to make that decision at such an early age, but the world was telling me that my father was a piece of shit because he was a Communist, a Marxist—he had these beliefs that you could change the world, he believed the world could be a better place. It was the fifties, and the whole scenario was that he was the worst, and ought to be sent back to Russia.

But I loved my father, so I had to decide right then and there who I was going to believe. Even at that point I couldn't violate my own experience. So I started choosing to believe my own experience very early, and I began to see that how one experiences the world and how the world experiences you are not necessarily the same.

I remember years later, when I left the Women's Building in L.A., a group of women came to see me and said, "Well, Judy, everybody thinks what you're doing is wrong!" And I said, "Guess what, girls, 'everybody' has been wrong many times and 'everybody' is wrong now." Now where did that certainty come from? Probably from having learned to have courage in the face of the world's disapproval. It's a place women have been very defeated. We have assertiveness training, now we need courage training. Courage is what women need.

JODY: Your art is full of courage, it communicates courage. When I see your work I have very intense emotional responses and it makes me cry a lot.

JUDY: Isn't that what you're supposed to do?

JODY: Yes, but art doesn't always elicit that response.

JUDY: It usually doesn't, but that's because most artists have forgotten what art is supposed to do; they think art is supposed to make them rich. They have totally forgotten what the purpose is of art.

JODY: Well, if that is the response of somebody seeing it, what is the experience of working on it? How can you bear to work on such overwhelmingly large and intense projects over an extended period of time? What sustains you emotionally? What allows you to work at that level of intensity?

JUDY: When I was working on *The Dinner Party*, I was working in a support community. That was very essential.

I built a support community because I needed a support community to be able to sustain the level of work. Now the question is, what allowed me to *leave* the support community and sustain myself, which is what I did when I left and went back to work alone in my studio?

First of all, the ten years of working in the women's community and in the community I created strengthened me enormously and helped me believe more completely in my own point of view. Whatever doubts I had came not from my childhood, but from my experience in the world of being told I was wrong all the time: "Wrong, wrong, your subject matter is wrong, your color is wrong, what you want to do is wrong, everything's wrong, you're wrong!"

When I went to Australia and gave a talk at Perth, this critic wrote: "Judy Chicago is wrong." He was specifically referring to one fact, i.e., that Mary Wollstonecraft did not die in childbirth—she died two months later from childbed fever—but he meant much more than that. That was the headline: JUDY CHICAGO IS WRONG. I thought, 'Well, at least he came right out with it.'"

Actually, that happened with *The Dinner Party* too. When *The Dinner Party* was at the Brooklyn Museum causing this big hoohah (because as it moved further east, they got more and more upset in the art establishment), this guy from *The New York Review of Books* went to the Brooklyn Museum three times. Each time he went he had to stand in line because there were long lines of people waiting to see the piece. So what does he say? "All of these people are wrong. This is a piece of shit and all of these people are wrong and, of course, Judy Chicago is wrong, WRONG! Unbelievable, right? Unbelievable, which is still the art world's stance toward me: I'm wrong. But even if it takes fifty or a hundred years to be recognized, *I'm not wrong*.

After ten years of working with other people, I just sort

of wanted to be left alone. As much as I liked being in a support community, I didn't need to do it anymore and I didn't want to do it anymore. I wanted to bring all my energy to bear on the work, only on the work, and I was strong enough. When I first came to Santa Fe I didn't want to see a soul; I just wanted to be alone. *Power Play*, my series of work examining male power, was very painful to do, and it was particularly painful because while I was dealing with these images of male violence, I was being harassed by some guy in the alley who would come and sexually harass me in the window.

I think that the thing that sustains me, and I know I'm taking a long time answering this question, is being in the presence of the truth. For a lot of people the truth is horribly, terribly painful and they do everything they can to get away from it.

I don't feel that; I feel the truth is a relief. Even if it's painful, it's a relief to be in its presence. There is something about being in its presence that gives you back a lot. So when I'm painting these images, the truth about what happened to people in the Holocaust, as hard as it is to paint them, the truth of them helps me. I don't know how else to say it.

The process of making a work also involves a tremendous amount of decision-making: color, surface and form. *The Holocaust Project* is very challenging visually and esthetically, integrating painting and photography and making them work together. I spent a lot of time figuring out how to do that. On the other hand, it's true that when I'm painting I have to really *be* with the material, and it's very draining. A lot of times I just want to rest after my studio day, I don't want to do anything else. My studio life is so intense, I just want to take it easy and prepare to go back in.

I don't know how it's fallen on me. It's how I used to feel about *The Dinner Party*: it somehow fell on me to tell this story, and that's what my life was about. And it's fallen on me to speak for all these people who haven't been able to speak for themselves, and I don't think about it very much, I just do it.

But I must say, *The Holocaust Project* has been the hardest thing I've ever done, the hardest, definitely, beyond anything I ever undertook. I said to Mary Ross recently, "When I finish this project, if I ever get another idea I'm going to cut off my head. That's all. I'm just cutting off my head, I'm not listening to it."

JODY: You have been involved in many births of different sorts: there was the Women's Program at Fresno State, there was Womanspace, there was the Women's Building, there was *The Dinner Party,* there was *The Birth Project*, and most of that involved women's communities and creativity (perhaps I should add "generativity"). What moved you from *that tremendous emphasis on creation and* life to the Holocaust, which focuses on destruction and death? Is it the theme of truth-telling, or is it evil on a mythic scale?

JUDY: First of all, the process of going from *The Dinner Party* and The Birth Project to Power Play...let's start there. I came to a point in 1982 where I couldn't make images of women anymore. I got to a point where I had actually said what I had to say: I had explored the nature of female identity, I had looked at women's history, I had looked at what it means to be a woman, I had looked at what makes us into women as opposed to men—which is the fact that we can give birth. I don't think there are very many differences between men and women except that, and what then comes out of that and how the culture deals with it.

In my "Women and Tikkun" paper that I did for the *Tikkun* conference, I talked about what happens when somebody individuates beyond their class or gender, which is what happened to me. If you grow there comes a point where you think, "Gee, I don't want to spend the rest of my life talking about what it means to be a woman. I mean, there's other things here, folks: that's part of who I am, but I don't think about myself as a woman all the time." I don't think, "Oh God, I m going to paint from my womb." I am a woman in the way I see the world, but I'm also a lot of other things…I'm an intellectual, a philosopher and a thinker.

For so many years, working on the nature of female identity I got interested in men and why men act the way they act. If women have been powerless (although I don't think like that anymore, that's an old way of thinking), but if on class levels women have been powerless and men have been powerful: what is the effect of power? The question that gets asked all the time, "How come if women are so great, they end up being Margaret Thatcher?"—you know, the same old question—it has to do with what happens to anybody who has the burden of more power than one human being should have. It's not gender specific, given the nature of power as it exists today. What happens when somebody, any human being, has that much power? What happens to them? Of course, mostly it's been men who have been in that position, so *Power Play* was an examination of that.

It was during the course of doing *Power Play* that I got interested in doing *The Holocaust Project*. I never really thought about the Holocaust, I didn't know a thing about it. I was at a party in 1984, and I met this poet who wasn't Jewish. He had just finished a long poem on the Holocaust, which had obsessed him since he was very young, and he had made a trip to Auschwitz and Treblinka. I read the poem and got really interested.

I guess something about what I was doing was leading me there. I believe that the Holocaust is a direct outgrowth of the way in which power has operated on the planet. I did not expect that perception to develop when I got into this because I came at it from a Jewish perspective, I was interested in it as a Jew. But after several years, because it took me such a long time even to learn, it was such a difficult process, I began to feel that the Holocaust was a path. Learning about the Holocaust was teaching me about the world we live in.

Now I feel very convinced of that, and what we are trying to do in the work is to show how understanding the Holocaust helps us to face the world we live in. It is very painful, but transformation is only possible after you face the truth. First you have to face the truth, as painful as the truth might be, or you cannot evolve.

I've made a choice: I have chosen to believe that we can evolve to a place as a human species that we can transform ourselves and the planet. That is what I believe: if I didn't believe it, I would flush myself down the toilet. There was a time when everybody believed that the sun revolved around the earth: somehow or other, human beings evolved to the point where they realized that was not true. That was a pretty major transformation of consciousness: everybody believed that false idea, just like a lot of people now believe there's nothing we can do.

JODY: Let's go back to *Power Play*.

JUDY: That's the first body of work I've done that was greeted by silence.

JODY: It seemed pretty radical to me. Didn't it generate controversy?

JUDY: Silence, really silence. It's too far ahead of its time. The female audience has not individuated to the point where it's become bored with talking about the nature of female identity. There are a lot of women who are still a long way from feeling confident in themselves and their own point of view. Those women still need a lot of affirmation and support. I support them in having that, but I cannot stop as an individual in my growth because other people are not as evolved as I am. So I can't expect them to be able to support me at the level I'd like them to, because they themselves are too needy. It's like someone who is so personally needy that they can't help you yet.

Of course, men don't want to hear what I have to say about them. They're not accustomed to looking at themselves operating as a class, they see themselves as individuals. In order to understand their behavior you have to understand how they have been shaped as men the way we say how we, our individual actions, were limited by our role-conditioning. Men have not gone through that yet.

Nonetheless, I had some pretty interesting things happen around *Power Play*. I was at an art educator's conference showing slides and some woman stood up and started attacking me. How dare I be so angry at men? Guess who defended me? A man stood up and he said, "You've got to be kidding; she's told the truth about us, those images are the truth. Let's hear applause from the men for this woman who has told the truth. She's confronted us with what we have become." There ensued the biggest dialogue. I just sat back and let it happen: what could I say? I'd already said what I had to say in the art. Interestingly, the few works that have been sold mostly were bought by men.

Someone told me just the other day they had gone with a group to see *The Dinner Party* and walked in and all started crying. People have said that about *Power Play* too; it does seem to be a typical reaction. The other thing people said was that the work was beyond them; it reached in some place and was coming from a place they had not yet been able to bring to their own consciousness, but they knew it was true.

Susan Griffin and I are on the same track here: she's working on war, and she's interested in widening her audience, she can't just speak to women. She's also decided that men are the more disfigured human beings on the planet. This is very much the conclusion I came to

in *Power Play*, that they have been very disfigured by
power...terribly, horribly, humanly distorted.

JODY: It's been my experience generally that women are
cooperative by nature. In *The Birth Project* book you talked
about women's sharing as a possible model for a global
community based on cooperation as opposed to competition. I recently heard someone define competition as
repressed anger: I think that's a very good definition, and
it brings to mind some of the images from *Power Play*.
How do we accomplish that paradigm shift from competition to cooperation?

JUDY: I wish I knew. I think we would be angry, too, if in
order to take our place in the world as women we had to
completely disconnect from our feelings and our fathers,
as men had have to disconnect from their mothers. That
is what is required of men, and we have not even begun to
assess the damage that has been done to the male personality. We as a species have to go through another change
and shift. One of the things that will have to come in
order for that to take place is a redefinition of what it
means to be a man.

The last image in *Power Play*, "What do women really
want a man to be like...as soft as a woman and as strong as
a man"—that's true, that *is* what we want, that's no big
mystery, right? How to accomplish that, how we help men
come to a point where they put down that old concept and
that old idea and move to a new place? I don't know. I'm
an artist, I can see it and I can describe it, but I haven't a
clue how to get there except for us all to keep working at it
and contributing and insisting on it personally, politically,
professionally: but we're a long way from it. Also, it has to
be global; it can't happen in one little corner of the world.
We have to believe that we can transform ourselves. That
we can see at a certain point what we're doing.

When this conversation comes up with my male
friends, which it does, they always say the same thing—

you know men have a crisis mentality—"It has to be a terrible crisis before it will happen." God forbid they should anticipate crisis and say: "Well, listen, guys, if we keep sending this ship with a drunken captain through the Alaskan waters, sooner or later there's going to be an oil spill." No, wait for the spill, maybe it won't happen. Men are very stubborn in this place.

JODY: Actually, we *are* in a terrible crisis relative to the environment.

JUDY: The question is, at what point will the crisis become clear enough to enough people? There are certainly signs of it. One thing I think is very important is for women to insist on a central role in the dialogue. Generally, women's issues are shunted to the sidelines as most men do not realize that the only revolutionary thinking today is being done by women. Our examination of gender has led many women to an examination of the way in which the world is organized. A number of women thinkers, artists and writers are in the avant garde in terms of the work being done, but men are so used to ignoring women they don't see it, and hence much of the new information is not being integrated into the culture.

Most men don't have a clue because they don't understand that the personal is political, and they don't understand that they have to start with a redefinition of what it means to be a man and come to a whole other relationship with the world—re-connect. It starts with re-connection: re-connection to other people, to the planet, to other species.

For example, the ability to experiment on animals is the same thing that allowed those Nazi doctors to experiment on people: it's no different. Every day perfectly sensate creatures are hideously experimented on, day in and day out. It's completely admissible to us until we cross the line and do it to people. Then we say, "Oh my God, how could this happen!" If you can do it to a chimpanzee you can do it to a Jew; it's just a matter of defining who is important and who is not and what creatures we consider "other."

JODY: Men often see women as "other", as outsiders. Does this imply that women's art will always be outside the social, cultural and economic structure in that to be "other" threatens the established world view?

JUDY: Which women's art? There are very few women who have had the courage to accept their otherness and to transform it into centrality. Women are just like everybody else; they want the rewards. Why shouldn't they? In fact, it's very seductive. Women can participate now, so long as they participate within the terms that men establish. They can even be rewarded for it. When I started out you couldn't. I tried: it didn't work then, it does work now.

If I were a young woman now, would I come to consciousness the way I did? Part of the reason I came to consciousness was that I was being a good old boy, I was doing just what the boys were doing but I wasn't getting the rewards, and that's what got me pissed off. That's what began to get me to challenge and to think about these issues. It wasn't that I was some better person, it was that I wasn't getting the goodies, and I was doing the same things.

If I were a young woman artist now and was getting the goodies for being a good old boy, maybe I wouldn't feel so obliged to challenge the system. Now it's true that women don't get it forever or at the same level, and also it requires a level of disguise—you have to be a boy.

JODY: In *The Birth Project* book you said you squeezed your personal life and needs into the little crevices left over in your workdays. Didn't this take a toll on your personal relationships? How do you, or *do* you, find a balance between your art and your personal life?

JUDY: I had no balance for many years. Like I used to say, my personal life wasn't of consequence, so what if I had a personal life? That was how I felt about it. As long as I had all these people around me all the time, all I wanted was to be left alone at the end of the day. I could hardly get involved in some other human being's process. Creation comes from a silent place inside and if you're giving, giving, giving all the time it wipes you out.

When I came here to Santa Fe, those several years when I was working by myself and spending months and months by myself, that was extremely healing. Then one day—I was coming to the end of *Power Play*—it was the oddest thing, it was like I turned a page in a book and it was a new chapter. Up until that point I just wanted to be alone, and then all of a sudden I didn't want to be alone anymore. I just came to another place.

It's amazing that when I got to that point in my life I actually was able to find somebody. The first time I met Donald was at the opera opening, but that was not a time I was interested yet. It took over two years of meeting him before I got interested. Donald was extremely persistent. And then, I had come to a pont where I felt I had achieved enough in terms of my own personal goals that I could begin to think about other things for myself. I had certain goals that I wanted to achieve in terms of my work; I really was driven by it.

That's how I lived my life for thirty years. I started working six hours a day even as a student, I had a studio of my own from the time I went to New York in 1959, and I was in my first show in 1961. I have been making art for thirty years: that's a long time, you know? So now I feel I have a right to take Sundays off and have fun and not work twelve or fourteen or seventeen hours a day an more. I can still do it, but I don't really like it. I can accomplish now in seven hours what it used to take me twelve or seventeen hours to do. I can really focus now, so seven hours of work is a lot of work for me. Also, the material is so painful I can't be in it all the time; I need breaks.

JODY: At some point did you make a conscious decision not to have children? Is that a decision you are comfortable with now?

JUDY: When I was young it was very clear to me. You have to remember that I came up at the time when they would say to me, "You can't be a woman and an artist too." I looked at the women artists who had succeeded, and guess what? None of them had any children, so I modelled myself on them. That was one of the things that was very different between me and a lot of other women. A lot of other women would say, "Oh well, I'm different and I'm going to be able to do everything."

I didn't believe that. I believed that I was just like other women who desired to achieve and if Georgia O'Keefe and Anaïs Nin and Simone de Beauvoir and those other women whose achievement I admired (and I wanted to achieve at the same level) felt they couldn't have a kid, then they had given it plenty of thought and who should I think that I was different? So I figured, forget it.

When I met Donald, I think we would have had a kid except it was too late in our lives. When I married Donald I was forty—six years old. Donald and I say it's probably a good thing, because we are enough for each other. We are full time jobs for each other, but if we could have, we probably would have done it anyway.

On the other hand, in a recent essay in *The New York Times* Ursula LeGuin attacked the idea that you can't be a woman and an artist too, and I think she is absolutely right. It is a totally untenable requirement for women that we have to make that choice, absolutely untenable. Then again, driven people are not necessarily the best parents.

JODY: That's true, but it doesn't excuse the fact that there is no place in our culture for women to have both. Speaking of motherhood, you haven't mentioned your own mother. What was your relationship with her like?

JUDY: My mother is actually the one who supported my art-making. My father wasn't really interested in that. I should probably have given her more credit for that. I was a really gifted kid and she was the one who always made sure I got art lessons. So my mother is the one I'm beholden to for that. My mother's alright, she's seventy-nine and lives in a retirement home in Los Angeles.

JODY: I wanted to ask you about honoring women in her own terms (that's your phrase). You said: "To honor a woman in her own terms would require a fundamental change in the culture and in the cultural values as they are expressed in art." Are there women in our culture who have been honored in their own terms. As opposed to honoring ourselves in our own terms?

JUDY: I'm reading an article in which the writer argues that it is not incompatible to deal with both O'Keefe's femaleness and her technical achievements. If that idea is accepted it would be a first step in the direction of honoring a woman in her own terms.

Gertrude Stein's writings are now being unravelled by lesbian critics. It turns out that Gertrude Stein's writing has absolutely nothing to do with Picasso, cubism or modernism. It has to do with lesbian content: descriptions of her relationship with Alice, descriptions of their sexuality, descriptions of orgasms. Unbelievable, right? It's taken fifty years. They are beginning to deal with Stein in her own terms and if they are right, which they probably are, that would be an incredible thing to establish her as breaking through on so many levels, again both technically and in terms of new content. There has been such a resistance to this.

JODY: You have pointed out that the idea that if you're really good you'll make it is a lie in relation to women and that those women who have made it were linked either to a period in time when there was a tremendous amount of feminist activity and feminist struggle or they had the

support of a group of women or, like Stein, the companionship of another woman. So is it male dominance that
has eradicated women from history?

JUDY: Decontextualized them, too. When they haven't
been eradicated they've been decontextualized. Stein is a
perfect example, completely decontextualized so that her
achievement couldn't even be perceived.

JODY: With the result that the struggles of one generation
don't guarantee the success of the next?

JUDY: That's what we're struggling with right now with
The Dinner Party. With the erosion of Roe versus Wade a
lot of women who thought I was overstating the case
when *The Dinner Party* came out are finding to their surprise and horror that I was telling the truth. They're
watching the erosion of our gains happen right in front of
their eyes. That is the story *The Dinner Party* tells: go forward go backward, go forward go backward. The next ten
years are going to be used up fighting a battle we fought
already.

We haven't even begun to understand the ways in
which we are not in control of our destinies. When Roe
versus Wade was decided, it defused the women's movement. I believe the decision was consciously or unconsciously about that, because the lynch pin of the whole
organizing of the women's movement was around abortion rights. It pulled the carpet right out from under
everybody and the political process could not be completed. Also, the national education process of women
confronting this country, of forcing a confrontation with
whether or not we have a right over our own bodies, was
interrupted.

Maybe it's going to happen this time. It's a shame, to
tell you the truth, because there are a lot of issues which
we would have been better off fighting. God, is it frus-
trating. But anyway, that is the story *The Dinner Party*
tells, and it's all the more reason for *The Dinner Party* to

reappear, because it could be a foundation to build on. For it to be the victim of the story it tells would really be a horrible loss.

JODY: Do you yourself have personal heroes, and if so, who are they?

JUDY: Of course. It used to be more important to me than it is now. When I was younger Anaïs Nin was one, and O'Keefe was one, and Virginia Woolf was one. When I was a little kid some of the great male artists, because I didn't know any women artists then. I saw Etta James the other day and thought she was fabulous. I get a charge out of seeing people who hang in there and who keep working, who keep doing it. That's actually the only people I'm interested in, to tell you the truth, people who keep at it for a really long period of time and don't swerve. Those are my heroes.

JODY: Doris Lessing said somewhere that she thought men and women came from different planets. I don't know if it's a humorful or a despairing comment, but what do you think about that?

JUDY: I think it's true experientially and totally untrue biologically. I can understand how one would come to think that, but if you've ever been close to a man, you know that they're really not all that different. There have been a lot of men I have been really close to. You're different in the world, that's for sure. Donald and I walk out that door and what happens out there is different, but we're not that different at heart.

JODY: Certainly men have the affirmation of society and women live their creative lives without it.

JUDY: Which makes us stronger personally but weaker spiritually. One of the things I have come to personally is, what can I do and what can't I do? What I *can* do is I can go into the studio every single day and I can paint, and I can say what I have to say and I can find a way to get it out into the world. And that's all I can do, folks.

JODY: Some years ago you said your goal was to make your form language reflect your feelings as a woman. What is your artistic goal today?

JUDY: For my work to last.

JODY: And how do you wish to be remembered?

JUDY: As a woman of vision whose images changed the way we see the world.

Lucy Lippard

Although Lucy Lippard and I were in the same class in college, we barely knew each other. However, I had followed her career and loved *From the Center: Feminist Essays on Women's Art*, which came out at a time when my own consciousness was changing. More recently I had read *Overlay*, a powerful book about the relationship between prehistoric and contemporary art. So when Esther Broner suggested I might consider interviewing her, I read more, was very excited and got in touch with her in July of 1989.

We met at Lucy's home in Maine and sat on the beach and talked for several hours. It didn't feel like over thirty years had elapsed since we had seen each other. The interview she gave me was excellent, but one of my cassettes got in with my son's music tapes and half the interview was recorded over with rhythm and blues before we discovered the mix-up. This was so upsetting that I couldn't even talk about it for two weeks. When I finally called Lucy and told her what had happened she was very generous about it, having a musician son herself, and we agreed to redo parts of the interview at some future date.

When we next met, Lucy, Esther and I had lunch together in New York. Major shifts had occurred in all our lives relative to dealing with aging parents and losing parents.

Lucy describes herself as a writer and an activist. She doesn't like to be called an art critic, although for many years she contributed to *The Village Voice,* wrote an early book on pop art, is considered a pioneer in the field of feminist criticism, has been responsible for the discovery of obscure artists of quality and for introducing them to the public and wrote ground-breaking books on political art and multicultural art.

Among her books are: *Pop Art*; *Dadas on Art*; *Surrealists on Art*; *Tony Smith*; *Changing/ Essays on Art Criticism*; *Six Years: The Dematerialization of the Object*; *Ad Reinhardt*; *From the Center: Feminist Essays on Women's Art*; *I See/You Mean*; *Eva Hesse*; *Overlay: Contemporary Art and the Art of Prehistory*; *Get the Message? A Decade of Art for Social Change*; *A Different War: Vietnam in Art*; *Mixed Blessings: New Art in a Multicultural America* and *Partial Recall: Photography of Native North Americans.* Her latest book is *The Pink Glass Swan: Selected Essays on Art.*

Lucy Lippard is a pioneer whose work is continually growing and changing. She has one son, Ethan Ryman, and is expecting a grandchild. She continues to be politically active, writes and lectures. Having lived in recent years in New York and Boulder, Colorado, Lucy now divides her time between Galisteo, New Mexico, and Georgetown, Maine.

The Varied and
Comfortable Spaces
of My Own Life

An Interview with Lucy Lippard
Georgetown, Maine
July 1989

JODY: A visible and vocal feminist, a founder of the political art movement in New York, former writer for *The Village Voice,* author of many best-selling books on art and
several novels—you've had a rich professional life! How
did all of that happen?

LUCY: It's been a long process! I grew up in the pop, but
mostly minimalist and conceptualist movements—those
were the exciting things happening when I was coming
of age professionally. I worked at the Museum of Modern
Art Library doing paging, indexing and research for the
curators...the only actual job I've ever had. It lasted a year
and a half; I've free-lanced ever since. I met Robert
Ryman, who was a museum guard and already painting
the all-white paintings he's now famous for, eventually
married him and learned an immense amount about art
from him and other artist friends.

In 1968, after I'd had one kid and two books and we
were divorced, I was radicalized through another minimal
artist and got belatedly involved with the anti-war movement and artists' organizing. I wrote a novel and by 1970
fell wholeheartedly into the feminist movement. I'd gotten pretty disillusioned with art objects and the way they
could be manipulated, but I got back into painting and
sculpture through women's art. Ten years later, a similar

thing happened with artists of color…this was after years spent concentrating on activist art outside the gallery context. Political awakenings have been consistently what opened things up for me. Process, populism and consciousness-raising have been my touchstones.

I've always found myself trying to bridge things, dualities: I can look at myself hopping from period to period in my life trying to reconcile contradictory positions and tastes and friends. First it was being a working wife or lover, mother and writer. Then art and politics—it's always art *and* politics! I got involved with art in college because I saw it as a place to be free. (I learned more about *that* later.) I was constantly arguing that you can be an artist *and* be involved in politics, an artist *and* a responsible citizen, a social envisioner. Then it was art, politics, and feminism. And then, within the feminist movement, it was socialist feminism and cultural feminism.

I did a show years ago called "Both Sides Now," and my book *Overlay* is another way of dealing with everything at once, in layers. I never want to give anything up: when people tell me, "You have to be this or that," I'll insist on being this *and* that. I was interested in the stones and historical goddess material, but I was also on the streets as a socialist feminist.

Now I'm trying to integrate politics and spirituality in my personal and professional lives. Working with people of color has made this easier, but I still often find myself in the middle, with a hand out in either direction, trying to get people to talk across abysses. It seems like I'm always standing up for people who are disliked and mistrusted by other people whom I also adore.

JODY: In *From the Center* you said you were alone in a fishing village in a foreign country with your son when you first realized you were ashamed of being a woman. Where were you, what were you doing there, and what led to that revelation?

LUCY: It was March of 1970, and I was in Franco's Spain. There has turned out to be a kind of seven-year cycle in my life that I do this, but I didn't know it then. I just decided that if I was really going to write any fiction, I'd better do it. (I'd been writing criticism all this time.) I was thirty-one, I had nothing to live on; I don't know what I was thinking. I had been divorced for a couple of years, and I was living with someone, so it wasn't anything to do with my private life.

I had met a French critic, Jean Clay, in Argentina, who used to write for *Réalité*. He had said casually, "I have this house in Spain on the Mediterranean, if you ever feel like going somewhere and writing when we're not there." I remembered that and called him, and the poor guy had to say yes. My five-year-old son and I took off on Luxemburg Air and had a real adventurous time finding the place. I went to write a novel, which I had started before I left New York; I was there for I think three months.

This was pre-feminist for me (and for most people in the art world). It was the heyday of conceptual art and I was *very* influenced by *very* male conceptual art. The book was a terribly obfuscatory conceptual exercise: I took one look at it and thought, "This isn't going to be much fun to work on for three months." So luckily I dumped that brilliant idea and just started writing. The only person I spoke to was the maid, who came with the house and was the baby sitter. I did a lot of reading and walked on the beach, and it was heavenly. It was the first time I'd ever had that kind of space. The feminist movement had already started in the art world, and I had been approached by people in it. I kept saying, "I'm a person, not a woman." Then I got over there and discovered what bullshit that was. When I came back, I just fell into the arms of the women's movement.

JODY: When you started writing did you have a certain form in mind or a certain content? Or did they come together?

LUCY: I never know what I'm going to do until I do it. I just realized this summer that the fiction always precedes a burst of creativity in some other direction. In the case of that book, it was feminism. In 1977, when I went to England for a year and wrote another novel (never published), I came back and wrote *Overlay*. I've gone past my seven-year cycle because of my father's death and the responsibilities I had then, but I went to Boulder for a semester last year and a semester this year. I've gotten fascinated by rock art and petroglyphs and in early June I went on a river trip in Utah for almost two weeks. It was an incredibly interesting trip. I went down with one man and came back up with another, but that was the least of it. We weren't on the river the whole time; we hiked in canyons and found rock art.

I was talking to a friend about power struggles between men and women on the trip, and she said, "Well, why don't you write a fiction/non-fiction piece out of this?" And I thought, "What a good idea!" So I came back here to Maine and am doing that. Then, the next book is multicultural, about the intercommunication in art and culture. I hadn't thought about it, but this fiction is totally preparing me for that.

JODY: Is there a balance or equilibrium which gets set up?

LUCY: Yes. I love to write. I never particularly wanted to be an art critic, but it seemed like a good way to make a living, and I got to write. At one point I realized that I wasn't going to write fiction for a living; I didn't have that total passion to write fiction. I like being involved in the so-called "real world"—politics and the politics of art—and I seem to go back and forth, come out and go in, which is probably the way most people would live if they were lucky enough, as I am, to be able to make a living in that way.

JODY: Why does women's art seem to be saying something different from men's art? Why does it feel different?

LUCY: It goes back to the fact that you can't change society until you figure out who you are and from what base you are going to move. Otherwise you are just going to be knocked off your pins all the time, you can't get anything done. The whole relationship of the individual to mass consciousness is something I have yet to figure out. I've read a lot of the Seth books. (I'm starting to quote them to see what response I get from scholars. "What do you mean by quoting an entity!") Working on yourself as an individual is the most powerful thing you can do. That doesn't mean you shouldn't work on changing the world. Focusing on the negative is not going to be the way it gets done. That all makes very good sense to me, and it was very nice to hear somebody out there say it.

JODY: Is there a link from one of your books to the next? When you decide to do a book, how do you actually go about doing it?

LUCY: I can look back and see where these things come from, and what is going to emerge, and what is a book and what isn't, but I don't know why certain ideas keep going and others don't. This multicultural book is going through endless changes; it is totally unrecognizable from the idea I began with, which was about Central America and the history and politics of various Central American countries, starting with pre-Colombian cultures and going up through modern times and how they have all split off into different places. It's no longer that at all, and it keeps changing.

Sometimes it's the form that dictates the book. *Six Years* is an annotated bibliography of conceptual art. The form was just right for that: it's not really a written book, it's an anthology of bits and pieces with a weaving process. With the Hesse book, there again the form just came, and it's a slightly innovative form, perfect for that book. The form definitely has an influence. Sometimes I get a picture of the form before I know what the content is going to be. I just get led. I'm always telling people I don't make decisions: obviously I do at some point, but I'm led into decisions in mysterious ways. Going to Boulder, for example, turned out to be just the right thing to escape from what was going on here at home. When I hung up the phone I said, "God, I said I'd teach for a semester, what am I doing? I'm not interested in teaching!" But the money was very tempting, and it turned out to be the place I was apparently supposed to go. Both pairs of grandparents on one side lived in Colorado. It's so interesting to think of the biological and genetic influences as well as the cultural influences you can perceive from your lineage.

JODY: That brings to mind *Overlay*, and the overlapping of and fascination with time periods.

LUCY: I have a feeling I had really intended to do that book for a long time, maybe hundreds of years. That was a great surprise, and it was a book that a lot of people wanted. I hope the multicultural book can find a way of also doing that; it's going to be the same sort of book. For years I've been looking for a way to get back into *Overlay* and just haven't been able to find it. It's interesting to me how these things come about. I've always dreamed a lot, and in the novel I used real dreams. But now I'm writing them down, which I've never done before, and making an effort to remember them and look for patterns.

JODY: Is there a relationship between the fiction and the non-fiction other than in terms of how the books come?

LUCY: This time I'm seeing a clear relationship I didn't see before. In a way the art provided an impetus for *I See/You Mean*, then the feminism provided the impetus for the novel I was writing when I was in England about three generations of women and how politics affected their lives. One of the characters was a sort of witch, and that has led into some of the *Overlay* material, although I wasn't aware of it at the time. I also was affected by feminist

artists, and the witch is the artist figure in this book. She
was the one I identified with least, and the other two were
more me. When you are writing fiction, these characters
sort of make themselves up.

JODY: I'm quoting from one of your books now: "Five more
years after the birth of my feminist consciousness, I still
have to question every assumption, every reaction I have,
in order to examine them for signs of pre—conditioning."
Are you still questioning assumptions?

LUCY: I don't think I'm past that point so much as that
what I've been thinking about in the last few years has
been racism. Feminism is not *just* a preparation for
racism, obviously, but it has been a great preparation for
it. I think every white person in this country is a racist,
period. There's probably not much changing that in one
generation, but I can question my own racism in a way I
never could have questioned it before feminism. And I
can use some of the same questions, I can feel the things
that people have said and done about women and apply
them. A lot of the questions I'm dealing with in this multicultural book came up first within the feminist context.
So I don't think it has so much stopped as that it is
expanding and continuing. The world hasn't changed
that much, let's face it.

I know somebody I have to work with off and on who
came late to feminism and is still in that stage where
absolutely everything has to be picked on and torn apart
and worried away. I must say that gets kind of irritating
after a certain point, but I know I did exactly the same
thing, I *remember* doing exactly the same thing. I have
young male friends who complain about the way young,
early stage feminists are treating them; and often it *is* very
unjust, and I can now see some of the injustices. These
guys often are trying really hard to be feminists and doing
pretty well, but I have to keep saying to them, "I did the
same thing, and I understand exactly why they're doing

it." And then, there's that funny business of men complimenting you as being more reasonable than other women. That just pisses me off and I say, "Well, I'm not reasonable, I totally sympathize with them." There is a certain mellowing that comes with age, which is really pretty pleasant. When it comes down to it, I've never been a very tolerant person. I'm a little more tolerant now.

JODY: What's your view of the hostility toward Judy Chicago's work: is it because of her feminist perspective or her overtly sexual imagery?

LUCY: In Judy's work they are inseparable. It's also Judy herself. She is such a powerful person; she is immensely threatening, powerful and smart—and is threatening to women as well as to men.

JODY: Isn't her authenticity a part of this as well? How do you define authenticity as it applies to art? Politics? Life?

LUCY: I still use that all the time, "cultural authenticity:" let's see, what do I mean by it? A sort of honesty, unpretentiousness, all the things I like—coming straight from the heart and not being too mediated by socialization. Things that aren't just borrowed. In an odd way here there is no one white American culture, or the culture is so all-pervasive that it doesn't look like culture anymore, so there is a lot of borrowing from other cultures. I have to plead guilty to the same thing because I'm very interested in other cultures and have been for a long time. I'm also interested in my own family's history, and I like history and oral history, but I'm hard put to say exactly what the authenticity of my own work would be in terms of this multicultural stuff.

JODY: Esther Broner said that your work is characterized by both change and constancy: change in that you are always willing to grow, and constancy in your view of quality. Does quality have anything to do with cultural authenticity?

LUCY: Quality is one of the things I have a terrible time

with. I call it "aesthetic integrity" instead of quality because I can't stand the word, it is so class-bound. My *quality* isn't going to be what your *quality* is anyway, so let's just forget about the word and let me talk about what I'm interested in and let it go at that. Or cultural authenticity, or some other euphemism. But unfortunately it doesn't mean the same thing. I find myself backed into corners sometimes and having to say, "And these also are very good artists," or something like that. I think to myself, "Why did I say that?" Because what I'm talking about means that she or he is a very good artist anyway, so why am I having to fall back on the old *quality* thing? It's hard to avoid.

I have finally gotten sick of the word *art* itself, and I say to people, "Let's just talk about these things. We know we are talking about what is called art. Instead of worrying about whether it is good art or bad art, let's see how we respond to it and whether it gives us what we are looking for in the so-called art experience." I'm also aware that frequently when I say that, the person I'm talking to does not get the same thing out of it that I do and isn't looking for the same thing I am. Consequently, just because I have a certain amount of power because I've written books, I can say, "This is good art, and if you don't see it's good art, then something is wrong with you," like Clement Greenberg always did, but that doesn't interest me much. I'd be much more curious to find out why they think it isn't good art, or is. I guess ideally I just like to bust down the categories so that people really have to look at the experience itself and figure out what it is and what it's doing for them, and if it's moving them. I keep saying, "Does this move you? Is this something you ever want to see again? Is it going to change your life at all, even in the slightest perceptual kind of way?"

JODY: Are you still an activist? Is that difficult? Does it require courage?

LUCY: Yes, I'm certainly an activist, but I don't think that's so much courage as conviction. Again, I'm very lucky I can make a living. Courage in this life often seems to have to do with whether you are taking tremendous economic risks or not, and I never have. Luckily, I found that when I change, there are enough people who change with me that I can still go out and lecture, which is really the main thing I support myself on.

JODY: For many years now you have been doing shows of protest. How did you become involved in this, and are you still doing it?

LUCY: Yes, I'm still doing it, very much so. I was always a liberal, but I started moving to the left in '68 with the anti-war movement and then with feminism, and then back into feminist left politics. Now I call myself a socialist-feminist or a feminist-socialist, whichever mood I'm in. I sort of enjoy being out on a limb. I'm writing a column called "Sniper's Nest" because I've always said that I like being a sniper. I much prefer being outside sniping in than inside being sniped at. I've been accused of being a moving target, and I say, "What target in it's right mind wouldn't move?" When I lecture and they ask, "What are you?" I say, "I'm a writer and an activist."

JODY: What were the circumstances leading to your first protest show?

LUCY: In September of 1968 I went to Argentina as part of a jury and for the first time ran into artists who were politically active. I had been so embroiled in the art world I just didn't have much contact. Outside I met artists who said, "We won't make art when the world is this much of a mess. We're going to do something about it, and we can do it with our art." That was a revelation to me. I was being gradually politicized in New York, mainly through conceptual art, through trying to democratize an art form that lent itself to that and had that as part of its reason for being. Then I came back—I always seem to go away and come back—and a friend of mine asked me to help put together an anti-war show. We put together a really beautiful, minimalist show that had nothing overtly to do with politics. Then the Artworkers' Coalition started, and from then on I've been one of the founders of every single political artists' group in New York, and still find that immensely rewarding. I don't think I could live with myself without that. But for almost nine years I worked almost entirely within the feminist community.

In about 1975–76, some of us tried to move back into the left community and discovered that the men still couldn't even use the female pronoun. There was a group called Artists Meeting for Cultural Change, and cultural change involved pronouns, it seemed to me. Even though they were well-meaning people they just couldn't do it yet, so I went back into the feminist community and we founded *Heresies*. At that point I was becoming much more of a socialist. In 1979 I started PADD (Political Art Documentation and Distribution) as one more attempt to see if men and women could work together, and because I really felt that the art world needed a political art community again. This time it took.

JODY: Can men and women work together? I still don't see a significant shift in men's consciousness.

LUCY: I work well with men. I have had a working partner for years who is a man, and the person I work most closely with in cultural organizing is a gay man. I find a lot of feminists either want to stay in the feminist community or have gone back into art and are not interested in political organizing. Because I feel very strongly that feminist principles have to be carried out into the world, for the last decade or so I've made that something I do. I don't work well with all men, but I just don't bloody well work with the ones I don't like. Men on the left can always be called on their mistakes, and if they are good people— most of the people I work with are—you can say to them,

"O.K., did you notice what you were up to?" They tend
to lean over backwards, and although they don't always
like it, I think they do pretty well.

JODY: Do you know many men who accept women and
women's values?

LUCY: I think so, and it was nice to get back to working
with men. I'm the only founding member still in the
Heresies collective, and that continues to be a base,
although now I'm away a lot so I don't do much. I was
really pissed off about three years ago; some woman called
me from the Midwest and asked me to speak at a conference about two weeks away. I said, "I would love to, but
what in the world made you think I could do this with
two weeks notice? Have you been planning it for a
while?" I was just curious, because usually when they
want you they get in touch with you ahead of time. She
hemmed and hawed and then said, "Well, I have to admit
that somebody out here who knows you (they obviously
didn't know me) said that you weren't a feminist anymore, that you were more interested in the Third World."
I said, "Isn't that interesting: I hadn't heard that the
Third World is all men." I was just enraged by that, and I
hear it fairly often. I think that's a very unprogressive
feminist attitude. There's no question that there's things
you can get out of working with women; I would miss the
feminist community terribly if it wasn't there, but there
are also things about working with men.

JODY: How are you viewed by people in the traditional art
world? How do you view yourself in relation to that community?

LUCY: I see myself as not really in the art world anymore,
but I do still make my living by being an art critic. I am
asked to lecture about art so I see a lot of things; I just
don't do the social aspect of it…meeting people and so
forth. I go and look at art and say what I think and use
what I can use of it. I'm completely out of the power

structure, although I can still call on aspects of it. But outside of New York I'm apparently perceived as a famous art critic with a whole lot of power in the art world and very much *in* the art world, which allows me to keep making a living by lecturing. Inside of New York people think of me as just some kind of crazy commie. I know a lot of people who think first I was this feminist, and then I became a—I've been called a didactic Stalinist several times—but at the same time, political art in watered-down form has become popular in the art world in the last few years, and they can't avoid the fact that I was there first. So they've had to pay a certain amount of lip service, and this goes for feminism, too. French feminism, the very intellectual brand of feminism, that's also in the art-and-politics realm. While I have nothing against those people, it isn't what I do; I don't have the patience, and it doesn't interest me that much. I'm asked to do plenty of things. I've got more than I can do, and at the same time I don't get bothered any more by people wanting me to advance their careers.

JODY: In a letter in *From the Center* you said: "I hope you remember that being a feminist carries with it a real responsibility to be a human." In all the years I was in graduate school nobody ever cared if a writer was an honorable human being or a shit, never even mentioned it. Yet that is such an important question, the links among life, politics and art. Consider, for example, Jean Jacques Rousseau, who used to expose himself in the streets of Geneva. Also, he wrote *Emile*, the great treatise on children's education, yet he sent his own six illegitimate children, whom he fathered with his servant, to the orphanage! How do you reconcile that? Aren't honor, integrity and treating people decently legitimate political concerns?

LUCY: I think they definitely are. One thing I got out of feminism and socialism was the notion that you live your life and you make your art all in one piece; you don't split things off. One of the things we talk about a lot in PADD is that the work we are doing is of a piece in terms of leafletting and going out to rallies and putting together sculptures for rallies. And my lecturing and my doing performances with my partner—all are part of a single body of work and part of my life, and the lines blur a lot. I refuse to make that kind of distinction. That certainly has something to do with your question. Then all of your relationships are part of your professional morality or your personal morality.

JODY: You referred to art criticism as not being a primary form. Was it your intent to make art criticism more accessible to people, to reinvigorate it? The art criticism I've read, you have to drink an awful lot of coffee to get through.

LUCY: I don't think about criticism that much. It really has always been the art and the writing. Once I'm interested in the art, I want to write about it clearly enough to get across what I want to say. I'm also bored to tears by certain kinds of writing and can barely plow through it. It takes me a day to read an article in some of this language that I don't understand, and I've never been interested in philosophy either, which sounds weird because a lot of the things I'm interested in have philosophical overtones. I like nattering away at things, but there is some level of that I just can't get into. So yes, I do still feel criticism is parasitic. I've developed a plain, journalistic style that is somewhat idiosyncratic to deal with art that I'm fond of. I don't think it's great writing, but it pleases me if somebody thinks they can understand it.

JODY: In *Sexual Politics, Art Style* you make a list of things that must be changed: for example, disregarding women or stripping them of self-confidence from art school on; refusing to consider a married woman or a mother a serious artist no matter how hard she works and what she produces; labelling women unfeminine and abnormally assertive if they insist on maintaining the values of their art; treating women artists as sex objects; using this as an excuse not to visit their studios, not to show their work; using fear of social or professional rejection to turn successful women against unsuccessful women; ripping off women if they participate in the unfortunately influential social life of the art world; identifying women artists with their men; galleries turning a woman artist away without seeing her slides...

LUCY: Frankly, I would be surprised if any of these changes have come about, aside from the fact that there are a lot more women in the art world—which did change, primarily from our changing it. I don't think any of those things *don't* still happen, but at least we know these things exist and can call people on them; how many people *do* call others on them is something else. I'm always quoting Herbert Schiller, who said something to the effect, "A raised consciousness is the greatest weapon for institutionalized change that we'll ever get our hands on." It's very sad there aren't women's groups and artists' groups going on in New York. Those support groups were so valuable: you don't need them your whole life, but we keep them our whole life; we continue to see the people we were particularly fond of out of those groups. Young women still need that; people starting out in the world need that just as much as they ever did. They may not think they do, but when they do, the framework isn't really in place anymore.

JODY: Are there more women in museum shows in New York, in Los Angeles, across the country?

LUCY: Again, I'm very much of two minds. On one level when people say, "The women's movement hasn't done anything," I get very annoyed and say, "Don't be silly. There are millions more women working and visible." And that's perfectly true. If people say, "Oh, it's all been done, there are women in museums as much as men," well, then I say, "That's bullshit, of course not." That's where it is. In the last six years or so there has been a real backlash with fewer and fewer women in museum shows. Susan Rothenberg is one of the few women picked up by the Neo-Expressionist movement. Although she doesn't call herself a feminist, she did publicly say she had refused to be the only woman in these shows. Museums being stodgier and being supposedly more involved with "quality"—which, of course, women just don't quite have—all that shit keeps on going. The art world is a microcosm of the real world.

JODY: Isn't all art political, one way or the other?

LUCY: I go back and forth on this one, too. I often say there is no such thing as neutral art. Whatever you are doing, it can be used for the status quo, and if you're not doing anything, then the status quo uses it. There certainly is a lot of apolitical art, but I can't have it both ways. If I attack apolitical art I can't say that all art is political. So what I'm really attacking is artists who aren't aware of how their work is used. Then, there are all kinds of so-called political art that work on different aspects of the audience, different audiences, and so forth.

JODY: A lot of people find their path, proceed ahead and the path gets more defined, i.e., narrower and narrower. With your work there is a continual expanding and widening.

LUCY: I'm either blessed or cursed: being both restless and impatient, I have to be moving out or I get bored and nasty and nobody wants to be around me. Actually, I'm very excited at the moment: I just turned fifty, and I feel like I've got a whole lot of exciting things coming up.

JODY: As an only child of fifty, how do you deal with caring for an aging mother? Are you like your mother or different from her? Were you close earlier in your life, and is it different now? Is your mother supportive of your work?

Lucy R. Lippard

LUCY: We've had very different lives. I'm not really like her in many ways, but I have a lot of her mannerisms and she's the word-person in the family. I guess everybody's mother becomes a part of them one way or another. Since my father died five years ago, our very dissimilar lives have become much more entangled, which isn't easy for either of us. Even though I'm an only child, I wasn't prepared for this new responsibility. After the first flush of being a "wonderful daughter," the crisis mentality wore off, and I thought for a while that my life as I'd known it was virtually over. Her friends were suggesting that since I was "unmarried" with "no job" I should go up to New Haven and live with her! But my son was a terrific help and emotional support, and in the last year or so mother's health and spirits have improved, and she's really very independent, so it's better. I live with her for two months in the summer and see a lot of her in the fall. Then I'm in Colorado for five months.

Being involved with my mother's life has actually taught me a good deal about life in general, and probably about my own. Turning fifty somehow made it all easier to handle. You do take stock at that point—half a century! For the most part I'm living exactly the way I want to: I love living alone, after some twenty years living with men, and I have tremendous freedom and flexibility. I feel very lucky. I always have.

JODY: How about your father: what were his gifts to you, his legacy? What have you internalized from your father?

LUCY: I got a lot of basically good stuff from both of them, about honesty and caring and a concern for social justice and respect for creativity. It's easier to think of the things I rebelled against, like the tremendous anxiety about what other people think of you and having to measure up to some imposed standards. My mother was the daughter of a Congregational minister and was raised to constantly be good at what she was doing, but she was rarely praised for it or for being pretty, which she was. That's the unhappy part of her childhood, I think, and I live with its residue or resonance and probably passed it on to Ethan.

My father also had to measure up a lot. He came out of a small-town, working-class situation to go to Yale on a scholarship and move on up in the world. At the age of twelve, I announced at dinner that I wasn't going to live like they did. I don't know what the hell I thought I was going to do, be Forever Amber or National Velvet or something. They were appalled because they thought they had built themselves such a nice life, and they had…but I somehow knew it wasn't for me.

So for a long time I've been trying to pry myself away from something in my parents' lives while staying very close to other aspects. I'm still not clear what it's all about. They made me the way I am; they were both immensely proud of me and not always too happy about the way I went about my life, especially my father, who took everything I did—books, relationships—more seriously than I did, in a way.

JODY: Do you approach your work differently now? How has your relationship to your work changed over time? Do you feel more intensely or less intensely about it?

LUCY: My work has changed. It's changed quite drastically, but it's also been consistent. I've always loved to write ; that's what I like to do, even if I'm writing basically fast things, as Esther Broner so kindly put it. As I said, I find that when I'm just about to launch into something new I write a little bit of fiction and it loosens some bolts and makes a lot of things possible. Maybe I'll never write fiction full-time or seriously, but it plays a definite role in everything I do.

My relation to the art world? I used to be rooted in it, as a community. Then it stopped being a community, for me at least, somewhere in the early '70s, when I realized what the art world was all about—partly through feminism, partly through politics. And then there was just an increasing lack of interest in spending my life looking at objects. You can only go around rooms looking at one object after another for so long and maintain any connection to the real point of art-making—no matter how beautiful they are, no matter how much of somebody has been put into them.

I'm lucky because my work has always led me. The next thing has always become apparent—sometimes through dreams or a series of events and "coincidences." I never make decisions, I just organically let myself be drawn into the next project. I love the moment when I'm finishing a book or organizing a project and have absolutely no idea what's coming next. But with each project that I finish, it's an opening; it's like being laid bare again, reborn even.

Ten years ago I wanted something to happen that would make me not be an art critic anymore. It never actually happened that neatly, but now that I look back, it's been happening in a lot of different ways. I write some non-art journalism, some fiction. I've always curated a lot, organized a lot. I've made "public art" for demos, performances, comics. So there really are no boundaries I'm forced to respect. It's a matter of making connections, not giving anything up, but finding the added ingredients that help it all to merge, or emerge.

I don't need much money to live on. I can do whatever I want, and if I'm not doing something I think I want, then I obviously don't want to do it yet. I have nobody to blame but myself. And I'm not blaming myself, I'm just waiting to see what comes next. *Mixed Blessings* may be my last "art book." Then again, maybe not.

My relationship to my work is primary, since I made a first unconscious and then conscious decision not to be involved in an all-consuming relationship with a man— partly because I haven't met anyone "consuming" for

years, but also because my own life is so full already.
Maybe later, when mother dies, when Ethan has a place of
his own, maybe then I'll want a relationship, but for the
time being I can't imagine having anybody around all the
time. I love the varied and comfortable spaces of my own
life. More and more, nature seems to fill the gaps.

JODY: How did you come to terms in your own life with
the conflict between your creative drive and your need or
desire to be with family? How did you put it all together?
Is it even possible to put it all together? Where have you
been frustrated, in your creative work or in your private
life or both? Do you ever feel torn between your work and
your personal connections to others? Where have you
compromised in your life?

LUCY: I've always felt torn, and at the same time kind of
proud of myself for integrating as well as I have, which is
not the perfect integration. I've been torn between parents and friends, lovers and child, child and work, work
and other work, but it's *all* pleasure. Boulder's an integra-
tive place for me because, while I can write any place, I
have nature and an activist community there. In New
York the activist community isn't flourishing at the
moment, and there isn't a tree in sight.

I do my usual six hours or so of writing a day, hike for
an hour or two, help organize to raise some hell, see
friends and go to movies and stuff and read the rest of the
time. At this point that's what I seem to need. I don't
have the urge to travel to exotic places right now, and the
lecturing gets me around the country. But the conflicts
are constant about how every minute of the day is going
to be used. There's always so much I'd like to be doing,
and I'm very aware that there will *never* be enough time.
Then I think, well, do I enjoy just staring into space? No,
not particularly. If I do, I want a book, I want to be walking or talking to somebody. I want to be *doing* something.

JODY: Marilyn French talks about the overwhelming and

destructive drive toward power in our culture, which also drives the feminine principle underground. Women are devalued in a culture whose values are power, violence and ultimately death as opposed to love, pleasure and life. What can we as women do?

LUCY: I have mixed feelings about this, as I think every woman does about power. I feel that way politically. I was a leader for a long time in this very small puddle that I was leading, and I got very tired of that. I really don't like the notion of being powerful, but then again this is ridiculous because I grab it whenever I can to do what I want to do with it, so I don't know where that comes from. This hand-reader read me a whole long thing about my ambivalence about power and she was right on. She said that now I would only go so far in terms of getting power, and that's really in a funny way how I feel, that I'll never want to take the last step. I've never wanted to run for office.

I've always loved collective work and that's what saved me (I hope) from being a nasty little male-identified, power-grabbing woman, which I think I was headed well into at one point. I didn't know what it was, but, luckily, when I was politicized I was "feminized" as well. I love the feeling of potentially taking power *as a group*, whereas individually it scares me. As I get older I want less and less individual power, though I like the same stuff everybody's ego likes. I do want my accomplishments recognized.

I had a moment years ago when I was becoming a well-known art critic, which was what I'd thought I wanted, and then came the realization that this is definitely not it: I don't enjoy this; I don't like the way people feel they have to act with me; it doesn't give me any pleasure any more. In the last few years I have had a confidence in myself, in who I am—for better or worse—that I've never had before. It makes life a lot easier. Now all I expect in terms of power is the power to communicate to people, to convene people, to set seeds going in their minds, to raise consciousness. It always comes back to me in the most gratifying, satisfying ways when the seeds have grown.

JODY: In Marian Woodman's *Addiction to Perfection, or the Unravished Bride*, she said that in a culture that is no longer healthy enough to serve as a context or container, each of us builds a context or a container with the images that are most personal and meaningful to us. Is there an image or images from your own life that applies?

LUCY: I guess it's a journey, a walk. I'm on a long, long curving dirt road or path by myself, in huge landscapes that are vast and empty but beautiful—endlessly rolling hills, plains, mountains in the distance. I've the feeling of being out in a sailboat heading out to the horizon, or in a big field walking towards a little woods, or coming out of the woods into a meadow. I see it all in landscape terms, with very good people along the way, whom I love…but it's essentially a voyage of solitude.

Judy Dater

I first became aware of Judy Dater's work through her book on Imogen Cunningham, one of my personal heroes. Shortly after reading it I saw a series of portraits of women Judy had done that piqued my interest. What clinched my decision to interview her was seeing two nude studies she did of a black man named Nehemia. They are intensely personal and extremely sensual, but what really knocked me out is their obvious relationship to a long tradition celebrating the female body, i.e., the classic female odalisques of Ingres, Goya, Manet and others.

I felt that these photos make a very daring statement in showing a nude man posed in a purely decorative and highly erotic manner. They reverse the habitual relation of man as observer of woman and woman as decorative object. First handing over the authority of the viewer to the female and subjective self makes them highly subversive. Also, the female photographer is white, and the male model is black. Finally, they make a very strong statement about woman's appreciation of the male body and the assertiveness of female sexuality.

Body and Soul, Judy's next book, also had a big impact on me. There is an immediacy and an absence of masking in all of Judy's photos. The images in this book are so intensely subjective and easy to identify with that they speak about the lives of all women. Her most recent book, *Cycles*, con-

tains personal and autobiographical photographs presented in the context of her complete work and traces recurring symbols and themes. With a forward by Clarissa Pinkola Estes, author of *Women Who Run With the Wolves*, the book is once again intensely subjective, this time in relation to Dater as subject.

Judy Dater lives in Northern California, although at the time we got together in New York she was living a bicoastal existence. After the intensity of her photographs and the articulateness of her introduction to the Cunningham book, I was unprepared for Judy's straightforward manner and simplicity of speech. Bella Lewitzky says in her interview that she believes every human being has one sense more profoundly developed than the others, and Judy is a visual person. When she was talking to me I felt as though she was seeing what it was she wanted to say and translating it into verbal terms in order to be able to communicate those images to me.

There is a card in the tarot deck, the eight of pentacles, the card of crafting, which reminds me of Judy Dater. It's about being willing to do the crafting out of which comes the art you struggle with for so long. It is the transmutation of the everyday into art, her unabashed eroticism and her power to see that I like so much about Judy Dater. Judy Dater's photographic work can be found in 75 *Women and Other Visions: Photos by Judy Dater and Jack Welpott; Imogene Cunningham: A Portrait; Judy Dater: Twenty Years; Body and Soul: Ten American Women,* with Carolyn Coman and *Cycles* (in Japanese and in English). A freelance photographer, artist and writer, Judy Dater has also been the recipient of a Guggenheim Fellowship and two National Endowment for the Arts Grants.

Looking for
That Charged Moment

An Interview with Judy Dater
New York, New York
September 1989

JODY: What got you interested in becoming a photographer in the first place?

JUDY: I was an art major before I started taking photography. I'd always wanted to be an artist from as early as I can remember, and I did lots of painting and drawing. When I was a senior in college I had to take either print-making or photography as part of the art major. I wanted to take photography, but the photography classes were full so I enrolled in a print-making class. It so happened that semester that I was working on registration. My job was to hand out the IBM cards for the classes. There I was with all the cards, so I just decided to take a card for photography and switch myself out of print-making. That was the second semester of my senior year in college, so I just barely made it.

I took a class in beginning photography with Jack Welpott, and it seemed like magic to me. I thought, "This is it! This is what I've been looking for." I decided to pursue it and pretty much phased out everything else I'd been doing in order to concentrate on photography. Of course, I got involved with Jack, who was my teacher, and we married and then later divorced.

I had gone to UCLA for three years as an art major and then transferred to San Francisco State, where I took that first photo class in 1963. Then I got an M.A. in photography.

JODY: How important to your photography was being trained in painting and drawing?

JUDY: Very important. You got the basic elements of how to put images together and balance light against dark. I took lots of classes in design: two-dimensional and three-dimensional design, and painting and drawing. My favorite class was life drawing. It was an easy transition to go from that to photographing people, which is really what I was interested in. I didn't realize till years later, when I started thinking back, that what I had always liked the best about drawing was the life-drawing. It made perfect sense to me that I had this interest in the body, in people and in faces.

JODY: You had a one-woman show at the Witkin Gallery in New York in 1972. Those are hard to come by. How did it happen?

JUDY: That's an interesting story I had shown at Witkin's before, in a group show. Witkin had come out to California in 1968 or 1969...I was in a group show at the San Francisco Museum of Modern Art with three or four other Bay Area photographers, and he saw the work and liked it. He wanted to have a small show in his gallery of some of the same people that were in the museum show, and he picked three or four of us. That was in 1969 or 1970. Then, he decided he wanted to do a show of my work. Witkin usually did two-person shows at his gallery at that time, so he was going to have a show of me and Berenice Abbott. Berenice Abbott was going to be in the bigger room and I was going to be in the smaller room. I was of course ecstatic to be showing with Berenice Abbott. I thought that was fabulous and I was perfectly happy to have a small show.

It turned out that Berenice Abbott had never heard of me and was upset that she was not going to have the whole gallery to herself, so she pulled out of the show at the last minute, after the announcements were printed and everything. Lee Witkin, not knowing what else to do, decided that I should have the bigger show and that he would put some Camerawork gravures in the small gallery. So that was the show. Anyhow, the show was quite successful and got good reviews, and people were excited about the work.

JODY: Your photographs don't seem posed, but they don't seem spontaneous either. They feel more like studies, chosen moments, and very intense moments at that. Is it in fact the intensity of a particular moment that attracts you in a photograph?

JUDY: Yes, that is what I am looking for; I am looking for that charged moment. I'm not particularly interested in a likeness of a person. With the portraits I did earlier of both men and women—I'm not really doing portraits anymore—I was trying to create a kind of dramatic moment or setting. I thought of it as a kind of theatre, and I would pick people who had a dramatic flair about them.

Usually I would go to their house and I would set up a situation that was like a stage set. (I always think of the background and the setting and where they are sitting and the light as a kind of stage set.) Then I would put them into it and try to get them to react somehow—to me, to the moment, to the setting. I totally directed it. I would totally control it, but I would try to set it up in such a way as to allow spontaneous things to happen within that controlled environment.

Most of the earlier portraits I did I used a 4 x 5 view camera. I would set everything up...tell them how to sit and where to look and what to wear...but when it came to actually snapping the shutter, I wouldn't look at them. I would look down or I would look away.

I think what I was doing was trying to allow them to have a little space within themselves to do something for me that, if I was staring at them I might make them more self-conscous. So it was controlling it up to the moment of taking the picture, and then not.

That was something I did very unconsciously. I didn't realize for years that I wasn't looking at the people when I snapped the shutter. Once I realized what I was doing, I tried to force myself to look at them. I felt so uncomfortable and so self-conscious myself that I realized somehow I couldn't impose that much of myself on them at the moment.

JODY: I can understand that because your portraits are so intimate. It would be like being present at some terribly private event.

JUDY: Well, it *was* very intimate. I would spend several hours with these people, but basically they would be strangers to me, and here they would be letting me into their house and tell them what to do, and how to look, and giving me all this time. I didn't necessarily become friends with the people afterward. I did with a couple of them, but usually not...it was just this thing of the moment.

JODY: How did you choose your subjects?

JUDY: Sometimes they would be friends of friends. Or I would see them at a party or I'd see people at openings or in restaurants or standing in line at the bank. I'd see them everywhere. Then it was a matter of working up my courage to approach them and ask if I could photograph them. If I saw somebody that moved me a great deal and I couldn't help myself, then I would get over my shyness and my desire to not have to go do that, and I would just do it.

JODY: Members of certain native tribes believe that the camera captures the person's soul. Your photographs do seem to capture the very soul of your subject. Is that a goal of yours...conscious or unconscious?

JUDY: It's not so much capturing the soul of that individual, but trying to capture a kind of universal quality that

I see in people. Some person will have the ability to project a universal quality or emotion, and I *am* trying to get that.

I see individuals as being actors who have the ability, whether they are conscious of it or not, of projecting a certain something I see in them. Maybe it's my own soul I'm capturing because I'm the one who thinks I see something in that person, and that is why I pick them. So it *is* about that. But I'm really trying to show something I see as a universal trait in people.

JODY: What about the portraits of Nehemia? Who was he and how did you happen to photograph him? They are exquisite, erotic portraits of a man by a woman. And the scarf on the sofa: how did that happen to be in the photograph?

JUDY: He was somebody who lived in the Bay Area for a while and had done modeling for some painters in San Francisco. I photographed him two different times. The first time I met him was at a party at another woman artist's house; he was there with a girlfriend and they were like this fantastic item. Everything he did in life was really for show, he was very dramatic. That first night he was totally in black and wearing really skin tight black-leather pants, a huge sword and a kind of Rudolph Valentino headdress...just this increditble outfit. You couldn't *not* notice him. He was outrageous.

He was with a woman who was very, very white. Very, very blonde and all in white. She looked like something off the cover of a 1930s *Vogue* magazine. I wanted to photograph both of them, and I did. But the first session I had with the two of them, they had such a fantasy about the kind of little tableau drama they wanted to act out, that I was just recording for them.

They had arranged to have a speckled white horse with black spots; we went out to the countryside and they went through this whole thing with her nude on the horse and him leading her through the forest. I took pictures, and they were rather amusing, but they weren't anything that was for me. I lent them the negatives, which they lost in a taxicab, supposedly, so that was the end of that.

Then, about a year later I saw him again, and he was by himself that time. I don't remember what he was wearing, but he looked just as fabulous and I thought, "I *have* to photograph this guy. He is too incredible!" We chatted, and I asked him again and I said, "But this time you have to let me do what I want to do."

He was living in Mill Valley at the time, and I went over to his place. I didn't know what I wanted to do, but I figured it really didn't matter; there was no way that I couldn't take a good picture of him. I started doing portraits. I think I took two pictures in whatever outfit he had on at the moment, and then he just took his clothes off. I didn't even ask him to: he just took his clothes off and started posing for me in the nude.

We started working outdoors, and then went indoors, and I got into arranging him. That's when we started working on the couch with the scarf, which had been draped over the piano in the apartment where he was living.

He seemed to fall into amazing poses rather naturally. He was very aware of his body and how beautiful he was and how well he moved, and he was very at ease with himself, which is why those pictures worked. He was a dancer and a musician, so he had great self-presence about what he looked like and how he presented himself. He was right there.

That time I got several photos I liked, but the two that have been reproduced are probably my favorites. My first favorite is the one where you can see his face. I really like that one because his face shows his confidence and how easy he is with himself physically. It *is* erotic: he is amazing to look at.

JODY: Many of your portraits of women are nude from the waist up. Why not completely nude or completely clothed?

JUDY: On some level it's more erotic to show part rather than all. Sometimes if the person is completely nude it's actually less erotic. So there is a desire to play with the potential of the erotic by partially revealing and partially concealing. That's the whole reason for doing anything nude. Whether the man or woman is completely nude or partially nude, there is the whole idea of adding an extra dimension of eroticism and that charged sexual tension that you get.

I always think of them as portraits though. I don't think of them as nudes, except for a very few pictures. For example, the picture of Nehemiah from the back is a classic nude but the one from the front to me is a portrait, as are all the ones where the women's faces are showing. They are usually looking into the camera and there is a certain look on their faces. When they have their clothes off, that creates within them and within me a kind of tension that wouldn't be there if they were totally clothed. Clothing is a kind of costume—it protects you—so when you have that taken away you become more vulnerable. I like playing with that vulnerability.

JODY: In an erotic photograph is it the fusion of your personality, your own sensuality, with the subject? Is it the result of that particular moment? Is it *your* eroticism that is being projected, or is it an erotic quality inherent in the person who is being photographed? Or both?

JUDY: It is a combination of things, just like portraits are a combination of the photographer and the subject. You can't separate them. Another photographer would photograph that person entirely differently, even at the exact same moment, and the person would respond slightly differently to a different personality. It's always a blending of the two.

JODY: Recently I interviewed a woman who worked with Moshe Feldenkrais, the great scientist and body worker. He said that he didn't heal people, he danced with them. And as he danced with them he felt their pain and so knew how to help them. I have the sense that you dance visually with your subjects, and that as you dance with them you draw out their essence. There is such a strong sense of dialogue in your photographs: do you work specifically for that?

JUDY: You have to be in tune with the person you are photographing. You have to pay attention to what they say and how they move. You have to be sensitive to all that and work with it. You have to very quickly figure out something about this person in terms of their personality, or their life, or whatever it is, and try and get yourself in balance with that somehow, so that you can work with them. I guess it's just being empathetic to who they are. You can't just go in and take a picture.

JODY: Are you aware of what attracts you to a particular person?

JUDY: It's not always the same thing, but it's a certain presence that people have, a certain flair for the dramatic. Sometimes there is a kind of knowing in a face—wisdom or experience. Most of the time those are the things I'm drawn to, or a kind of mystery. I'm less interested in the naive than in the knowing, which is probably why I don't normally photograph children. (I'm leaving out children who may have had illness, or some extreme thing like that.) I'm more interested in a face that's had more life experience.

JODY: What kind of camera did you use for the portraits?

JUDY: All those portraits you have seen were done with a 4 × 5 Deardorff.

JODY: What effect did your father's owning and operating a movie theatre have on your becoming a photographer?

JUDY: It had a lot to do with it, on a lot of different levels.

When I was a kid I used to go to the theatre with him. All the lights would be out, and it would be completely dark in there. I would play this little game with myself to see how far I could walk down the aisle in the total darkness. My goal was to get to the stage, and I was terrified. I think I did make it up to the stage a couple of times, and then I would run out as fast as I could.

Of course, seeing all the images—and they didn't censor anything—I saw zillions of films when I was a kid, plus my dad made home movies. I was always playing in the home movies and going to the movie theatre with him and playing with all the movie posters and publicity pictures. I was very interested in the images on all kinds of levels.

I remember as a kid taking the movie still posters; they would give out 8 x 10 glossies of posters, and he would always have tons of those around. I used to play with them and put them in order of my favorites. I don't see how it *couldn't* have affected me, plus the whole idea of growing up in Hollywood...All of that had to have had a major effect.

JODY: Speaking of major effects, how did you meet Imogen Cunningham, and what was she like?

JUDY: She was fabulous, completely outrageous, very feisty, very outspoken...a real showman.

JODY: How old was she when you met her?

JUDY: She was eighty. It was really something to meet someone who at eighty was so alive and out there. She was very flamboyant, and she loved to be the center of attention. She always dressed in some wild get up so that you would have to notice her, and if you didn't, she would make a point of engaging you in conversation. I was twenty-two, I think, and she was eighty. She amazed me; I had never met anybody like her before.

I met her at a conference in Big Sur Hot Springs, which later became Esalen. I had just started in photography; I'd been doing it for maybe six months or so. There was a gathering of people who had known Edward Weston, so she was there, and Ansel Adams, Brett Weston, Cole Weston and a bunch of other people from the Bay Area. Mostly, they were sitting around talking and reminiscing about him and about his work.

During that gathering she asked if she could photograph me. She took me out somewhere and put me up against some funny old building and took some portraits of me. Then she said when I came back to San Francisco I should call her up and come over and she would give me a print. So how could I not do that? I did call her, and she invited me for lunch. I went over and she asked me questions about my photography and what I wanted to do.

She befriended me. She drew me in to part of her circle; she did that with lots of people. She liked young people. I think she liked having them around her. She was interested in me because I was one of the few people who was photographing people; everybody else was pretty much involved in doing landscape. She was not a landscape photographer, she was a people photographer. I think she saw something in me that interested her because I am interested in people.

Our friendship was one of my going over often and having lunch with her. Once in a while she would come out to my house or we would go places together, but the majority of time it was me going over there and having lunch and hanging out for several hours and talking.

JODY: Did you consider her a mentor? Was the talk over lunch about photography?

JUDY: It was not all photography because she liked to talk about everything. She loved to gossip, and she was into gardening and had many, many interests. But we did talk about photography, and on a few occasions she looked at my work and would give me these very funny critiques. They were never very intense, but they were usually to the point. There wasn't a lot of that. I always felt like I didn't want to impose on her, but if she asked me enough times I would bring her things to look at once in a while.

She was very much a mentor and a life teacher, more than anything. Every time I would go over there I would feel inspired in some way. There is no way you can be depressed or feel sorry for yourself when you are around somebody like that who is just working and doing and thinking about what to do next.

I knew her for thirteen years, from eighty to ninety-three, and she never, ever seemed old to me until the last time I saw her, when she was ill. It was a shock to see her because she never seemed like an old person to me. I don't know what she was ill with but she died shortly after that. You just never thought about it because she was so lively and had so much energy. A living example of amazing human-ness, that's what she was.

JODY: How lucky you are to have had her in your life.

JUDY: Really lucky. I haven't met anyone like that since, and I doubt I ever will in quite the same way. She was unique.

JODY: Imogen Cunningham used only natural light. Do you work only with natural light, or do you use artificial light as well?

JUDY: I prefer natural light. When you live in California it's a lot easier to get away with it. Since I moved to New York, sometimes I have to use other kinds of lighting, but I prefer to use natural light if I can.

JODY: Why did you move from black and white to color?

JUDY: I really started it just because I wanted to try it. I had been doing black and white for a long time. Around 1978 or 1979, a lot of fine-art photographers were beginning to use color. It seemed exciting, and it seemed like something new to do. The technology had changed quite a bit so that it was possible to do it better and easier and more permanent.

For a while I was shooting everything in both black-and-white and color. I did a lot of black-and-white land-scapes in color, and I thought, "These are just not work-ing in color." But then when I came to do the ones in the costumes—I did those also in black-and-white and color—they were just much more effective in color because a lot of it was about the color in the costume and the detail of the color. Now I'm back to black and white. It doesn't mean I won't do color again at some point; it just seems like for some things it's really appropriate and not for others.

JODY: How did *Body and Soul* come about?

JUDY: The publisher, Tim Hill, originally had an idea to do a book about men and women in non-traditional work. He had known me for a long time and wanted to work with me again. He also knew the writer Carolyn Coman and thought we would like each other and would get along. So he approached us about doing a book on that subject. I would do a single portrait of the person, and she would interview them.

Initially, he wanted both men and women doing cross-over jobs. We started to make a list but came up with very few jobs that men would do which had been traditional women's jobs, and they all seemed pretty boring. We thought: "It's not happening, except for a token house—husband or telephone operator. So let's not do men, let's just do women."

We found lots of interesting women doing tradition-ally men's work. We talked with a rabbi, a deep-sea diver, a sports writer, a wine-maker, an orchestra conductor and lots of others. But, when we started to interview them, it seemed that wasn't the issue any more. Women who were working in what had traditionally been men's jobs had already fought that battle.

The only one from that first group who is in the book was Barbara Bane, the sprinkler fitter. She ended up staying in the book when we changed the concept because she had so many other things to talk about. We were interested in having full-life stories; we wanted the whole picture. What we found out was that an interesting job does not necessarily an interesting woman make. So we decided to drop the idea of non-traditional work and find ten very interesting life stories with as much variety as possible within that limitation.

It was not supposed to be a book about every sort of woman in America. We also knew that by picking only ten we were going to limit ourselves, but we were very limited budget-wise. We tried to find ten interesting stories with women of different ages, different religious backgrounds, different parts of the country, different types of jobs, some married, some single, some gay, some straight, some with kids, some without, some successful, some not successful—just to get a range of good stories.

JODY: It is such a powerful book, it's a shame you could not have done a hundred more.

JUDY: It was a ton of work even doing those ten!

JODY: How did you decide on the series of photographic frames across the page, like parallel portraits? Did you arrive at that as you worked on the book or did you decide on that technique ahead of time?

JUDY: It was something I worked on with the designer, Lance Hidy. He also happened to be the husband of the writer, so the three of us worked very closely on the whole project. He wanted to do some radical things in relationship to the book design. I had taken hundreds of head shots of all these women as they were being interviewed and we could never decide on just one. That didn't seem to be what it was about at all. We wanted to show a range of expression, of feeling and emotion, as these women were telling us their stories.

Since then I've been using that idea in my own personal work. For one thing, I was using thirty-five-millimeter a lot on that project, and I really loved using it. The head shots led to a whole new direction in terms of the variety of expressions. It was a really good take-off point for me.

JODY: What did you intend to communicate with the blurred close-ups that you used in the book?

JUDY: That, too, was something I am now doing in my work; it came right out of that project. It started with the pictures of actress Geraldine Fitzgerald...she had such intense expressions! I couldn't believe it when I looked at the contact sheets because the conversations we had with her weren't heavy in the same way as some of the expressions that appeared on her face.

Because she was an actress, I got the idea that if I put them out of focus I would create a theatrical mask, like masks of comedy and tragedy. There was something in her face that made me think of that: I wanted to distill the expression to the essence of what I saw in her face, those really intense emotional expressions of anger, fear and surprise. I thought, "If I make them out of focus, that will come through stronger."

It didn't work with everybody, but it did work with those intense expressions. It was almost like making a visual vocabulary of expression. Also, I liked the idea of putting them out of focus to get rid of the particulars and get to the essence. Most of the work I've done in the last couple of years now I've done out of focus in order to get to what I think of as the essence of what's there.

JODY: Barbara Bane, the sprinkler-pipe fitter said, "It's not important that your life be easy; it's important that you be happy and that your life be interesting." Those are certainly words to live by. Has your life been easy? Has it been interesting?

JUDY: It's definitely been interesting, and it continues to be interesting. Certainly, parts of it have been easy, relatively speaking, compared to a lot of people, but no life is ever just easy. There have been plenty of bad times, horrendous times, but when they are not happening none of it seems so bad. Basically I think I'm a very lucky person, and my life is very good in comparison to 99% of the people on this earth. So I feel I can't complain...but there's been a lot of shit.

JODY: I loved the way antiphonal themes arch across the book. In a way, all the women were connected, with the exception of the woman who accepted her fate passively and removed herself into a fantasy world for gratification. She was the only one who seemed to feel she had no choice about her life. Why did you choose her?

JUDY: We wanted someone who worked in an assembly-line plant of some sort. Carolyn found a shoe factory where they were willing to let us come in and talk to some of the women. We went at lunchtime. We didn't know quite how to start talking to all these women, or how to decide whom we should approach. I decided to walk up and down the line and take pictures of the women at their sewing machines, hoping that would evoke some kind of response.

Gloria was way down at the end of the line. She started making wisecracks, calling attention to herself. When we worked our way up to where she was, she asked what we were doing, and we said we were working on this book. Then Carolyn came up with the idea of asking, "Is there any event that happened that had a profound impact on and really changed your life?"

We went back and Carolyn asked her that question. She said instantly, "Yes. My husband had his leg amputated, and I had to come back to work twelve years ago to support my family." We made an appointment to talk to her later. The only place she felt comfortable talking to us was at the Dunkin' Donuts, so we met her at the Dunkin' Donuts and did the interview there.

We felt she probably represents millions of women in

this country. It's a story that is tragic and very real, and she is not an isolated case. Who was it who said that most of us lead lives of quiet desperation? That was her life. That's why she's there.

She *was* different from the others because she was very, very unhappy. When she read the interview she made one tiny change, but basically said it was fine. Then she began to tell us another fifteen pages worth of horror that had happened since we had last seen her. The continuation of that hideous saga went on and on and just took our breath away.

So she was in the book because she called attention to herself, but she was probably a good choice. In a way, although it was a tragic story, on a certain level she is a survivor. She was getting up in the morning and going to the shoe factory and taking care of the children, and she was holding it together. She was self-destructive with her smoking and her eating, but she was still going to work. However miserable her life was, however pitiful it was, she was still doing it.

JODY: The other women seemed so full of hope, whereas she seemed so full of despair.

JUDY: After reading about Gloria, Doreen, the woman with dyslexia, said, "Well, you should send her to me...at least she can read!" Doreen thought that nobody had a right to complain if they could read.

JODY: What about Belle de Jour, the woman who provides S&M services to her clients and who said that she hated the word "normal"? I loved her philosophy: "Each person do what's good for him, live and let live, try everything once if it's not harmful, be happy and loving, be wide open and optimistic, eat plenty of fruits and vegetables." What's your own philosophy of life?

JUDY: I don't have one that poetic. I wish I did!

JODY: Who were your favorites among the various women?

JUDY: I loved Belle; she was my favorite. The nun also. She

was so intense that she took my breath away. She was the one woman who initially didn't want me to take any pictures of her; she thought she needed to be anonymous. Then, as we went along, she changed her mind. After I sent her all those pictures, she told me she felt like she had gained a totally new realization about herself and what she looked like.

I thought I did some of the best pictures of her. When I first saw her I didn't think I would be able to photograph her, because she's not the kind of person I would have picked off the street to photograph. But as she talked, there were so many things that happened in her face, that I just loved watching her through the camera. She was willing to act for me—twirling in the church, climbing the tree, putting in those false teeth—she really got into it. There was so much energy coming out of her. It was really intense.

Belle was the most fun to photograph because she was the most flamboyant visually, and that was very enjoyable. But I liked my trip to Alaska the best. That was great, in terms of all the places we went.

JODY: To me the solitary, Maggie Ross, was a saint, because she seemed to be at the heart of life. She reminded me of those women in the eleventh and twelfth centuries who went into the convents, became great abbesses and had tremendous learning and spiritual power. She emerges right out of that period. Tell me more about her.

JUDY: Now she is in London at Christ Church, although she is originally from Southern California, from a well-to-do family. I don't think they wanted her to be a nun: it was her calling, and she had to follow it.

JODY: She certainly appears to be a lot more than just a nun.

JUDY: She loved being in the book with all the other women because she felt her profession was related to everyone else, even though she was a solitary. She said she wouldn't have accepted if it was going to be a book about nuns; she wasn't interested in that. But the fact that there were going to be all these different kinds of women, she liked that aspect as being part of life, not apart from it.

JODY: I was struck by the need for solitude on the part of some of the women and the need for connection on the part of others. For me these are boundary issues having to do with time and space. Are you aware of these kinds of boundaries when you work with people generally? What about with these women?

JUDY: You have to know how far you can push someone or what you can ask them to do and not do, even if it is just in terms of how long you can continue to photograph them. Some people will be willing to be photographed in the nude and some won't (and sometimes I don't even want to!), or sometimes they will suggest it. Or sometimes there will be something about them that you just know you wouldn't even dream of asking. I guess it is a matter of knowing what is appropriate and what isn't and being sensitive to who people are.

JODY: What is your current work like?

JUDY: As I said, in a way it grew out of *Body and Soul*. The variety of expressions I was getting in the head shots led me to do some work that was beyond the single image. I would take five or six or even nine images and put them together in various kinds of grids. They are totally fictional, but there is a kind of implied narrative, so that the viewer looking at this group of pictures together thinks it is telling a story. A lot of the story is what they bring to it from their own past experience and how they interpret the combination of images.

Some of the images have faces in them, usually with very strong expresssions, in combination with objects or scenes that seem to imply something about these expressions on the women's faces. I know what the narrative means for me at an intuitive level; there is a reason in my own mind why I put these particular pictures together and how I feel about them, but there is no right way to interpret them.

I wouldn't expect anybody to get the exact same thing out of them as I do, even though lots of people looking at them see some of the same things and then tell me things they see in them that I didn't see. And that I like, that's exciting to me.

It's not that different from when I was doing the single portraits and people would look at them and get an idea of who this person was and maybe make up a story about that person. These are similar in that way; it's just that they are more complex because there are more images and there is a longer, more implied story.

As I said, they are totally fictional. I will put pictures together of people who have never met each other but who seem to be related. I'll put landscapes in where it seems like the landscape has to do with this particular person. So when you look at them in the image, there is a reason why they are together, but that person may never have seen that landscape or this object.

Some of it is based not on the truth about that person but on some other kind of truth, or some story that someone may have told me. I'll end up using someone else's face or some other object to tell some tale I have heard from someone, or to express some feeling that I have experienced myself. That's about the best I can describe verbally what they are about.

JODY: What aspect of photography is the most pleasurable for you?

JUDY: The high moment is when you make a print of something for the first time, and you look at it and say, "Yes, that's great, I like that." That's even better than when you finally get it printed and framed and up on the wall. They never look better than when they are wet in the fixer. That. Also, taking the pictures. Those are the two highs.

JODY: Of all your body of work is there a particular image or series of images you like the best, or of which you are the proudest?

JUDY: I like what I am doing right now. I'm sure that's not surprising. I feel like it's a sort of synthesis of a lot of what I've done up to now: it's gutsy and it's strong and it's different. I like it a lot, and I like the fact that I've done it now. It's not that I don't like what I did in the past: it was really good at the time, but I'm interested in what I'm doing now.

JODY: That implies that you have continued to grow and evolve in your work. It's a wonderful way to feel, isn't it?

JUDY: Yes, and it doesn't always happen. There are long periods when you are stumbling around trying to find your way, and there are always transitions from one project to the next. But once you get into a project, and you are in the middle of it, and you know that you like what is happening, that's always a good place to be.

Marilyn French

The day I interviewed Marilyn French in New York I stopped to have lunch with my uncle, who lived in the neighborhood. I had bought a brand new tape recorder for the event, and after lunch I decided to walk the ten blocks or so to Marilyn's and buy her some flowers on the way. The sky was gray, but the day was warm, so I strolled up Amsterdam Avenue, looking in store windows until I came to a flower shop. I had a bag with a bunch of audio tapes and the recorder on top, which I leaned on the counter while choosing some flowers.

By the time I arrived at Marilyn's rain was falling and my paper bag was disintegrating. Just as I arrived at the elevator, it broke, spewing out cassettes and flowers—but no tape recorder. I searched frantically, but the machine obviously wasn't there, so I ran back to the flower shop (no tape recorder) and then all the way back to my uncle's apartment. He gave me his tape recorder and I ran back to Marilyn's, arriving on time but having lost most of my cool.

I expected to meet a formidable woman, and Marilyn is indeed that; however, she was also warm, concerned for my plight and extremely hospitable. It is her fine mind and her great gumption that make her formidable, and the several hours we spent together were very exciting and passed like ten minutes. At the time I felt that some of her statements about her difficulties in getting published and the hostility to her work were slightly paranoid. However, hers and Judy Chicago's interviews really were the most difficult to get published. I am convinced that the refusal to support their work is because of the hard truths these women tell in combination with their assertive and non-apologetic style.

Many of the women in this book have similarly difficult content, but their styles are more conciliatory, so they have an easier time getting away with strong, inflammatory or subversive content. French and Chicago are completely uncompromising, aggressive and sometimes even strident in their approaches. As a result they meet considerable resistance and take a lot of lumps.

Marilyn's French's *Beyond Power* is one of the most powerful books I have read. It is distressing (and revealing) that this work, which should rank with Simone de Beauvoir's *Second Sex* as one of the classic feminist texts of this century, has received little or no critical acclaim, publicity or support from its publisher. At the very least it should be required reading in every Women's Studies program in America.

Marilyn French lives in New York City and has two grown children. Her works include *The Women's Room*, *The Bleeding Heart*, *Her Mother's Daughter*, *Beyond Power* and *The War Against Women*.

It's Up to Us

An Interview with Marilyn French
New York, New York
September 1989

JODY: Is there a consistent theme or concern in all your work? If so, were you aware of this when you started writing? Or is it simply the natural outcome of a progression in your thought?

MARILYN: Theme is not something I started out thinking about. As I look back at the things I've written, early novels that have not been published, I'm always concerned with the interplay or sometimes the mutual exclusion of power and pain and the way they seem to be assigned each to one sex. The surface, of course, is always deceiving; men have more pain than they appear to have, and women have more power than they appear to have, all in sub rosa ways, but our images are certainly mutually exclusive.

I guess I'm just trying to look into the nature of power: what does it mean; what does it cost; what does it give you? What do you get out of having power? What do you get out of having pain?

JODY: Anaïs Nin commented in the *Diaries* that she envied Henry Miller's ability to write down his life as though it was a story, to make a simple event seem like an adventure. You seem to write about life as it is, without trying to transmute it into an adventure. I'm curious about the writing process and how you get from the facts and events to the novel itself?

MARILYN: My writing may seem to be descriptive of everyday life but of course it isn't. There isn't any way you can do that. There's no way you could put the character of a single human being, even yourself, whom you supposedly know, on paper. It's all much too complex. The art that comes closest to being able to express the complexity of experience is music, where you can do contrasting things at once, but even there you have to simplify.

I don't know that I started out with any kind of exalted idea. My first novels were very traditional women's novels, sort of a la Virginia Woolf, although there was more male-female violence in mine...emotional, mainly. I don't know when it came to me that the actual texture of women's lives is what creates them and that that texture had never been described.

If you read most novels about women it seems that all women do is go shopping. If you read Jane Austen the girls are always shopping or sitting around the house waiting for the men to come in for tea. Virginia Woolf is the same way: in *The Years* she has women who work, but the working women always live in these dreary, grim, bleak little flats, and they have no clothes, and they are wallflowers, and they are certainly not enviable. Well, most of our lives are probably not enviable. But the actual texture of going around a house all day cleaning it, raising children, doing the laundry—what does this do to you? What kind of psychology and emotionality does this produce?

So while my novels may seem to have that texture, it is a carefully selected texture; it's simplified. It's not reality, but it has a different kind of rhythm from, let's call it a traditional male novel, just as if you look at Shakespeare, the comedies have a different texture from the tragedies, the comedies being female-centered and feminine, in my terms, and the tragedies being masculine.

I try in my novels, without giving it any fancy name or without saying, "I am now doing thus and such," or producing some kind of a manifesto, to do something different. I don't think that has been recognized. It would be nice to have one's craft acknowledged, which it is not. Reviewers act as though I wrote novels with my uterus: you know, it all comes pouring out like menstrual blood and I don't have a thing to say about it. All I have to do is open my legs.

The rhythms and the structures of my novels, therefore, are different in some way from the traditional male novel because they're not built like the five-act play with the crisis in the third act and the denouement gradually occurring. There are lots of crises and lots of denouements, and none of them is ever final and nothing ever really ends and you never live happily ever after. But on the other hand no tragedy ever completely does you in either. You do go on, which I think is the experience most women have in life.

So you could say I was trying to create a female rhythm and a female texture in the novels. Now I really believe that men's lives are the same as women's, but that they impose upon them this other structure. They have one, large, ambitious goal, and they achieve it or they don't achieve it. That's their tragedy. And then the end comes, and of course they do die younger than we do, so they are more likely to see their endings as final. We don't see our endings as final because many of us have children we see ourselves living on through. And tragedies, which occur to us with great regularity, do not destroy us.

JODY: How did you come to write *The Women's Room?*

MARILYN: I had written other novels. I'd written short stories, and I know I was a good writer. I'd been writing for twenty years, but I wasn't getting published. My novels were lyrical, art novels or whatever, and of course they were very, very feminist, but there was no feminism at the time. It didn't exist. There was no common language. My novels just seemed to puzzle the editors who read them, all of whom admitted that they were well-written, but were discomfitted by them.

I was in a certain amount of despair. I thought, "I'm going to be fucking Emily Dickinson and leave behind these things tied up in pink yarn." Mine weren't even tied up in pink yarn. They were too thick. So I thought, "I'm just going to write it down straight. I'm not going to be oblique, I'm not going to be lyrical or poetic or any of the things I was in the earlier books. I'm just going to tell it the way it is."

The major problem in writing *The Women's Room* was finding the right voice for it, and it took quite a few years before I did. But once I did, I wrote it quite fast. I showed it to some friends who said, "It's good, Marilyn, but nobody's ever going to publish this." It was just one of those things: my publisher said had he gotten it two years earlier, he probably wouldn't have published it. But things had happened in his life that had changed his awareness, so it was timing.

JODY: Mira, one of the characters in *The Women's Room,* said that "people were essentially not evil, that perfection was death, that life was better than order and a little chaos good for the soul." Are those your own personal values?

MARILYN: I wish they were.

JODY: She also described choosing her own life as "the shocking, divisive, arrogant rending of the social fabric that it was." How much leeway do women have today in America, in this last decade of the twentieth century, to choose their own lives? Have things gotten better?

MARILYN: Any woman who was alive in the 1950s has got to know that things have gotten better, and every single inch of that betterment is attributable to feminism and the feminist movement. That feminism has done its job, that the movement is over, that women now have what they want, is a joke. They have more options, more choices, and they can live on their own.

The one thing that women have never been allowed in any culture, at any time, is independence. (It's even been made quite explicit: "Don't let women have jobs or they won't get married, and if they don't get married, they won't have children.") The ability to live independently, to survive on your own, to support yourself and to live—not like Virginia Woolf's poor dreary people up in their little attic rooms, but in a decent place. To have a car, buy a house, get a loan, have a decent job, a job that uses your abilities: all of that is wonderful. But the feminist movement set out to change the world, not just the lives of educated women. I think the change includes women of color, not just white women, but they have to be educated. If you're not educated none of the benefits of feminism currently really help you.

When we say "change the world," we mean change the course, the direction, of governments, affect government policy, change this terrible power race and struggle for profit and domination that has characterized all of patriarchy, and turn the world around. Now this is not something you can hope to do in twenty years. It is kind of a joke even to suggest it. You know, it sounds like something utopian, and it may be, but it seems to me it's the only thing worth doing if you're going to be alive. Why go on with it the way it is? You can't hold yourself apart from your culture, but why foster it any more than you have to? It's conceivable that societies, that nations, that the world, could live somewhat differently. There is enough food to feed everyone, and that's basic.

JODY: At one point in *The Women's Room* you ask: "When people starve to death because of the policies of governments and corporations, is that murder?" What do you think? Is it murder? As you have pointed out, the majority of those who starve to death are women and children. What can we do about that?

MARILYN: I don't know what can be done. I feel that nothing can be done, truthfully, at this moment. Dick Snyder of Simon and Schuster said about ten years ago, "In ten years there will be five publishers in New York"—and he's not far from right. I'm going to oversimplify: by the turn of the millenium there will be five corporations in the world, and there will be one farm, and one corporation will own it, and it will cover the globe.

Peasants who lived on farms and were self-sufficient for hundreds of thousands of years will become wage slaves like the rest of us. They will grow carnations if they are ordered to grow carnations, and if there are bad times they will starve. They are dying, and all of those who have lived for hundreds of thousands of years in subsistence economies are going to be wiped off the face of the globe. It's happening in Africa and South America and Asia. By the time our grandchildren are adults, I don't think there are going to be any subsistence economies left either. The quiet pride and dignity (and hardship) of the subsistence life will be a very dim human memory. So will the autonomy of that kind of life. Nobody will be autonomous and that's a problem, because when people don't have autonomy, they get angry and become violent. I don't know what can be done about it. I don't know how it can be stopped. These people are too powerful, too unscrupulous. They don't care, and I don't think we care enough to be able to stop them. And I don't know what we would have to do to stop them. What are you going to do, stop buying their products? That means you stop buying everything, because they're all the same: there's no real choice.

JODY: Although *The Women's Room* is depressing because of the content of women's lives there were passages that left me hopeful. For example Mira, again, said that "there was no justice, but maybe there could still be love." Do you still believe in the possibility of love?

MARILYN: Of course: when you stop loving, you stop being alive. Clarissa in the novel said, "Isolation is death." It's only love that takes you out of isolation, no matter to what degree the love is expressed. It could be friendship or love of children, or it could be sexual love or whatever.

JODY: Did you reconstruct *Her Mother's Daughter* from memory? Did you have to do research in order to be able to describe the intimate details of your mother's childhood and your grandmother's life? Perhaps what I'm asking is, how much of that book is true?

MARILYN: I wrote it from memory. The details of my mother's remembrances of her mother are all things she told me. I don't think they are all accurate, but the major things are. I did a series of interviews with her and taped them to make sure I got the details right. It was amazing to me how she censored herself when that tape recorder was on. Where before she would have said, "My father, I hated my father!" now she said, "Well, my father was thus and such," very much moderated and toned down, and all the force of life gone out of it. So the tapes were useless to me.

But she was a great help because she read an early draft. In one scene where she was a little kid I had her turning on the light, and she said, "We didn't have electric lights." I hadn't thought that they didn't have lights because there was electricity in the early decades, I think, but in her house there were gas lamps.

JODY: What did she think of the book?

MARILYN: She loved it. She never saw the very end, because she died. She was terrified, she said, "You're going to write another *Mommy Dearest*." I couldn't say there wasn't any criticism of her in the book because there is, but certainly what I was trying to do wasn't to "blame mommy" but to show how hard it is to be a mother, and also to show that all mothers are daughters and, they all suffer from their mothers.

This placing of all the responsibility for children on one poor soul's back, and half the time she is trying to support them at the same time—it's just not a job that can be done. It's not humanly possible, not by the standards they hold up for us of what kind of people we're supposed to be if we're mothers. Again, I was trying to do something I felt hadn't been done, which was to examine the nature of motherhood and daughterhood—motherhood, mainly.

No one has looked at mothers because for the first three-and-one-half million years of time on earth, we had the kids, whether we wanted to or not. This is the first century in which we've ever had a choice about whether we want to become mothers or not. And some women are saying, "I don't know if I want to do that." There's very good reason for saying that, because being a mother is a thankless job, and it's not a job you can quit. You can't suddenly say to your children when they're forty (which my children are coming up to), "That's it, I resign." You still have the job.

What's it like, and what does it feel like, and what does it cost you, and what does it mean, and what does it do to you, and all those things we haven't really ever examined—that's what I was trying to do, especially in this age when mothers come in for so much flak and are blamed for everything.

JODY: Both Belle and Frances are inconsolable. Is it built into motherhood, is it the role, or were they as personalities inconsolable? Where you saying that motherhood is so difficult that inevitably it leads down that path? Or did they just happen to be two women who were inconsolable?

MARILYN: I don't know what Frances was like before she lost her children. She was just worn down when I knew her, but I don't think she was by nature a depressed person. She could manage cheerfulness and she could manage to be pleased with herself—not that I could understand most of what she was saying, because she would be speaking Polish—but I could see that she was.

My mother was totally inconsolable. She never got over her childhood, never. And I was inconsolable for much of my life because I got it from her, because I was raised within her psyche, as it were. I put myself there. I'm not saying she did it to me, but that's where I was.

JODY: I am interested in something you said about women's rape fantasies. I've been reading a book by Marian Woodman, a Jungian analyst, *Addiction to Perfection, Or The Unravished Bride*. She says: "Rape suggests being seized and carried off by a masculine enemy through brutal sexual assault. Ravishment suggests being seized and carried off by a masculine lover through ecstacy and rapture. Rape has to do with power; ravishment has to do with love." Do you have a comment on that? You are one of the few women who has discussed it at all. I believe that most women have ravishment fantasies, not rape fantasies.

MARILYN: I think that some women's rape fantasies do have to do with rape and are sado-masochistic, but I don't think they have anything necessarily to do with men. I think that rape fantasies, or sado-masochistic fantasies, or enacting sado-masochism, which some do, have to do with power. They represent one's own juggling in one's own brain of very confused self-images of power and submission. Who are you submitting to when you give in to sex? You're submitting to yourself.

I've been involved sexually with an awful lot of men in my life, and they have exactly the same fantasies women do. So do men want to be raped, too, then? I wish we didn't talk about "women's rape fantasies:" there are sado-masochistic fantasies, and both women and men have them. I think it has more to do with how hard it is to give up control of ourselves and surrender to that kind of feeling. I think it has more to do with that than anything else, although I do love that distinction between rape and ravishment. Of course, we all want to be ravished.

JODY: Why is sex more threatening than aggression?

MARILYN: God knows, and that is a well chosen phrase.

JODY: *Beyond Power* is an incredible book, not only for the encyclopedic information it contains and its clear and articulate language, but also for the thoughtful way in which it is put together. Then, too, it is difficult to find elsewhere all the information that is in it. What inspired you to write *Beyond Power,* and how did you move from fiction to non-fiction? Also the range of the book is so broad, and it spans so many disciplines, how would you categorize it?

MARILYN: I would categorize it as a history of ideas or philosophy. I thought I was going to write a little essay... that's what I started out to do. I was going around giving speeches after *The Women's Room* was published, and women would always ask me, "How did things get this way? How did it happen?" And I would say, "I know the answer, but it is so long and complicated that I'm going to write an essay on it." I set out to write a thirty-five page essay, and five years later I finished it.

JODY: What was going on in your life at the time?

MARILYN: Nothing—that's why it almost killed me. It took me five years. I worked seven days a week, roughly ten hours a day. I did almost nothing else. Once in a while, I'd go out to dinner and I'd sit there and think, "Why am I here? I'd much rather be working," because I was consumed with this book and that's not good for you, psychologically or physically. I got really not well from it.

JODY: Your own academic discipline is literature. How were you able to work in such breadth and depth in so many different fields?

MARILYN: That's why it was so hard to do. And I don't feel that I did justice to those fields; at the time there wasn't enough written from a feminist perspective on the sociology of law, the sociology of medicine. I did talk to lawyers and doctors and people who taught those fields for references, but they just didn't exist.

I feel that *Beyond Power* is not a complete, finished work. It's kind of a rough outline for somebody else, or maybe many somebody else's, to build on. The morality of law and what is really going on in the entire legal structure of this country, or the medical profession, with these huge machines and the kind of treatment one gets from doctors—all of that is fascinating, but if I had tried to find any more material than I did find, I probably never would have finished the book. I just had to call it quits and stop, but I'm hoping other people will pick up where I left off and finish the job.

JODY: In the introduction to *Beyond Power* you said that many feel we are living through the death throes of what has been called "western civilization." You wrote that several years ago: how do you feel about it now? What if anything has changed?

MARILYN: I think there is no question about it: we are living through the decline and fall of the Roman Empire, and most of us know it. Virginia Woolf wrote, "On or about December, 1910, human character changed." I think future historians will date the end of western civilization as 1914. The 1914 war, which killed off the male aristocracy of Europe, was the end of western civilization as it had been. The thing is, when you are in such a tumultous, chaotic period, that's the time, if you write, or are a political activist, that you can change the focus of the next age. It's a very terrible time to be alive, as in the Chinese curse, "May you live in interesting times," but it's also a very vital time and a time when things aren't fixed yet. The next age could be the age of the greatest totalitarianism the world has ever known, or it could be the feminist age.

JODY: You have pointed out that the compartmentalization of knowledge in the eighteenth century actually banished certain knowledge as well as certain approaches to experience, and that resulted in the dominance of linear thinking. Don't we as a culture suffer enormously from this particular problem?

MARILYN: Yes, and it's not an easy problem to solve. One of the reasons Nobel Prize winner Barbara McClintock's work was disparaged was because it was based on a theory of non-domination among the elements in a cell. Science can only go so far with this domination theory. Sooner or later they are going to have to admit that most things don't function that way. Only human society functions that way. Ethnologists love to look for dominance structures among animals, but the most recent and informed work on dominance structures points out that they have very limited application and may also be transient. For example, among Macaque monkeys there are clear dominance structures in the male, but they inherit their status from their mothers.

Among some other simians they thought, "Aha! This mother has dominance," but then they realized that when the next one had a baby, she became dominant. Now that's just like human life, the mother with the most recent baby gets all the attention. Of course! It has nothing to do with domanance, it has to do with centrality, which is a totally different thing, and very transient. Anyway, they look for dominance structures because they need to believe that they are dominant, because if they didn't believe they were dominant, they would have to think they were inferior.

I don't know when men are going to get beyond this. The change has to be in action, in behavior. But I do think it is possible to build a society that emphasizes service, cooperation and sharing more and emphasizes power, success and domination less—yes, I do.

JODY: The categories into which history is usually divided, like the Renasissance, the Reformation, the Middle Ages and so forth are, as you point out, basically meaningless to women's history. How do you look at traditional historical categories? Have you considered developing an alternative set of your own?

MARILYN: In the course of writing my latest book it has emerged that certain forms of government are better for women than others in the sense that they admit women to a greater voice. But the form that's best for women is monarchy. Rule by an aristocracy is best for women simply because rule by an aristocracy involves rule by a family, and in families women have power. In the late days of the Roman Empire women had tremendous power behind the throne. In some cases in Europe, when women were allowed to inherit the throne, women ruled; but that doesn't do a thing for the mass of women.

As I wrote I found I was not just writing about women, although women were my main focus. But I had to include slaves as a group, peasants as a group and the poor as a group—all the groups that fight against or are affected by power one way or another. And women are part of those groups. Class consciousness or group consciousness is essential: it's the essential thing in the twentieth century.

No, I don't have any categories. I place a lot of emphasis on the rise of the state because I do think that's when women really got it. But it didn't happen the same way in every state, although it did happen in every state eventually.

Women retained enormous powers in Egypt until it was colonized by the European powers. Women retained enormous power in Japan until about the fourteenth century, whereas in China there's not a time within recorded history when they had any power. Why? Who knows? In India women seem to have had informal power, but it wasn't written down, and the rules read as if they were very oppressed. I don't have categories and I don't have periods; I have to follow male periods to some degree.

JODY: How did you write all these amazing books, raise your children, earn a living and stay sane?

MARILYN: Well, I'm over sixty years old. You do your life in bits and pieces. I was writing when the children were little, and I could write only a couple of hours a day. I'm very efficient in my use of time, I have to say that. If you're raising children you just have so much energy left over , and if you're also supporting them it's very hard to do much more than do your work and take care of the kids.

JODY: What do you consider to be the successes and failures of your own life?

MARILYN: I think my major success was getting out of my marriage, which almost finished me and I thought would finish me, through violence of one sort or another, either murder or suicide. That was the hardest thing I ever did, and it was the necessary thing.

I'm pleased with things I've done: I'm pleased with my children; I'm pleased with how they turned out, and I'm pleased with my books. To the degree that I can claim I had a hand in that, I'm proud of it. I don't feel especially proud of myself. I don't feel not proud of myself either; it's not an emotion I live with very much.

JODY: Do you ever suffer from self-doubt?

MARILYN: Emotionally, all the time. In my work, not a whole lot. Self-doubt? Every page is self-doubt, but you deal with it, and once it's done it's done. It is what it is, and I can't spend emotion on it. I don't have enough to spare.

Sometimes I think I would really like to go back to writing the way I used to write in the beginning, this lyrical, much less didactic, much less obviously socially focused work. And sometimes I think, The next book I'll do that!" But the next book never comes out that way. *Her Mother's Daughter* was supposed to be that kind of book, but it didn't become that kind of book. I've been planning for some years now to write another novel, and maybe that one will be.

I think that probably I would like most to write poetry, to boil everything down to a few perfect lines instead of writing these reams of things. But I think I also have to accept that that's not my gift and let it go.

JODY: From your own point of view which of your works is the best written and why? I haven't asked anyone that in a long time.

MARILYN: I have two children. They are very different, but I love them profoundly for what they are. That's how I feel about my books: I love each of them in a different way. I like different things about them, but I can't say I favor one over the other. I find it more fun to write fiction: hard as it is and draining as it can be, I find it much more fun than all these research books. After *Beyond Power* I swore I'd never write another one, and then I did.

JODY: There are so many great quotations in your books, my refrigerator was plastered with them. One I particularly like is: "Loneliness is not a longing for company, it's a longing for kind." In my life "kind" has been pretty rare. What about in yours?

MARILYN: It's not so rare that you despair. The trouble is, if you're someone like me, and perhaps you, or many of us in this world, you've moved around a lot in your life, so you meet someone who is "kind" here and someone else there, you have a friend in Paris and a friend in London and a friend in Portland, and it's not much use to you.

JODY: You said that a feminist vision of the world won't be realized in our lifetime, our century, or this millenium. When I read that I felt wretched until I realized that's only a few years away. Are you optimistic or pessimistic about the future?

MARILYN: I'm fifty per cent of each. I do think it's up to us; it's up mainly to women because even those men who claim to be feminists and who help us often have their own little power games going on. We need men's help and we need men's participation, but I absolutely believe the future is up to women.

Laura Huxley

It was Rupert Pole who initially suggested Laura Huxley's name to me, but it was through photographer Nancy Ellison that I eventually made contact with her. Laura Huxley is in her eighties, but she has the energy of a thirty-year-old. Her expressive green eyes dominate the features of her beautiful, patrician face. She is very slender, almost birdlike, and moves with rapidity, flexibility and grace, undoubtedly the result of years of yoga and tai chi. The day I came to her house she made me a vegetarian pasta with an incomparable pesto sauce. Good food evokes more subtle forms of nurturance, and I definitely felt nourished in my several meetings with this delicate, passionate and informed woman.

Laura Huxley is best known for her involvement in the human potential movement, but she started her professional life as a concert violinist. Born in Turin, Italy, she made her debut at Carnegie Hall in New York at the age of eighteen and studied at the Curtis Institute in Philadelphia. With the outbreak of World War II she says she realized she knew little of life beyond that of the concert hall, and so she put her Guarneri into its case and stopped playing. Over the following years she produced documentaries, played in a major symphony orchestra and intensively studied health, nutrition and psychology. She became increasingly involved with body/mind/spirit therapies, which at the time were still extremely unorthodox.

After the war Laura met Aldous and Maria Huxley, both pioneers in the human potential movement. After Maria's death, Aldous and Laura began to see one another socially, and eventually they married. Together they explored ways of opening the mind to new levels of consciousness. After Aldous Huxley's death on November 22, 1963, Laura continued to work as a therapist, give seminars, write and study. Her books include: *You Are Not the Target*; *This Timeless Moment: A Personal View of Aldous Huxley*; *Between Heaven and Earth*; *Oneaday Reason to be Happy* and *The Child of Your Dreams*. She is also the guardian of a teen-age girl and has organized Our Ultimate Investment, "a foundation for the nurturing of the possible human." A resident of California since the '40s, she lives in the same house where she and Aldous Huxley lived and where he died, overlooking the Hollywood hills.

You Have to Continue
the Dance

An Interview with Laura Huxley
Los Angeles, California
November 1990

JODY: In *This Timeless Moment*, the book you wrote about
your life with your husband, Aldous Huxley, you described him in the following way: "Aldous maintained
throughout his life the best characteristics of youth: openness to ideas, an ability to let go of old habits, a desire to
travel and learn first-hand from new cultures." Isn't that
an accurate description of yourself as well?

LAURA: Well, some of it, but I don't travel easily. At least now
I don't. Yes, I do like to know things directly. That is true.

JODY: That statement also reminds me of Anaïs Nin's
description of the source of her own energy as a quality of
responsiveness, of remaining alive to whatever was going
on around her. You knew Anaïs Nin, didn't you?

LAURA: Yes, I met her in Paris years ago. I had been told,
"This lady is wonderful; you should go and talk to her."
At that time I was studying with the great violinist,
George Enesco, and violin lessons cost one thousand
francs and therapy cost one hundred francs; so I cancelled
a violin lesson and went to see Anaïs ten times. I remember I lay down on a couch. That was the only official therapy I ever had, really. I often recall that first session
because I remember saying, "All I want is peace."

   She wrote me some wonderful letters later on, and we
went to a night club once or twice. I stayed one evening

in Louveciennes, at her house outside of Paris. And once she took me to her boat, and to Henry Miller's. He gave us wine in egg cups. At the time I didn't know anything about the strange world in which they lived. She and her husband, Hugh, came to a concert I gave in Paris. Then I saw her here in Los Angeles, but very little.

JODY: Was it your work with her that sparked your own interest in doing therapy?

LAURA: No, that is a much bigger story, which marked a turning point in my life. I was working on a film in New York that summer. Virginia Pfeiffer, my best friend for many years, was in Connecticut, so I would go back and forth between New York and Connecticut. She became very ill, and I took her to the Mayo Clinic in October 1949, where they removed a large tumor. The surgeon said, "There is nothing more that can be done for this woman. She has the two worst kinds of cancer one can have." They gave her six months or, if some miracle happened, maybe two years.

I knew the Mayo family; in fact I was staying with them, so I put a note in every file and spoke to every nurse and every doctor. I wrote, "Do not tell this patient her prognosis," because if they had said, "You are going to die," she would have said, "Fine." Ginny had an extraordinary mind, brilliant, very much like a Zen master. She told me many times "You don't understand: there is not such a great difference between death and life." It is remarkable that years later, speaking about death, Maria Huxley, Aldous' first wife, said: "It is just like going from one room to another." But I didn't want Ginny to die, I was very attached to her! So I asked them not to tell her anything.

In 1950, Ginny and I came back to Los Angeles. I told only Ginny's sister Pauline, who was Ernest Hemingway's wife, of the terminal prognosis of Ginny's illness. One day, by chance, I went to a heath food store and there was a book called *The Grape Cure Will Cure You of Cancer.* With complete naivete I thought, "Why worry? Here is the cure!" So I said to Ginny, "Why don't we eat grapes for a week?" I could do that and later on suggest all kinds of therapies because she had migraine headaches. Although she wouldn't have minded dying, she didn't like having migraines. So we ate grapes for one week and felt wonderful afterwards.

At that time I was working for the motion picture producer Gabriel Pascal. One evening he and his wife invited me to their house for dinner, and their other guest was Professor Szekeley. Pascal had told me he was inviting a man who was going to teach him how to get thinner, and here was this big man! Szekeley talked about Rancho La Puerta, his ranch in Tecate. He also talked about the grape cure and said that there were about 800 books on the subject. I thought maybe it would be a good idea to see what this grape cure really was, so Ginny and I went to visit.

The place was totally primitive. There was hardly even a bathroom, and it cost five dollars a day. Professor Szekeley's wife, Deborah, was very young and very sympatica. I told Szekeley the terminal prognosis given to Ginny by the Mayo Clinic and asked what he would advise. He had his own method of healing, which little by little became better known. His theory was that the illness, in this case the cancer, and the patient are like two fighters, two enemies. If you weaken the person by using certain therapies which weaken the general organism, the cancer can win. But if you strengthen the person and somehow starve the cancer, then the person wins.

That was fine with me, as I had no other options. We started with a very specific diet, a vegetarian diet. Anyway, after eight days of only grapes you can't face meat anymore, you get so clear. I never again did smoke or have cocktails. Then another book came out that promised a cure for cancer and arthritis, so I studied that too.

For five years I practiced on Ginny. I used many of the methods employed now at Esalen and elsewhere that use the impact of the imagination on the body and the physical release of negative emotion, plus some kind of meditation, although I didn't know at the time that it was called meditation. I just did these things because I didn't know what else to do. I never read a book on psychology, so I didn't know the orthodox approach at all. To me it is this basic energy that you either use in a good way or it kills you. It's one or the other. So I practiced on her and invented more and more recipes, and strangely enough, people began to come to me for therapy. Then, when I met Aldous and his wife Maria, they were interested in those same subjects.

So, that is how I became a therapist. It was the most unexpected turn in my life, and it felt so natural. From those experiences came *You Are Not the Target* and *Between Heaven and Earth*. I found I was very comfortable with it, and I felt I was doing something that was working. Lots of these techniques, which earlier I called "recipes for living and loving," are in *You Are Not the Target*, which was published in 1963. But in the meantime I had become more and more interested in the organismic approach, and after I met Aldous, I learned a great deal from him. Ginny got better; in fact, she lived another twenty-three years, and when both Ginny's and our house burned, we all came to live in this house.

JODY: Were you ever involved with re-evaluation or "co-counseling"?

LAURA: Yes, in fact I taught it a bit at the Southern California Counseling Center. Co-counseling is wonderful; it is basically teaching people the art of listening. Dr. Ben Weininger, the eminent psychiatrist and founder of the Southern California Counseling Center, showed that counselors without degrees are sometimes as successful as therapists as those with degrees. For some people it is much less threatening than working with therapists who have all those titles.

When I was first practicing I had a room in our house. Then, when we all moved here, I had a studio down the street. The studio was two or three rooms, one of which was completely empty, so there was no indication of my status. I had no title, and people knew that. When I worked at the Counseling Center with Weininger I had groups of young people, but instead of seeing them in the office, we went to the park and held our groups there. In that way there was no overriding sense of authority, only a great freedom of expression.

JODY: Do you have a sense of the creative will as an active and driving force in your life?

LAURA: As a young woman, following the thrust of the creative will seemed like an absolute impossibility. I come from Turin, Italy, and at that time it was very conservative. One didn't even think *if* it was conservative or not, it *was* that. Also, I come from a family that loved me as much as anyone can love, but I wasn't even allowed out of the house. The first time I was allowed to go around the block by myself I remember I had a little dog and my parents said, "Alright, you can go around the block." It was a peak experience! And I was then around fifteen years old!

So what could I do? I went to school until I was thirteen. I was an average student, doing just what one had to do to get by. My father was always taking me to hear concert violinists, and I was given a violin when I was very little. He loved music, and he hadn't had the opportunity to study as he had to start working when he was very young. When it appeared that I had talent, then I knew I *could* do something, that I could express myself through that talent. I put more and more effort into it, which impressed my family, so it became very serious. Then I could say, "I had better not go to school, because I have to practice five hours a day."

The most difficult part was that I could not hurt my mother and father...that I could not do. Suppose I had gone out and sought employment? People would have laughed and said, "What can you do?" I could do nothing, of course. Asking for a job not only would have humiliated my family, but they would have thought there was something crazy about wanting to work instead of going to school.

But, because I had this thrust toward music, and the talent, and the will, little by little I was allowed to go and study. "I have finished with this teacher in Torino," I said, "so now I have to go to Bologna." Then I had to go to Rome, and of course they had to help me, because it was such a reasonable request, and then to Berlin, and then, later on, to Paris.

I didn't reason so much then. I just knew that I had to do two things: express myself, give some voice to this urge which I didn't even know what it was, and not do anything to hurt my family in any way. But those two things were in such seeming contradiction to one another! For example, I had the idea that I would become an actress. At that time it would have been like announcing that I was going to become a prostitute! So, fortunately, I had this talent and I had this will, which is what brought me to America.

JODY: Was it the fact that the second world war broke out that caused you to remain here?

LAURA: I came to America four times before the war. Twice I studied and concertized in New York, and twice I received a scholarship at the Curtis Institute of Music in Philadelphia. Then on May 20, 1941, Italy entered the war. I had my ticket to go back at the beginning of May, but something very dramatic happend that redefined my life.

At the time, Italy had two big ocean liners, the *Rex* and the *Conte di Savoia*. One would leave from New York as the other left from Genoa. I was leaving on the Conte di Savoia. Those were very dramatic times: Hitler was invading one country after another, and Mussolini had made his fatal alliance with him. When I went to the boat, I had the feeling that maybe I wouldn't come back. The boat was to leave at twelve and I arrived late, with twenty-one pieces of luggage. Also, I had spent all my money because I thought I wouldn't need any on the boat and my family would be picking me up in Genoa.

I hurried to the boat with all this luggage, and as I watched it going up the ramp an officer came rushing up to me. He said, "You cannot take this boat!" "What do you mean?" I replied, "I am here and there are still three minutes left!" He said, "No, it's not that. We received a cable from your father asking you to stay here." He gave the order for my luggage to come back down and said, "If you want to change your mind, you have thirty seconds!" I watched my suitcases come down, all twenty-one of them. I never even saw the cable that changed my life because the officer couldn't show it to me as it had just arrived and was in the company office in Manhattan.

What had happened was this. That morning, the boat that was supposed to leave for New York from Genoa was stopped, so my father thought they were afraid of torpedos. Italy was not yet in the war, but war was imminent. He thought his daughter would be better off in America than under the sea. It was a tremendous decision for him, because he was very anxious to see me, and he had no idea how long the war might go on. So there I was in New York, just like that! I had a very nice suit on that day, and three cents in my pockets—that's all I had. So I was stranded! The *Conte di Savoia* arrived in Genoa safely, and two days later war was declared.

People were wonderful to me. That weekend I stayed in New York as the guest of one person and then another. Then I went to Arkansas for the summer with my best friend, Miriam McHaney, whose father was a Supreme Court judge in Little Rock. It was a very strange summer. There weren't many foreigners in Arkansas, so I was taken from one party to another, a strange Italian violinist stranded in America.

JODY: How old were you at this point?

LAURA: I was twenty-three.

JODY: What happened next?

LAURA: Something happened to me at that point. Actually, it had been happening over the preceding year or two. Here the war was going on, in '39 and '40, and I was feeling uncomfortable because so much that was happening in the world was reverberating in me, yet here I was continuing my own little specialized routine. When you are a violinist and you give concerts—unless you are an exceptional person like Yehudi Menuhin, or like my husband, who was both a specialist and a generalist—if you don't have that kind of mind and talent, you just have to be a specialist and put blinders on and work all the time.

This feeling of being so separated from the rest of the world had become more and more compelling. I could also see that there were many interesting things I wasn't doing. The violin had been my liberation, but now I felt as though I was its prisoner. So I decided I was going to finish with all that. I gave a last concert in Philadelphia, and it was very painful. Later on, when I told the story to Aldous he said, "What courage!" It *was* sort of courageous but also it was like courage seems to be—inevitable. I couldn't do anything else. It was as if someone works hard for twenty years to earn a million dollars and then one day throws it all in the fireplace.

After that it was interesting, though, because I did *everything*. I did become an actress for a while; I would get scholarships in acting quite easily. I wasn't good at it, but I gave the impression that I was. I remember one time reading for the Pasadena Playhouse: I was always given parts as a spy or a baronness, always the same thing. I got the part and the play was unsuccessful, so it ran for eight days. I thought, "How horrible, if I am ever successful I will have to play the part for two years!" Also, I realized I had no technique and no special acting talent, just general talent.

JODY: Your modesty reminds me of a passage in *This Time-less Moment* in which you describe a weekend in New York with Aldous when you told him you felt that all the things you had done hadn't added up to much. His response was at once a statement, a gesture and an understanding: "But what do you mean? What you have accomplished is this—*what you are.*"

LAURA: I miss Aldous more and more as time passes. It's strange you mention that incident: no later than yesterday I was thinking about that. It was late afternoon, it was still light, we had had a pleasant dinner, not at a swanky restaurant but at a nice restaurant, and I always remember that beautiful gesture he made with his hand: "It's what you are." Yes, I remember that. I've been very lucky.

JODY: Is it really a matter of luck? Or does each of us have a path that we affect by our beliefs and our actions?

LAURA: I think both are true. Obviously, you feel those days when you are lucky and those when you are not— whether it is our merit or our destiny or somebody sneezing in one of those planets we have not yet discovered. I am one of those people who believes in the perfectibility of human beings. That makes life not always easy. If you believe in human perfectibility, then you always have some work to do, which is not always welcome, or suitable.

Then you think about very high people like Ram Dass and others who say, "Everything is just right, just as it should be." How can that be true when you see what is happening in the world? So it is very difficult in the sense that you cannot take too many vacations from responsibility if you believe in the possibility of improvement in yourself and others. It does not make for a quiet life—a very interesting life, but not a quiet one.

Also you have doubts because there are many great people with their theories saying that you cannot do anything, you cannot interfere with the karma. What do you mean, you can't interfere with karma? Maybe that *is* the karma, to interfere with the karma! It seems to me the only definitive answer is that there are no definitive answers. It would be nice to have one, of course, but you have to continue the dance, even when there are no answers, even when you are exhausted or doubtful. There is a saying in Italy, "When you are at the ball…dance!" Well, you and I are at the ball…

JODY: Another passage in *This Timeless Moment* that moved me deeply was your description of Aldous' death. I'd like to know more about what happened and how you look back on that experience. It seemed to be a moment so full of love…

LAURA: The reason I could do what I did is because I knew that Aldous had thought and spoken and written about the fact that death is a moment of tremendous importance, of possibility for clarifying a lot of things. Also Aldous had spoken in this beautiful manner to his first wife. They had an extraordinary thirty-five-year marriage, and there was much love between them. Yet he could say, "Go on. Don't worry about the past. Let it go, go towards the light." He had written about Maria's death, and we had spoken about it. Also, he had suggested giving LSD to a physician in Chicago who was working with terminal patients. So I knew that was what he wanted.

Aldous didn't speak about his death; he never did. I was always ready to encourage him to speak about it, but he was living so much in the present, even when he was sick, that he didn't speak about it until a few hours before he died, by which time he could hardly speak at all, and then he wrote his last prescription. It was his own prescription and I did exactly what he asked me to do, which was to give him a shot of 100 micrograms of LSD, which I had there, I was ready for it.* You might have some doubt in different circumstances, but for me there was only the difficulty of actually doing it. Mentally, intellectually, I knew that was what he wanted. There was no doubt. So that was his decision, and, with a man like Aldous, you accept it. In retrospect, if I had *not* done it I would feel badly today.

JODY: What was Aldous's view of death? What is your own view of death?

LAURA: One's views of death are different when one is well or when one is sick. When I am well I think it is the greatest adventure, to go into it. Aldous said, and even wrote, that he had a lot of things still that he would like to do. That was clear. But he would not want to go on unless he was really capable of doing them. He felt badly about being sick, although he was not sick very long.

Aldous said even publicly that death is a continuation, that you might even learn after death. In one talk he said that the process of learning goes on all your life, from the moment you are born until the moment you die, and afterwards. He never eliminated the possibility that there was something left, some kind of vibration, some kind of vortices—he spoke of vortices.

That was his view, and I think my view as well. It is very simple, you know; if there is no after-life, we will not know it, and if there is something, we will find out what it is. There is a difference between the process of dying and the fact of being dead. We know that dying might be painful and difficult but that it is different from being dead. Either we'll have a surprise or we won't.

*In 1963 LSD was legal

JODY: Don't you think that people fear the idea of everything ending, of nothingness—not to mention the possibility of hell and damnation.

LAURA: Well, of course, if you believe in that! I'll never forget one episode when I was a therapist. A Catholic man came to see me because he was so afraid of hell. We discussed this on a rather intellectual level. I said, "How can you possibly believe in hell? The longest time you can sin is a hundred years, yet hell is eternal. You can't believe in a God that is so unjust, who would punish you eternally for just a hundred years of sin!" We discussed it, and he was convinced and seemed fine. I walked him to the door and waited as he went down the steps. I had given him all my wisdom, and I thought he was at peace and convinced he didn't have to fear hell because hell is right here, etcetera, etcetera. There were about fifteen steps altogether. At about the fourteenth step he looked up at me and said, "But what if there really *is* a hell?"

Those beliefs become cellular. I believe you really have to go very, very deep if you want to work that out. You see, when I said "lucky" before, that was one piece of my luck. I was brought up Catholic, I was given my first communion when I was nine years old. I had my period of religiosity where I would light a candle to the virgin. I knew the catechism and all that. Then one day, when I was probably thirteen or fourteen, I thought: "But this doesn't make any sense! I cannot go to hell for eternity." That was no drama at all for me. I didn't even tell my family. I still went to church on Sundays, but I knew there must be other points of view, although I hadn't encountered them yet.

I can believe in a very extraordinary essence that has created all of this, but I cannot believe in a God who, when you do something wrong, punishes you for eternity. That is not right. So, that was that. But I meet people for whom getting rid of such a belief is a lifelong struggle. I feel that I am lucky to have a measure of inner freedom.

JODY: In terms of Aldous's death, do you ever feel an almost palpable presence at times, an energy, a feeling of love around you?

LAURA: That's it! Sometimes I feel it, yes. And if I don't feel it I scold Aldous and I say, "Where, where are you? I need you now, come on!" That is probably what Aldous meant by vortices.

JODY: What we are really discussing here is the nature and importance of energy: in one's life, in one's relationships and in therapy. Are you yourself very sensitive to other people's energies?

LAURA: You can call it intuition or whatever; yes, I feel I am aware of other people's energies and of my own. Often when I am tired my own energy is not right, so I try to stay by myself. Energy is the constant element in everything, isn't it? Blake said it, "Energy is eternal delight."

Probably that is the basic point in therapy, too. I know that years ago, when I started, it was no wonder that people got better because of the way I prepared for each and every session. How much energy I would put into it! I would be quiet or meditate for an hour; then, I would give them two hours or more, and after the person was gone, I would write up the session.

JODY: In your opinion is channeling an authentic phenomen?

LAURA: I think there are all kinds of things in the air and some people sort of catch some, but they never know if they catch them from inside or if they catch them from outside. That is for each person to decide. But the experience I described in the epilogue of *This Timeless Moment* was absolutely extraordinary and would not have been possible unless there really was communication.

A medium named Keith Milton Rhinehart came to the house—right here where we are talking, in fact. He gave a session to six friends of ours and said something to each person that he or she could not have known. One person said it was not significant; however, the next day he found out how significant it really was, because certain things had been happening at exactly that time. When all this was finished Rhinehart said, "Aldous said something. Here, I better write it down." He wrote:

seventeenth page sixth book from left, or sixth shelf,
third book from left, twenty-third line."

He then handed me the paper and said, "Aldous wants you to look up those books."

I went upstairs to Aldous's room, where the reading had taken place. The walls of the room are covered with bookshelves. I went to the small wall, which has six shelves about four feet in length. I counted to the third shelf from the floor, counted to the sixth book from the left and took out *Coloquio de Buenos Aires*, 1962, 257 pages, in Spanish, published by the PEN Club of Argentina.

I opened the book to page seventeen, and before I even counted to line twenty-three the name Aldous Huxley leaped to my eyes. The paragraph said in English: "Aldous Huxley does not surprise us in this admirable communication in which paradox and erudition in the poetic sense and the sense of humor are interlaced in such an efficacious form. Perhaps the majority of the listeners to this conversation will not have a complete idea of the spiritual richness of this communication through the summary which the faithful translator and learned scholar in scientific disciplines, who is Alicia Jurado, has just made for us."

I had never seen the book before, which is a report of a literary meeting to which we were supposed to go but did not. The paragraph quoted refers to Aldous's last book, *Literature and Science*.

Having recovered partially from the shock, we began to think that there might be another book that fit the indications. We had counted from the floor up: now we counted from the ceiling down. On the bottom shelf we took out the third book from the left, *Proceedings of the Two*

Conferences on Parapsychology and Pharmacology. On page seventeen the paragraph read as follows: "Parapsychology is still struggling in the first stage. These phenomena are not generally accepted by science, although many workers are firmly convinced of their existence. For this reason the major effort of parapsychological research has been to demonstrate and to prove that they are working with real phenomena."

One more book met the requirements of location and page. It was *My Life in Court* by Louis Nizer. The paragraph containing line twenty-three described a man bearing no resemblance to Aldous, *except* for his unusual height of 6'5". Aldous was 6'4". It was as though the intelligence that motivated the two previous events wanted now to give also a physical proof. All three of those books were pertinent, yet nobody knew they even existed. I didn't know because my sister had put the library together; I didn't even know I had those books. And out of a book of 257 pages, to pick out one paragraph that was so absolutely pertinent to Aldous!

When you ask me if channeling is authentic, how can I answer yes or no? There are so many different phenomena in parapsychology, and only a few are incontestable.

JODY: Continuing on the topic of energy but of a different sort, it takes an enormous amount of energy to raise a child, and you are doing that now, aren't you?

LAURA: Yes, I have a child now, Karen, who is Ginny's granddaughter. Karen's mother was ill and died, and I took the guardianship of Karen. She has been living with me since she was a baby.

I, of course, am one of those people who worries about kids. I was brought up so differently! She has so much freedom, and it is a very difficult world. She is offered the opportunity to do hundreds of right things but one thousand wrong things all the time. For instance, young people have access to nicotine, which is one of the most addictive drugs...even more than drugs that are currently illegal. Nicotine kills more people than the combined number of all the deaths of suicide, homicide, accidents and AIDS. And now the clever advertising has induced younger and younger teenagers to start smoking.

Anyway, it is an incredible situation. Just imagine a woman of seventy-eight, which I am, and a girl of sixteen, which she is, coming from such different cultures, and she being immersed in a culture that I hardly know. It takes enormous energy, particularly because she has no other family. I am everybody. So it is a difficult situation: difficult for her and difficult for me.

She is a very wonderful girl, and we are making it, not without a great deal of struggle. The other day I was insisting on a certain point—because I don't give up easily—I asked her, "Darling, I wonder if you will write on my tombstone, 'She never gave up!'" And she replied, "Unfortunately!" So it is that kind of relationship: very open, very humorous, and very dramatic, and of the deepest love and loyalty.

JODY: Is there any relationship between your own personal situation with your daughter and your public concerns?

LAURA: Yes, in 1978 I founded Our Ultimate Investment, an organization "for the nurturing of the possible human," beginning with conception. "The possible human" is a term invented by Jean Houston.

The unjust and frightening question whether to abort or not to abort must be changed to: should I conceive or not conceive? Unless we make that change, mindless violence will continue and the realization of our potentialities for intelligence and compassion will proceed at a snail-like pace because of the unconsciously inflicted damage to the human being at the time of conception and thereafter.

Piero Ferrucci, who co-authored *The Child of Your Dreams* with me, is my nephew. We have been close all

our lives, and every summer he comes to be with me and
Karen. Two years ago he married. This Christmas I went
to Italy to see the birth of their child, and they were here
for one month this summer. I saw everything in that book
applied, and it was so beautiful! You see how right it is
that a child should be given total attention and total love
for at least one or two years. You can see also what the perfect diet before conception has done for this boy. It is such
happiness to see the joy and the beauty in him. That is
what I was speaking about before, the recognition and
development of our latent potentiality, particularly if you
begin very, very early.

So far as I am concerned, that book may be the most
useful thing I have done. It is about beginning early
enough to have respect for the fact of creation. You speak
about the creative urge: conception is probably the most
important thing you can do. What is more creative than
that? Why not do it consciously?

JODY: You feel so deeply yet your passion is tempered by
great lucidity. If a very young woman were to ask you,
"Laura, what should I do with my life? Where should I
begin?" what would you tell her?

LAURA: I am faced with that quite often. I think it is the
same whether you are young or old: you have to be aware
of your motives and know what is happening inside of
you before you follow somebody who is outside of you.
Choice is the difficult thing. So, listen, listen, but finally,
listen to yourself as honestly as possible.

Actually, I suggest the following:
1. Respect your body.
2. Focus your mind.
3. Love your heart.

And cooperate with those people who do—and even those
who don't do—the same.

Bella Lewitzky

A friend once told me that we are never more than ten people away from someone we wish to meet. I met Bella Lewitzky thanks to Catherine Saltzman, a wonderful woman in one of my classes at Irvine Valley College. She asked if I knew of Bella Lewitzky's work and wondered whether I might be interested in interviewing her. When I responded enthusiastically, she told me that her brother Brahm van den Berg had danced with Bella in the early years, and she offered to get me her address. When I wrote to Bella, she accepted graciously.

Bella Lewitzky is 5'2", striking and youthful at seventy-six with luxuriant, short gray hair. The day I met her she was wearing a tailored, bright-red blouse and skirt. As I sat down at the dining room table I recalled the descriptions I had heard of her as matriarchal, impressive and even intimidating. The woman across the table from me was warm, intelligent, honest and completely present. The latter two qualities she says she inherited from her father. She was also intense passionate, and alert.

I knew that Bella had a great fondness for chocolate, so on my way to Los Angeles I had stopped at the local chocolate shop and bought fresh, hand-dipped chocolate-covered strawberries and raspberries. Bella lit up when she saw them: she even called her husband, who must be a chocoholic too, to see them.

A native Californian, Bella was born on the edge of the Mojave desert and raised on a chicken ranch in San Bernardino by Russian immigrant parents. Married to architect Newell Reynolds, she gave birth to her only child, daughter Nora Reynolds, at age thirty-nine. Pioneer of West Coast modern dance, she founded the Bella Lewitzky Dance Company in 1966 and is the company's choreographer and artistic director. Bella has been the recipient of a Guggenheim Fellowship, a member of the California Arts Council, a member of the Women's Building Advisory Council, a member of the Board of Directors of Dance/USA and Vice Chairperson of the National Endowment of the Arts Dance Advisory Panel.

In 1990 Bella Lewitzky rejected a $72,000 NEA grant and filed a lawsuit against the NEA, seeking to have declared unconstitutional a clause prohibiting artists from spending NEA funds on works the Endowment chairman determined to be obscene. Shortly afterwards, Congress rejected renewal of the obscenity clause.

Bella Lewitzky's work is nationally acclaimed. I like critic Dierdre Kelly's description of her art as "movement pared close to the bone." For me, Bella's work is innovative, full of variety and play. It strikes me as intensely physical, athletic, unlike many other dance forms, which seem almost ethereal. Inspiration for her work often comes from other disciplines, for example painting and sculpture. She incorporates these into her sets and costumes as well. I recall a piece she wrote which she introduced with a quote from Albert Camus. It sums up what I felt in her that day in Los Angeles: "We have art in order not to die of life."

Dance is the Center
of My Being

An Interview with Bella Lewitzky
Los Angeles, California
March 1991

JODY: You wanted to be a dancer at an early age. What
made you want to be a dancer, and how did you know you
could do it?

BELLA: I never saw anyone dance. When I decided I was
going to be a dancer I had never seen a dancer; I think I'm
being honest in saying that. I cannot verify this scientifi-
cally, but no image comes to mind. I cannot say that yes,
I saw something, I experienced something, and that motivated me. Far from that. I have arrived at a very fanciful
answer to that question based on an educated belief, so
let's say it's semi-factual. I believe that every human being
has one sense more profoundly developed than the others.
Some people are oral, some are visual, some are tactile,
some are mental processors and some are kinetic. There is
no question in my mind but that I was a kinetic child; I
know that to be a fact because I can trace my impressions
to kinetic experiences.

These facilities and emphases, which are individual and
developed with a little more certainty in one way or other
in different individuals, are not valued much by society;
therefore, they are permitted to die before being born, as it
were. This is hard to verify, but educated guesswork tells
me that there must be an element of truth in this. I was a
kinetic child: I lived in the country; I ran; I jumped; I fell;

I rolled; I tried to fly. Most children do, but I can specifically remember the incidents. I remember trying to jump off our roof at home—a low one, because it was a chicken-shed roof—and being terribly surprised that my coordination (this was what I attributed it to) was not exactly right. I never really allowed the fact that gravity was involved to dissuade me. I knew that if I just did it correctly, I would be able to sustain myself, be air-borne. It's a common experience and a profoundly kinetic one. I can remember when a wind would come up, and I'd turn my back on it and think that I should be able to sit down in it. Many a bump I took! So, a lot of my sensibilities were strongly based upon being country-reared, and upon movement.

Also, my father was an excellent amateur painter and his easel and canvases were always in our living room. I saw form at a very early age without knowing that there was a word that was *form,* or that colors placed together created more than the sum of their parts. These things were not intellectually clear to me, but emotionally they were very clear to me. My father never talked to us directly about what it was like to be a painter, but his own love for art was so effusive and abundant and contagious that it was something the family shared. I remember him saying, as he was putting paint on his canvas, "Look, Bella, look at the hills, look at that mix of colors. Look at the pinks and the blues and the browns and what they make of a color we see!" I was the one kid in school who knew you didn't paint a mountain brown.

And there was always music in our house. I attribute that to the fact that we are of European origin, an older culture and a culture which in the main (even for very poor people, as my family was) treasured art and ideas. As a very young girl I heard Mary Garden sing *Carmen* on a record. I heard Schialiapin, I heard Caruso, I heard wonderful instrumentalists on records because they were always in our house.

I grew up in San Bernardino, a town at the edge of the desert in Southern California, with not a lot of culture around. It was a railroad town, a citrus-farming place and had some very repressive, reactionary elements in it. Next to us was a city called Redlands, and it had the same group of people, only a little more churchbound, I think. For a community that small, it must have had a church on almost every corner and almost every faith was represented. (I doubt that the Jews were too well represented.)

A socialist family named the Smileys lived near Redlands. I don't know how they earned their money, but they were rich and we were poor, that I could discern. They endowed Redlands with a library, a park and a small outdoor Greek theater. This Greek theater was run by a remarkable woman, Grace Mullen, a visionary who thought that everybody in Redlands should experience art at its best. She brought wonderful artists to this place, all internationally known artists in every form, including dance. I saw my own teacher, my own mentor, there before I ever knew I was going to have anything to do with him.

So our family had a very rich background in the arts, which they gave to my sister and me as a matter of food on the table. It was never considered something special that you sat down to do. It was there, and we always went to the Redlands Bowl. That was a very particular outing for our family. Life is interesting because it is unpredictable and because it has things that don't belong, in places where they shouldn't be. The culture that existed in an otherwise barren citrus-farm community was provided by a socialist family! So I had this kind of wealth in my early childhood.

Both my sister and I were considered by our family to be poorly reared if we didn't have some form of music to practice. My sister took violin, which she played very, very badly. We had a dog who howled incessantly whenever she hit a high note off key, and I played the piano, also very badly. The fact that I chose dance over piano, and before I ever really saw dance, was probably because I was a mover. I made up dances without knowing that they were dances, but that was my form of play, even though it was probably unrecognizable as a dance to anybody else. My family assumed this was a very healthy and very natural choice on my part, so I had the one rare thing that most people hardly ever have, and that was support and empowerment from my family. The career, the way of life I chose, was considered honorable, right, ethical and appropriate by my immediate family.

JODY: How would you gauge the importance of childhood influences as opposed to living and working with dance over a lifetime? Is creativity more a function of early inspiration or does it come out of a lifetime of discipline and performance?

BELLA: I think it is possible through a lifetime of discipline and experience to acquire tremendous bundles of creativity. But I think no one has yet been able to determine how much your earliest impressions color, affect, edit what you then learn in your disciplined years. I can only speak for myself and say that my earliest impressions are with me as actively today as they were when I first experienced them. I have added to them and accrued a whole set of disciplines and experiences I didn't have before, but the heightened emotionality of my earliest experiences has never been replaced; it's always there, and fresh, and like a guide. It's like the first note you ever heard, the first color you ever saw. Very often when other choreographers talk to me, their references are to their very early experiences. I think perhaps I am not singular in this. All of us have been affected very dominantly by our earliest experiences. Even if they are negative ones, they do something to shape you.

I do not believe in an innate, inborn psyche. I think all

of us are affected by our inheritance, which is altered appreciably by how you take these first genetic beginnings and nurture them or fail to nurture them. I don't think there are givens which are engraved in stone and will never change, so I find it difficult to accept complexes that are unalterable. I do feel there are early experiences and genetic engravings that define us very early in life and that one can recognize in an infant something about its personality, that there is something genetically embedded. How those first genetic setdowns grow and thrive or are hampered depends on how one's life is lived. So I would say that your earliest experiences are extremely valuable and significant in making you into a creative or non-creative individual, but equally important are the ways in which you hone the gift. How you dedicate yourself to the defining of it, the making of it, the service to it determines whether or not it will live, flourish and become an entity.

JODY: You are often described as both a humanitarian and an artist. How do you express your personal concerns and values through your art?

BELLA: I think the description is a fairly accurate one, but I would place as first on my plate of goodies, choreographer, and then educator and humanist. As I became a proficient artist, that is, after I had studied for a long time and had achieved a level I felt fairly good about, I found that I could apply my art form to education almost directly. It was one of the most exciting discoveries I ever made, and it occurred as I followed our only child into her early educative years.

Since we did not live in an extended family I had little experience with raising a child, so I needed education probably more than she did. The school furnished her with a scholarship, and I furnished the school, a private one in this case, with my skills as a dance teacher. It was amazing how directly applicable the dance art form is to basic fundamental educative subjects. That was revealing and exciting. I had developed as a dance educator earlier because in the days when I began, the way one earned one's living was not by dancing, but by teaching dancing. Whether one was able to dance, was skilled at it, was in love with it or not didn't make a lot of difference. You did it because that is how you kept yourself alive. So that I did, and learned to become a more gracious and, finally, quite good teacher.

The humanism came from my family. They were humanists by practice, not by preachment, and I didn't realize how rare that was. They never ever suggested that my sister and I should follow in their footsteps and reject other philosophies. As a matter of fact, I dipped into as many kinds of philosophies as my very curious mind would take me, from the supernatural to the spiritual to the materialist. I don't mean to make this sound as though I became proficient in any of these, but I tested them and arrived by my own choice at the same place I had witnessed my parents practice their lives, as somebody who does feel that indeed she is her brother's keeper.

How that addresses itself in the art form is by indirection, I think. I seem either biannually or annually compelled to do a ballet based upon the state of the human being in society, or the state of society as it affects the human being. It comes out in a variety of forms, but that's about as direct as it gets, I believe.

JODY: In your 1978 commencement address at Scripps College you said, "If I were to place a value on attributes I find of great importance, they would be commitment, passion, the capacity to rebound from adversities and the power to dream." Would you add anything to that list today?

BELLA: That's a damn good list! I still believe that.

JODY: You said that to dance one returns to the physical knowledge of emotion. What exactly do you mean by that?

BELLA: There are certain things the body does in response to pain, to pleasure, to confusion, to fear. These very profound human emotions that guide our lives are first manifested physically. All of us have experienced, long before we could verbalize, long before we could make symbols to identify meanings, that when you are hurt, your response is purely physical. So, we have a memory of them from very early times before we learned to speak. We knew pain, we knew pleasure, we knew fear, we knew a lack of understanding, which did not become those words I just articulated but became a physical expression. If you name the major emotions or mind sets, they all have physical equivalencies, the earliest ones we knew, probably. I am told, and I have no reason to doubt it, that before we are born this form of physical intelligence was being set down and continues to grow, and is there as a language too often hidden because it's not recognized or appreciated fully, too often hidden to make use of or to develop or to give due credit to, I guess. It's an expression of physical understanding, physical intelligence and, therefore, physical communication. I think that's what I meant by that statement.

JODY: I'd like to ask you about the creative process. How do you initiate a dance? Do you start with an idea you wish to communicate or a movement or an emotion that you want to translate into dance?

BELLA: If I had a formula for making dances it would be a far less painful process. A lot of it is at the unrecognizable, subconscious level. Something has impinged upon my consciousness, only it is still buried at this point. So I fuel it, I feed it. Then, a separating process begins, where all the things not relevant to this initial seed are funneled away, and all the things that are relevant to it are fed in. And then it comes to a very conscious level, and I begin to choreograph. I begin to make a dance. So the process is like begetting anything; it's a birthing process. Part of it begins at a level I may not even be totally aware of at its initiation. Sometimes it is started by a direct, conscious idea. Sometimes it is a response to something I've seen, heard, felt. Each dance for me seems to have a different birth and a different birthing process.

I'm a very kinetic thinker, so it is difficult for me to actually begin a dance without that element present, even if it is simply that I begin walking—I walk around in a closed room because I am easily distracted when I am at a heightened conscious level—until a motion symbol comes forward, and that will be something that I will then pursue. But as I said, each piece has a different origin and a different process in the making. In some dances I set every gesture, every inflection for my company. In others I do very little of that.

For example, I decided that because of my father's gift to me, my parental inheritance, I would like to do a trilogy about my impressions of the artists I have seen throughout my life and loved and who have meant so much to me, have been so fulfilling so enriching for me. I chose as the first the work of the English sculptor Henry Moore. I fell madly in love with Henry Moore the first time I saw his work and never knew much about him at all. Then I became a visual collector. I've never been wealthy enough to be an actual collector of a Moore piece, but it doesn't matter because I have the Moore in my mind and in my body and in my emotional set. I just love what he did. I love the fact that he looks classical and is anything but, and I love the fact that he is one of the few sculptors who has never presented woman as object but always woman as power, woman as a maker of things.

So I decided the logical thing to do would be to do the Moore as a work for my six female dancers. We began to look at Moore's books and we did some reading about him, but we were less concerned about Moore the man and more interested in his work. Almost all of the dancers had seen Moore's work one place or another, and photographs were reminders of an initial, three-dimensional experience. When we were on tour, as we were most of our lives, dancers would come to me and say, "Oh, Bella, there's a wonderful Moore in the plaza, you have got to go see it!" So we would continue to "collect" the Moores.

At this point I turned to Moore's own teaching, which he elucidated with great clarity. He had categorized his work and had titles for certain of his pieces. There was a whole series of things, like *Two Figure Forms, Interlocking Shapes, Three Rings, Helmet Image* and so forth. I said, "This should be the template for what we do. Let's use those headings: what can we do kinetically as two figure forms?" It was such fun! It was so exciting! We began a process of exploration. When it came to two figures, it was easy for the two dancers to choreograph for themselves because they had a good feeling for what they wanted. When it involved more than two figures I stepped in and did the choreography, because it's hard to be in that many places outside yourself. So basically we choreographed this together; however, we already had certain precepts set down so that there was always a touch of asymmetry. The figure or the object never touched the ground solidly, there were always spaces—for example, two points would touch, but not the whole. There was a whole stack of things that we understood about Moore and we had the luxury of choreographing this piece for a year, which is unusual because we have to earn our living by touring.

That's an example of a work co-choreographed by the six original dancers and myself. On the other hand, a work called *Spaces Between,* which has been called my signature piece, is an abstract dealing with spatial concepts, an inheritance I probably also got from my father. I choreographed every bit of that. So from one to the other the process varies, depending on the work.

JODY: You have said that you want your dances to be "slightly puzzling." What does that mean for you?

BELLA: It means that one can see many facets at one time.

I call it *layered,* so that you may be evoking a specific image for one person, but quite a different one for another. I have had people come up to me and say, "You have changed that, haven't you, Bella?" I haven't changed it at all, but on the third viewing they saw something they didn't see the first time. That to me is a mark of success. That is what I mean. And I don't like to spell things out too much because life doesn't spell things out. Life is interesting because it fails to do that, because your wit always has to be sharpened and your mind widened enough to accept what is unexpected. So I like that in my art forms as well.

JODY: Over the years what kinds of risks have you taken, and what did they get you?

BELLA: That's a very difficult question for me to answer because it assumes I function in a way that I do not. I never set out to say, "Now I'm going to do a risk-taking dance, now I'm going to do a safe dance, now I'm going to do a happy dance." I don't do that because things gestate for me; they have their own embryonic voice that has to be matured. I don't set out to do a risk-taking anything; I set out to do what that piece calls for. In some cases I guess it could be called that, but I really don't know what *risk-taking* means because it feels to me like someone sets out to do something outside of the art. Truth-taking is something that I understand. If it happens to be risk-taking, it is because the art demanded that of me. I suppose it is exciting for some people to say, "Nobody has done this. I'm going to shake up the establishment." But not for me; I simply don't function that way.

In *Confines,* which is one of my so-called social pieces— I don't know that it should be called a social piece, but its content deals with the human state within our society)— I was very interested in the confining things that happen to women in our society through what are considered acceptable women's roles. For example, teen-age pregnancy was so alarming and unsettling for me, I who wanted a child and had a child very late in my life, that I had to push myself to comprehend. Here is a baby having a baby: how can that be; how can that work; how can it have meaning? What a difficult place that is for a female! Having a baby should be tremendously exciting, rewarding. It's hard enough, God knows, to be responsible for somebody else's life. There are moments when I really say, "How did I ever think I could get engaged in this!" And then to have a baby this way, it's unfair. It's wrong.

In this dance I have what looks to be a young girl in a slip—the women are in lingerie in this, with a pregnancy pad—and a little rag doll that she holds. The imagery for me was multi-layered. Well, one critic saw this and said, "Ms. Lewitzky must really hate children!" Now what would persuade her to this conviction? I suppose one could say that was risk-taking; I don't know, and actually I don't care a whole lot. I was much more concerned with what I wanted to convey. These are the layers of life I would like to share, to communicate, and if somebody gets them as wrong as this critic did, then that's the truth of that. Most do not; that was very unusual.

JODY: Is costume in your dances an extension of your interest in graphic art?

BELLA: In some cases very directly. In other cases the costume becomes revealing of the body form and not an extension of it at all. My love affair is with movement itself; therefore, very seldom will I encumber it in a way that the costume is what you are looking at and not the movement. I have a work that I am just bringing back into repertory called *Inscape.* Again, landscape is something I understood from my painterly father, and I thought that because this was about people I would call it *Inscape,* about the insides of people. That's kind of an amusing thing, because I thought I had made up that title, and I found out that Virginia Woolf had used it long before I did! I shouldn't have been chagrined; it probably meant the same thing to both of us.

I collaborated with a very well known costume designer, Rudy Gernreich, the enfant terrible of the sixties. I first knew him as a member of a company in which we both danced. He had come to see a work of mine and said, "We must do something together," and I replied, "By all means!" We had a meeting and I said, "Why don't you do wardrobe and I do movement?" So, fabric became extremely important in this particular work, and the wardrobe did truly amplify what was being said.

Rudy set the stage in almost a Mondrian light through the use of fabric. He began with two shiny poles that went up beyond the top of the fly system and out of the audience's view, and two dancers down below wore what looked like black capes. As the dancers begin to climb to the top of these two poles, they leave stretch fabric in a tube behind them. Then, three dancers wander across the stage taking with them ribbons that are held at one end and then fastened as the dancers move from one side of the stage to the other. So the dancers have created the stage setting in motion and fabric. At the very end Rudy devised a false head that he put on the dancers so that the hair is literally covering the face and the face is at the back of the head. One's feeling of distortion is incredible because you see this backwards, and when the heads are finally removed you see these white masks with a little smile. I don't know what Rudy's statement was, but for me it was that too many people are masked and one seldom sees the true face of the individual who sits opposite.

The exact opposite happened in the Moore piece, where dancers had to look nude. I do not use nudity because it would change the content entirely. The dancers wear unitards, a one piece garment that matches their skin color so they basically look nude without the conflict of somebody's being more interested in genitals than in dance. Also, nudity, I discovered, has been distorted in our society so that its overtones are too multiple to really overcome. In my third and final impression, which is based on the work of Paul Klee, Klee's wardrobe—what he puts on his figures in his line drawings—is the statement, so we imitated that. For instance, he has a line drawing sketch of something he calls *Forgetful Angel,* where one wing is in the front and one wing is in the back. It's such a typical Klee—talk about layered meanings—that we replicated the costume. Here, too, costume had very specific importance, whereas in some other pieces you want to reveal the body.

JODY: You are known to give very positive encouragement to your dancers. What are your views on cooperation as the basis for a mode of teaching, as opposed to competition?

BELLA: I think that if people are encouraged to be the best they can be, then you get a cornucopia of wealth flowing from them. And if you set out to pit them one against the other, you get a real wealth of negativity, of things that are injurious. Probably, it produces too, but in a way that I'm not terribly interested in. It tends to dehumanize and to brutalize. So I practice what I believe as much as I can, and I hope that each dancer in the company feels encouraged to move as far as he or she can possibly go. I will help them as long as they help themselves. If they stop helping themselves I become totally disinterested in them.

JODY: How have you balanced your creative work and your personal life?

BELLA: I have been able to balance my life because my husband is such a remarkable man. Newell has always been extremely supportive. One of my fondest statements from him is that for me to go out and take a dance class was probably the most inexpensive and healthiest form of therapy, and he's absolutely right. When our child was born I took care of her while he was at work, and when he came home, I would go off to my work and he would have the opportunity to be the parenting member of the family. It's always been that way, a very sharing marriage that we have. We quarrel incessantly and in an aggravated tone of voice, which I contend is what keeps our marriage together. I have supported him in his work and he has supported me in mine, which has made it possible to be a full-time wife and mother and artist. Without the support of my second family I wouldn't be who I am, just as without the support of my first family I wouldn't have become the person I developed into.

My daughter is the same way: she is a very gifted teacher and dancer and choreographer, and she too is married to an architect. Amidst the things that don't go right, there are some things that do go right. My daughter was also very supportive of my being a professional artist and a mother; she never had a problem with it. When she was three years old she said, "Can I come take a class, Mommy?" I replied, "As long as you don't interfere with any of the women." And this little figure was barely able to reach the bar, her little hand stretching for it, doing leg swings!

She was quite wonderful; she improvised to records when she was about six years old. I think she thought that was the way everybody played; she just didn't know that everybody's family didn't dance all over the place! So she grew up already with that attitude toward dance and toward art and decided on her own, not by my persuasion, that she wanted to become a dancer. And she became an absolutely beautiful dancer. Here again, there was this very strong familial support.

JODY: Your daughter said you are a person of incredible strength and drive. What do you consider to be your own strengths and vulnerabilities?

BELLA: In terms of my personal beliefs I think she is accurate, because beliefs exist outside oneself, and they are one of the most powerful sources of strength. I find certain values in life to be terribly important to me, and I gain whatever strength I have from that. I do admit I am a strong person. There are probably other reasons for it, but none that I could articulate with as much clarity. Driven? I guess that might be accurate if it means that making dances and being part of the dance world is for me like breathing.

JODY: Actually, she said you had fantastic drive, not that you were driven. There's a difference, isn't there?

BELLA: A little. If you have drive, you are driven, and I have no problem with that. I would voice it a little differently, because I don't feel driven at all, I have never felt that, that I can recall. I think that my interest is so very directly tied to the work I do, and it is so high a priority for me that my life is much more fulfilled when I do my work and far less fulfilled and without meaning when I don't. That could also be construed as drive. Only drive seems to mean that I've got a separate motor that moves forward in that direction. I guess because I really am not competitive, I think there is a difference between how I feel and whether I am really driven. It is just that dance is the center of my being. If you say I am alive, I would say to you, I am alive because I make dances. I am an artist, and dance keeps me alive. They are so inseparable in my world that the focus on it is obviously very singular. So commitment and focus on a single issue would be accurate.

JODY: How does living in Southern California affect your artistic vision?

BELLA: I don't know how much it impinges on my work; how it affects me personally is very clear. I feel stifled in stone canyons—on Wall Street or our own downtown, where you can't see a horizon line, and when you look up and see unending tops of buildings you don't see land or earth. I love California; I love Southern California. Its sun is to me what the south of France was to the Impressionist painters. It fills me with the same kind of nourishment that they obviously got and that I get from the sun and colors of Southern California. The tall mountains represent a power I understand. I share that. They reach into the sky with a statement, a presence that is forceful, powerful, like strong arms raised to the sky, and always the promise of something beyond them.

That's another thing: I don't like endings; I don't like single visions. I like the unknown. I like the fact that you don't know what's on the other side. If I can see the horizon line as it falls away from me forever and ever, I get claustrophobia. I can see to the end—how awful! I miss my tall mountains, where mystery is always behind them, where the unknown is just over the other side, where you can be guaranteed that there will be the unexpected, something you didn't know. I love this landscape with a passion. I miss it when we're gone from it too long. Whether it affects my art or not, directly, I haven't any idea.

JODY: You made your first trip to Europe in the fifties. What impact did that have on you?

BELLA: A tremendous impact. I had never seen another culture, although to live in Los Angeles is to know other cultures very intimately. Europe was different in that it meant learning other history, ancient history. My first view of Europe that I remember with the most impact was our visit to Greece. My husband was like a young schoolboy, running around the Acropolis, lifted out of two dimensions into three and carrying the mantle of history, saying, "Here it was!" I felt the same sense but not as acutely, because after all, he is an architect and I am not. But I responded the same way to the temple of Poseidon. I remember pictures of Isadora Duncan holding her arms up amidst the pillars of that temple, and I suddenly realized what she must have felt. It was a very special outdoor esthetic experience.

But most of all, what I saw was a civilization that had died and about which nobody seemed to care very much: columns fallen to the ground, pigeons eating off the nose of a broken statue, an arm or a finger gone. I felt, "How did this happen?" Because the only images I had ever seen of Greek sculpture or buildings were as they were when intact. I was totally unprepared to see them fallen and broken. The fact that history dies had a very strong impact on me. Europe is a very good example of how history dies. I had never thought about it before because we live in such a young culture here.

JODY: You are considered a highly acclaimed choreographer, a superb artist and one of the greatest teachers of dance in the country today. Is it possible to say which has been the most pleasurable, or the most important to you: performance, choreography or teaching?

BELLA: I would have to put those on a time line. The first thing of importance to me was performing. I was really fanatically devoted to becoming a perfect performer—unachievable, of course, so you could always work at it until you dropped dead—a perfect technician and a perfect creator of a role, a perfect "performer" in that I could communicate what I felt, all combined into one. That was what I dedicated my performing life to, and I think I achieved it maybe four times in all of my years of performance, because it is extremely difficult to combine all those things. At that time that was my sole interest.

From that point I moved to becoming a choreographer. I happily gave away performance because I had had a very fulfilled performing career and headed into choreography with the same kind of dedication, I guess, and devotion to becoming an expert choreographer. But there was a big difference between being an expert performer and an expert choreographer. To become an expert performer, there were tangibles: did I have balance, fluidity, coordination, rhythm? Could I express it, could I make it flow? These were very specific things, and I could go on and on headed toward that goal of perfection. But I was always dealing with me, with "I," with the performer, with my body, with my ability.

Choreography was the first time I confronted the art

form: suddenly I was in a whole other world far larger and quite outside myself, involving space design, time design, motion design, rhythm and musicality. Now all the things I had learned long before about music and art came back to me with a much wider scope, with parallels I could learn. For example, why was I in love with Picasso? For the first time, I would examine this from a formal point of view: because he presents one object with four viewpoints. From that I realized I've always loved that quality, and that moved into my choreographic capacity. I've always loved space as a geographic attribute: how did one define it choreographically? So I was in a whole other arena where I the person, the instrument, was secondary if not cursory, and the form itself became my teacher.

Dance—the art form—grew for me to a place of tremendous dominance. If I had had to choose between the two careers I would have chosen choreography above performance. I was an absolutely wonderful performer, I need to say that, without any ego involved. I worked at it and I had a gift for it. But I would give you that for what happens to me when I become a choreographer. It's far broader. It's the difference between the playwright, the vehicle and the actor; one is totally dependent upon the other. In choreography the performer brings to realization the choreography, but without the choreography, the performer has nothing.

That was my second phase. My third phase was teaching. I began as an intolerant teacher: "Why are they here? They don't have the body for it. What is it they are attempting to do? Can't they see I'm standing in demi-point in balance? Why aren't they?" I was a very ignorant and intolerant teacher; ignorance makes intolerance, I think. It took me a very long time to become a teacher. Remember, performing is a very lonely act: I don't have to communicate; I don't have to interface. Choreography is this thing that is outside me: I interface with the tools of choreography, and the performers are tools of choreography. But teaching, that's a different thing: I must interface directly or I am not a teacher worth the title. So again, I had to learn a whole different craft, very rich and very rewarding.

Teaching did one thing for me that neither the art form itself nor the performing did. A performer has a very short life span: when she has stopped performing, that's it. A choreographer may or may not outlive her time; it depends on what she has done. A teacher will outlive her day because the only form of immortality is the inheritance. People invested in me and I added to that, I hope, things of quality and value which I pass on to the people I touch—and they pass it on, and thus it is passed on to future generations. So it became a very meaningful and once again very enlarging experience for me. But I realize it came in time increments: first as a performer, second as a choreographer, third as a teacher.

JODY: Writer Anaïs Nin said that the source of her creativity was a responsiveness that she never lost, that she still felt things as keenly at seventy as she did at twenty. What is the source of your own creative energy?

BELLA: Curiosity! Less responsiveness, although both my daughter and I share the same disability: we are vulnerable to over-empathizing, which performers acquire. It's taken for granted that you have this level of responsiveness to things that happen, and you can't have a performer who does not empathize. But curiosity was what kept my creativity alive. I'm still a very curious person. I still feel like a student in life. I measure my growth by things I have learned rather than things I have done. And I still will say, "What would happen if…?" Some of my dances have their beginnings that way. For example, "What if I were able to move the dancer off the floor plane into a higher plane?" That became a source of curiosity for me that developed into a dance. Not all my dances begin with unanswered questions, but a lot of my life does: what if, what is it like? Curiosity keeps my creativity alive.

Barbara Hendricks

As an opera lover I first heard of Barbara Hendricks, and then heard her sing, in France. Adopted by France as one of its favorite artists she has captivated the French, as well as everyone else, by her quiet, understated art and personal magnetism. Since the early '90s she has been constantly on the front page of the French newspapers, particularly in 1992, when she gave a concert in Orange to provide relief for victims of the terrible flood disaster in Vaison La Romaine. Considered one of the most impressive lyric sopranos of her generation, Barbara Hendricks is consistently praised for her elegance, refinement and style, especially in French art songs and German lieder. Herbert von Karajan compared her to Maria Callas in "her passion and interpretive possibility." Her activism and commitment as well as her glorious voice made her irresistible to me. I had been debating how I could contact her when a former student of mine came to visit from Montpellier. Her boyfriend's older brother had done some photographic work for Barbara Hendricks, and he was willing to provide me with an address!

The following interview was done preceding a concert Barbara Hendricks gave in San Francisco. Her beauty, her intense spirituality and her intellectual integrity are wrapped up in great personal warmth and a simple presentness. There is also in her character an innate feel for equilibrium or balance—between music and science, between recital and operatic performance, between performance and humanitarian activism, between career and family. The one surprise, when she initially opened the door, and again, when she gave me a goodbye hug, was her physical petiteness, so much in contrast with the immense person she is.

Born November 20, 1948, Barbara Hendricks' first exposure to music came from the church and school choirs in which she sang. Her early academic education was directed more toward science and mathematics, both areas toward which she was naturally inclined. In an interview she once described herself as "one of those people who really liked calculus." As a student at the University of Nebraska at Lincoln, she was a combined chemistry and mathematics major; however, by her junior year in college she had begun singing again.

A turning point occurred when a member of her church choir asked her to sing at a small community gathering in Lincoln. A prominent local lawyer named Richard Smith heard her sing and invited her to attend the Aspen Music Festival that summer. There, she found herself exposed to music and musicians in a way she had not experienced previously. She also met celebrated mezzo-soprano Jennie Tourel, who became her teacher and mentor. Barbara Hendricks attended the Juilliard School of Music in New York on a full scholarship and continued to study with Tourel. Jennie Tourel also provided Barbara Hendricks her first opportunity to travel to Europe, where Tourel conducted master classes every summer.

Barbara Hendricks has made appearances with every major orchestra in Europe and America. She has sung at the Metropolitan Opera, the Vienna State Opera, Glyndebourne, La Scala, Covent Garden and Salzburg and made over fifty recordings. With all of that, she has somehow found time to be Goodwill Ambassador for the United Nations High Commission for Refugees and has given many concerts to raise funds for humanitarian causes. She sang at the televised gala that preceded President Clinton's inauguration, and on New Year's eve, 1993, she gave a concert in Sarajevo. Barbara Hendricks has been married to Swedish born Martin Engstrom since 1977. They have two children, Sebastian and Jennie.

Staying Alive

An Interview with Barbara Hendricks
San Francisco, California
April, 1993

JODY: At what point in your life did your vocation become clear to you? Was there a moment of truth, a turning point?

BARBARA: Oh, yes. The summer between my junior and senior years I was invited to Aspen, Colorado, to study with a teacher and to participate in the music school there. I accepted because it seemed more interesting than the other prospect I had for the summer, which was to do research in Vermillion, South Dakota, which had been proposed by my organic chemistry teacher. I thought going to Aspen would be a lot of fun, and music has always been a part of my life and I think would have been even if I didn't do it professionally. I accepted it as a natural part of my life, like eating and sleeping, so I suppose I was never confronted with the decision of what I was going to do with the music. I was always sure this was a part of my life. It was nothing I even thought about.

The summer I spent in Aspen was arranged by someone who had heard me sing at the university and who had liked my voice and wanted to give me the opportunity. He had chosen the teacher, and he had gotten together with a group of his friends, some of whom I still don't know, and raised money for me to go that summer. These are people to whom I am still very close and to whom I am very grateful. We write, not very often, but at Christmas we have contact and when they come to Europe, they pass through and see us. They have always been almost surprised by what started there, happily surprised in the sense that it has more than exceeded their hopes. Yet, at the same time, they have never ever treated me as if they bought a piece of me, never, and I was always very grateful for that.

So that summer I met Jennie Tourel, whom they had chosen for me as the best voice teacher. You have to realize that I did not know how to prepare a voice lesson; I had taken voice lessons at the university as an elective, to keep my average up, but I didn't know anything about serious voice study. I must say, with somebody like Jennie Tourel I learned that very quickly, after the first lesson. But the decision—I don't even want to use the word decision because it was not a question in my mind when I went there—was easy. By the time I left it was very clear to me this is what I had to do, or at least this was what I had to try to do. It was as if I accepted that as my destiny: it was not agonizing, it was not frightening, it was just natural. So that's really how it happened.

JODY: Were your parents supportive of your choice?

BARBARA: Not at all. They thought I had lost my mind. Given my parents' background coming from the South, and the fact that both of them had gotten an education but with great difficulty—it took my mother years to get her college degree while we were growing up—for them, an education and a college degree were the key to the future. Even though I returned to the university and finished my degree, they saw my going off to New York as some kind of folly, that I was throwing everything away. So they were very unsupportive in the sense that they were frightened for me. I understood it. I didn't like it, honestly; I would have preferred them to be more supportive of my choice, but I did understand. They had never been further than Memphis, Tennessee, so New York City was all the sin and dangers that my father had been trying to protect me from all those years.

JODY: What was it like to go from Stephens, Arkansas, to Lincoln, Nebraska, to New York City? Isn't that a trajectory of major change?

BARBARA: Well, to tell you the truth, it was a very natural progression. Not only that, but to end up where I am now, from Stephens, Arkansas, to Switzerland, to Europe, to really being a citizen of the world was a natural progression. I never lived in Stephens, that's where I was born, my grandmother lived there. We lived in many towns in Arkansas and in Tennessee because of my father's work, which probably prepared me for this nomadic life I lead, and the ability I had to learn very young of letting go, letting go of things and, what was more difficult, letting go of people. But I gradually did, particularly as a child, because I got new friends at school. I have no childhood friends from Arkansas or Tennessee; I can't say I miss it because I have good friends, but no friendships that I've kept from sixth grade or anything like that. I tried, but it's very difficult as a child or a teenager to keep contact and to keep writing, and then when others stop writing, gradually, you know, there's the occasional Christmas card and then nothing. There was never any rupture, there was never any finishing high school and going off to college. I first went to a Methodist school in Tennessee that my father insisted on—I was sixteen when I went to college—but I found that the curriculum was just not up to what I wanted from an education, so that's why I moved on.

When I finished university I went to New York, and when I left New York I went to Paris because my husband was working there. He couldn't come and live and work in America, so it was easier for me to go and live in Paris. So again it was a practical decision. I loved Paris. I had been to Europe several times over the summer studying with my teacher, and I had always felt very at home there. When we left Paris and moved to Switzerland, it was never a rejection of what had been in the past. I have always carried where I have been with me. I've never left because I was unhappy; I've left because I had to move on.

JODY: You continued your studies at the Juilliard School of Music with Jennie Tourel. What did you learn there about yourself and your voice?

BARBARA: The period at Juilliard was a very difficult one for me because even though I had a full scholarship I had to earn my own living, and financially I was constantly worried how I was going to pay the rent at the end of the month. That was a development time of standing on my own that was very important to me, very painful but very important. Then, of course, I had to find the *devise,* as the French say, the reason why I was there, what I wanted to do with it. It wasn't substantial enough wanting to be famous, or wanting to make money, or being liked: that seemed to me too transitory.

Meeting Tourel gave me an example of the kind of artist I wanted to be. That meant really having to accept the fact that not only was it my duty to follow what my talent is, but that art is not a luxury. It is a necessity to life, and one cannot follow a more noble quest than serving one's art and serving one's talent, whatever that might be. It took me a while to accept that and then to take it on as my own banner of what I wanted to do. That was very important those years at Juilliard, much more than learning how to sing, because I sing just about like I always did. I had a natural voice and I really just had to nurture it and be patient rather than to make it into anything. So what I learned was really more about artistry than technique.

Tourel always worked through a piece of music; she and I both hated to do exercises. I'd come in, and she would say, "Have you vocalized?" And I'd say, "No," and she would say, "O.K., let's do a few." Where we really worked is when we started to work on music. If there was a problem then we worked on that problem, but in the context of the music, what the music had to say. What I learned from her also was the importance of being able to stand always behind the music. There is never a moment where you become more important than the composer or the music, or the reason you are there, which is to communicate.

My feeling about art and the necessity of art is that art speaks to us in a place where we are alike, and that language is actually necessary for our survival. It is more than doing entertainment or singing a dead music. Sometimes I'm asked about singing "dead" music. "How can you do it?" Because God's not dead: genius comes directly from the divine. So that was what I discovered and the most important thing I learned when I was at Juillard, besides the technical things—languages and studying the piano and solfege, which I never really got. It was the first time in my life I couldn't learn something just by applying myself.

There was a lot of that kind of work: daily work at school and working on the voice, but working on the voice in a different way...being patient, really, not making it try to do something it wasn't ready for. That was the hardest thing. I would say the most difficult thing in life for me is patience, is to be patient and keep faith and not want to make something happen before its time: living in the present.

JODY: What is it that makes singing effortless for you? Or, is it ever effortless?

BARBARA: I don't sing just from the throat, it's a whole body effort. It's integrated and it should be harmonious—what's the word I'm looking for, organic, yes—not just what is happening in the neck and throat. As I said, I always sang very naturally. I try to keep that. Very often with singers you see how they sing; that is one of the reasons why opera singers can be so unphotogenic sometimes because you see every bit of technique, you see them reaching for their notes...Maybe that's necessary for them; I've never had to do that, and I've always tried to have the sound coming from an inner core as opposed to just from the throat. That doesn't always happen: there are times when I don't feel well, when there are things that need to be worked on, but I've always tried to keep the way I sang as a child because that had the least amount of superfluous effort. It is the most pure way of singing.

JODY: How important is the emotional or mental aspect of singing relative to the technical aspect?

BARBARA: It's the most important, because it is the technical part: it's all in your mind. If you are convinced that you cannot sing the note you will not be able to sing it, no matter what you have in your throat. It is the mental as well as the spiritual aspect that is so important. You have got to believe that the note is going to come out. I listen to my daughter, who can scream notes that we wouldn't professionally think are possible, but those notes are there: so the mental part is really the limits we put on ourselves. Of course, there are physical limits, absolutely. But within the physical limits we have, we probably use only about ten per cent of what's available to us. And I think you unlock that only by having a free-flowing mental and spiritual energy.

JODY: How have your teachers influenced you, for better or for worse? And how else did you learn what you needed to know?

BARBARA: Well, I only had one teacher. I only had Jennie Tourel, really. I tried other teachers, and it didn't work. They were't bad teachers. They just didn't give me what I needed, so I found myself having to become my own master. I looked, I looked, and I was very upset that I could not find either a conductor or stage director, somebody who would take me under their wing and tell me what to do. I found that I had to do it myself, because there was no choice.

Jennie Tourel was like a second mother—although we didn't often socialize, we didn't chat on the phone or anything—but there was a mutual respect. When I met her I didn't know who she was, you see, so I never approached her as a famous person. I grew to admire her and love her for the woman I knew, and that gave us a very real relationship. Sometimes she had a certain kind of bitterness that saddened me because I felt she was greater than that. She had a difficult life, and there were things about her life that I didn't want to repeat: I didn't want to end up alone with two little dogs in an East Side apartment in New York. Some choices that she made also had to do with the time in which she lived. She has been dead twenty years. Next year I will do a recital in Alice Tully Hall in tribute to her. But she has never left me, because I don't think I could have gone on without that influence she had on me.

At the same time, I understand that if she had stayed alive, with us both having very strong personalities, there might have been a moment when I would have had to push her away and maybe reject what there was she had to give me. I really feel that she stayed alive the last five years of her life for me. When I had gotten what it was she was supposed to give me, it was OK for her to go on: that's how I looked at it long after she died.

But it was very scary out there, because the people I went to, the agents, the conductors, people you expected to sort of keep you in line and say, "You have to keep your mind on your music, and keep your mind on the goal," were talking bullshit. So I was the one who was having to set some standards, and that scared me to death, because I thought, "How am *I* supposed to know? I don't come from this world of music and performing and career."

I remember the first time I had to file my income tax the accountant was furious with me because I hadn't paid my installments. I said to him, "How do you expect me to know? I don't come from a family where anybody has money in the bank; there's always less money than there are bills going out." Nobody ever paid taxes in advance in my home; there was no money. I mean, all the things that there were to learn! There just came a moment when I recognized that I was going to have to be it. So I surrounded myself with friends, with people whom I trust. But I have had to have inner ears and outer eyes to see what I am doing and to feel it.

There was a point where I thought maybe I should record everything and listen to it and videotape my performances and watch them. I have all the equipment, but I never did it because I somehow feel that would take the awareness outside myself to something exterior—which doesn't mean that I wouldn't be able to learn from it, but not as a rule. I know some singers who record everything and listen to everything they sing. When I'm recording I do, and I learn a lot when I'm recording, but I don't do it on a daily basis, listening to every concert the next day and seeing how it sounds and how to improve it.

JODY: Has race or gender been an obstacle to your career?

BARBARA: No more than it has helped me. You know, I am not liked by everybody in this business. I mean, who is, thank God. Some of them I'm glad they don't like me, given their standards, but I assume first of all it is because they don't like my work; we have different tastes, that's all. If there have been instances where I have been not given something for reasons of race, there have also been others where people wanted to do something positive and probably did. But in everyday life, yes. The taxi that keeps going, the shopkeeper who treats you, no matter

how well dressed you are, as if you are going to walk off
with the shop. It doesn't happen all the time, but from
time to time it's still there, it's a part of life.

I see life as taking particularly what could be seen as
negative as the tools that I've been given, so there is a reason that in this life I came back the way I did, as a
woman, as black, as poor, as from the South, with the
family I had. The way I deal with that is to take it and use
it, take it as a tool for my life. What it has given me is far
greater than any suffering I have come from. And I certainly think that being a woman is the greatest thing in
the world. I look at my daughter and I say to her, "You
know, we are so lucky, you and I."

JODY: What was it like to sing for President-elect Clinton
the night before his inauguration?

BARBARA: It wasn't so much singing for him, it was being
a part of that atmosphere in Washington, which is something I've never felt in this country. I was too young to
remember what it felt like for Kennedy's inauguration,
although I remember the speech because the speech
touched me, but I was too young to celebrate it or do anything other than watch the speech on television.

When I arrived in Washington I was very tired because
I had arrived from Pnom Phen, where I had been visiting
with returnees from refugee camps in Thailand, and I
came by way of Bangkok and Tokyo, so I arrived pretty
dead. I came into the hotel and put on the television to
see what was happening and they were starting their trip
from Thomas Jefferson's to Washington. I had agreed to
do an interview for French radio about the time they
arrived in Washington, and the crew were there and they
said, "Well, let's just put it on." When Clinton started to
ring the bells, tears came to my eyes, first of all because of
the sincerity of his really wanting American reunion, and
because I saw so many different people from all over the
country ringing bells: it was very moving.

So more than singing for a person, I was singing for a president who stood for American reunion and this hope that I had never ever felt in the country before. It was not easy to sing because it was a highly emotional moment, but once the music started, it was alright. I must say that I did not at all expect that kind of reaction in the hall, because I was a token classic, with the exception of Alvin Ailey Dance Company, and it was an unknown piece, a little kitschy, but it had an effect. When everybody stood up—you didn't see it on the television because of course they cut, but the applause lasted quite a long time—the first ten seconds I couldn't do anything. I couldn't take a bow; I just stood there taking in all that energy. It was so fantastic, so incredibly positive.

It was an unforgettable moment, to be a part of that...Then the next day I went to the inauguration, and I'll never forget it, I'll never forget it. I really had to twist myself around like a pretzel to do it because I had to go back to Tokyo right afterwards for four more concerts, and I had planned, certainly, if the other guy had won the presidency that I would be on vacation in Thailand or in Vietnam those five days I had off so as not to kill myself! But it was worth it, it was really worth it, it was unforgettable.

JODY: You said once, "I am just another human being trying to live the way I believe, making mistakes and trying to stay vigilant and not become too comfortable." What mistakes have you made, against what must you remain vigilant, and what constitutes becoming too comfortable?

BARBARA: Oh, you know we all make mistakes—the daily ones—mistakes of judgement or lack of patience, lack of tolerance. The comfort is in settling in to a life where I would refuse to be aware. It would be easy because financially I am comfortable; I live in a country where I don't have to see poverty, and I don't have to see filth. You know what Switzerland is like, and I live in a beautiful part of it. I could very easily isolate myself. The vigilance is against that trap of having made it and thinking that I don't have to do anything more. The vigilance is being constantly aware, taking constant part in life, staying alive, looking into people's faces. The comfort is death, really.

I passed a girl on the street yesterday, and normally I don't give on the street mainly because I can't make the choice whom to give to and whom not to: you can't give to everybody. But just before I came to her she smiled at me, and I could not turn that smile down, I had to go back. Most of the time people walk around, and they wouldn't have even seen the smile. So it's staying alive, staying vigilant and having the courage in your everyday life to stand up for what you believe, to keep your eyes open and dare to look in the face of unpleasantness.

I don't consider myself a courageous person; if somebody is holding a gun to my child's head I'm not going to defy him. I'm going to do what I'm told. But in everyday life when people are gratuitously mean, I say something. "I really don't think that behavior was called for," I say to my colleagues, directors and conductors, without butting in too much. There are moments where you have to just stand up and say, "This is unacceptable behavior."

Or reaching out where it's not dangerous to people who are not threatening to you, to begin with—in your family, in your office. You know you don't have to be afraid of the lady who lives next door to you because she's been living next door to you for twenty years, and she's never done you any harm. I mean, being able to say hello, offer a hand—that kind of vision that we don't have, that kind of courage. Then I think it becomes much easier to see something that's happening a little further away from you and become concerned about it and want to do something. Often people say, "Well, Yugoslavia and Africa, what can we do? It's so far away, there's nothing to do."

Very often there *is* nothing that an individual citizen sitting at home can do, but there is often a lot that we can do where we are. Human rights begin at home.

I try to be vigilant with my children, I try to be aware of when I'm neglecting. It's not perfect; it's just that I'm aware of when I've done something or said something that I shouldn't have or that has caused pain or has been unjust. That vigilance, I think, keeps me alive.

JODY: In the various articles I read there were many references to your social activism. How do you integrate morality and ethics into your professional life?

BARBARA: What I do in music and humanitarian activism for me is the same struggle. The declaration of human rights comes from that same place; it is what connects us as humanity. They are not two separate things. They are just two different ways of fighting the same struggle. The whole thing is about me touching you and us recognizing that, somewhere, we are alike. And then dealing with what our differences can be, even appreciating cultural differences or being able to have a ground on which we can deal with our real differences—differences of opinion, differences that could lead us to war. Realizing that we have that ground to stand on, which is the declaration of human rights, for me is more important and precedes religion, nation, race, gender. Then we can respect each other and yet have differences without resorting to barbarism, without resorting to destruction. I find for me that is the only hope for the future.

We are going through a time now, an incredible transition, that is frightening but not without hope, because we have choice. During the Cold War we had very little choice because the superpowers were locked in a status quo. Now we have a choice to decide which direction the future is to go. Without its being based on human rights I think we will just go back to tribalism, or total destruction of the planet. My current activity is being a Goodwill Ambassador for the United Nations High Commission for Refugees, which I have been for the last six years. I visit refugee camps, I talk to refugees, I try to really be their ambassador. I try to speak about what a refugee is in human terms as opposed to in terms of statistics—there are over twenty million of them—or in terms of some faceless person asking for a handout.

My teacher, Jennie Tourel, was a refugee, and I wouldn't be here today without her. Our lives, particularly in America, have been enriched by so many refugees who have come to this country. I try to convey a more complete, comprehensible picture of the refugee—eighty percent are women and children—and try to get the message across that we are connected to that person too. When it becomes second nature for us to feel the hunger pains of a child who goes to bed hungry, then we will do what is necessary to see to it that he or she will be fed in emergency situations and also search for lasting solutions to some of the world's problems.

That's basically what I'm doing. When I finish this tour my kids are coming over to go to Disney World. I have concerts in Miami, and then we are going to visit my parents for Easter. It's going to be a trip, two days at Disney World! Before that I have four days free and I'm going to Washington and will try to meet with President Clinton. Once he gets my letter I'm sure he will receive me because he promised to, but where my letter is on the pile I don't know; it's very difficult to get through. Just to give him the benefit of my knowledge because I have been to more places than he has, and certainly know more about the refugee situation than he does, and I can give him some first-hand information in a different way than a professional diplomat or a Washington advisor who has never been in a refugee camp could.

I am also working very closely on the International Foundation for Humanitarian Action, co-founded by

myself and Dr. Bernard Kouchner (former Minister of
Health and Humanitarian Action of France and founder
of *Medecins du Monde* and *Medecins Sans Frontieres*) to continue on many different levels to push the idea of the
necessity of human rights. Of course, he has worked very
much on the *droit d'ingerance*, the right to interfere, and it
was because of him that at the end of the Gulf War the
Kurds were given assistance, which was a mandate he got
through the United Nations. I continue to work because I
feel that if we just sit idly by now, while things are sort of
bubbling, once they settle we won't be able to change
very much. So I'm mostly concentrating my time on those
two efforts.

JODY: You gave a concert in Orange not long ago to raise
funds for the flood victims of the Vaison la Romaine disaster, and I know the French adore you. What's the history of this great love affair between you and France? The
French don't normally adopt Americans the way they
have adopted you.

BARBARA: I don't know, I think it's coming home, that's
all, past-life stuff, I'm sure. There is just no reason for
how at home I am in French culture: the food, the wines,
the cheese. I would never have moved to the German part
of Switzerland; I feel very comfortable having France
across the lake from me, and I'm often in Paris. Most
French people know that I am American, but probably a
lot of them think of me as French.

JODY: Do you envision ever returning to live in France?

BARBARA: Possibly. We went to Switzerland because the
city was getting to be too much for me with the two kids.
We had a robbery in the apartment, and I always sort of
listen to things, and out of that I thought: it's time to
move. My husband thought, "move from the apartment,"
because we were in an apartment where we were alone in
an office building; but we had the ninth and tenth floors
with a terrace. We saw all of Paris; it was wonderful. Then

we thought, we love the south of France, and I thought, wonderful, we'll move down to the south of France.

Then we started thinking about the schools. We have very close friends who live in les Baux de Provence and they send their kids to school in Paris. I wanted the kids to have a school where they could have the opportunity for a bilingual education. So I thought, well, that's stupid. If we then have to get an apartment in Paris so the kids can go to school! That's where Switzerland came up. We made an inquiry, and it went like a snowball. Three months later we were living in Montreux. It just happened: somebody said, "I have an apartment," and then they said, "Well, we'll ask the commune and the commune said yes, and the canton said yes, and it was like we couldn't say no, now they'll be offended. But this wasn't a decision—we didn't say, "Let's go live in Switzerland."

Again, following my destiny—because I think I needed to be away, I needed distance too from that kind of—it's more than an adulation or an adoration that I get from the public, it's really an affection. I think I needed to be away from it, but it is quite incredible.

When we were in Cambodia, the morning before I left we went to visit Ankor Wat at sunrise. As were leaving, after the sun came up, there was a whole battalion of French soldiers with their blue berets who were leaving the next day and had come for a last visit to the temple. As we were walking along they all recognized me—I heard my name sort of going through the line—and I thought, "This is incredible, nobody will believe this." It was nice because it wasn't at all possessive: I'm treated like a member of the family, and that's very nice.

JODY: What is your husband like, and how did you meet him?

BARBARA: My husband is Swedish. He doesn't look Swedish, he's tall and has dark hair. I met him through my pianist, who is here with me now. Staffan and I knew each other at Juilliard, and he invited me to come to Sweden for a concert. He was very well known and still is, as he was a child prodigy in Sweden. I arrived six hours late, and Staffan had a concert that evening, so Martin picked me up at the airport. Then he turned pages, and that was the beginning of that.

JODY: What is he like as a person?

BARBARA: A very gentle person, a very good father, very laid back, not at all workaholic like me. He plays piano and likes music but is not as disciplined as me. He is the opposite because I'm always sort of plowing in all the time, and he teaches me a little bit how to stop and sit down and do nothing, although I don't enjoy it for very long. But I do it. He's a real play father—my kids are really lucky—and very supportive of my career. He was my agent—and when we moved to Switzerland, he just took care of me. Now he is starting a festival in Verbier that will be a little bit like Aspen, although he has never been there, so he is very very busy. I said to him that I didn't know how much longer he will still be able to be my agent, but that's fine, because this is something wonderful that he's doing, I'm very happy for him.

JODY: Do your children see your performances?

BARBARA: Yes, they have even participated. They were in Orange for *Carmen* last year. I thought it was going to be terrible. I thought, "Oh, they are going to be in the dressing room all the time; they are going to bother me." I never saw them except when Sebastian would come and change his costumes and leave them on the floor of my dressing room so that I had to hang them up!

JODY: Do you ever experience a conflict between being a mother and a performer attempting to do your own creative work?

BARBARA: Not a conflict, but the separation from them is very difficult. Having children doesn't hamper my work because they know that they are not in competition with my work: they always come first. If anything, it feeds me enormously. Now that they are getting older they see me as a person, not just as the mother who is there to give out. They can also understand my pain; they can understand when I am upset or stressed. The other day I was running around, as usual, like crazy, and Jennie said to me, "You should take it easy, you don't have to do all that. Sit down, take it easy." Because she sees me get up in the morning and I'm cleaning and I'm packing and she says, *"Maman, c'est trop."*

You know, it's wonderful to feel when it starts to become more of a relationship with the children. The difficulty is being away from them, but, again, I look at presence and absence in a different way because I think time is more than the way we normally deal with it. I try to have a connection with them that means that my presence does not have to be my physical presence and that a presence is there when my body is absent, that they know I am there for them. I think it goes in line with preparing your children for your death, really, from the time they come out of the womb. You start to prepare them to be separate at that moment, and you start to prepare them for the final separation—on this earth, in any case: to stand on their own feet.

JODY: I'd like to take that a little further, because all of the women I've interviewed have been driven by the creative will yet have been unwilling to sacrifice their intimate lives as women. They've had sexual lives, children *and* their careers, and that is a combination that is still the forbidden zone. So my question is on a practical level.

BARBARA: Difficult. I always feel hostage to the person who helps me out with my kids. I come home and they tell me, "Oh, Jennie missed you so much," and I say, "I know, I missed her, too." They do it to you every time, things they would never do to a man who was alone with children, never. That's really the hardest thing, trying to

have things go at home the way I would like to when I'm
not there. I'm still searching for it. But in the end, I have
to realize that my kids are in pretty good shape, and the
universe is going to take care of them. That whole thing
about Zoe Baird, the woman who was nominated for
attorney general? What she did was illegal—there's no
denying that—but what it brought up is how we look at
women who work and their child care. I thought she
should not have been attorney general because she had
done something illegal, *basta*. The fact is that if that had
been a single man or a widower who had done the same
thing, he would be attorney general today because in the
end, we are supposed to be staying at home taking care of
our own children, illegal or legal aliens or whatever.
That's the bottom line that is not accepted.

JODY: You are also a travelling mother: now you can give a
concert in Paris on Tuesday morning and another in San
Francisco on Tuesday night. How does that affect your
experience of performance?

BARBARA: In general, I try to avoid that kind of performing, mainly because I need the time for myself, to recol-
lect myself in order to give. We should go back to the
time when it took five days to cross the ocean, because
that was a time when you were more with yourself, more
centered. But it is like everything else today, I think. You
really have to make an effort to pull away and not follow
the crowd like a sheep. This instant way we have of doing
things means that what we tend to get is very superficial.
So I try and spend a lot of time with myself, to not get so
lost in this really fast world that we live in.

JODY: It's obvious from watching you that you give a
tremendous gift of yourself and that it must take an enormous amount of personal energy to perform. How do you
nourish yourself in order to be able to do that over and
over again? What is the source of your strength?

BARBARA: There has to be a replenishing of it. Some of it

comes from the audience giving back to us: without that you really go away empty. When the connection is made, and there are moments during the performance when the connection is not only made between myself and the audience, but when you feel like within the audience we are all resonating at the same place, that is very nourishing. From a personal point of view I do things for myself, I do yoga. I'm also very concerned about living my life on a certain level, being always in love, not just in the sexual sense, but being in love with life because love is energy and that keeps us alive. Being aware, being out there, walking that tightrope and not sitting on the sidelines, that nourishes me a lot. And going through the pain, whatever pain that life presents, the pain and the joy: that's all life is. Life is difficult in terms of the fact that most of the time we are looking to make life easy, but life *is,* and it happens to be difficult because being awake is difficult, and that's what it's about, I think. So, I get my nourishment from the people who are in my life, and I'm trying to live and experience love in a genuine way. It's not easy.

JODY: What gives you the greatest joy?

BARBARA: Overcoming obstacles, succeeding at something, having something that was difficult behind me— to get through that and to move on.

JODY: Our world today seems virtually bereft of wonder. That wonder was there in Clinton's inauguration: the music, the bell-ringing, the walk to Washington, the call to reunion. Is singing a way for you to return to that feeling of wonder?

BARBARA: Yes, that is it. That's the childlike effortlessness, that's how I sang when I was four. I see children when they sing; they are just completely transparent vessels that the music passes through. Too much effort can keep the energy from passing. The wonder happens when you give yourself completely for it to happen. I cannot *make* it happen, I cannot do anything of my will to make it happen except give it permission. That takes an enormous amount of faith. That's what life is about, keeping the faith. It's hard.

JODY: You are already very prolific in terms of your recordings. Is recording more consistent with childrearing? Does it involve a different kind of time commitment than, for example, singing opera?

BARBARA: Yes, recitals also make it much easier to be back home in a short time. For example, if I sing a concert in Munich, I'm home at lunch the next day. That's one of the other reasons I do less opera because to do it the way I like to do it, I really have to have rehearsal.

For me the creative process is the rehearsals, is what nurtures me, and the result of that is what nurtures the audience. What I need to get from my own work is trying, taking risks, failing, deciding that was the worst idea I ever had. That I cannot do in front of the public because they have paid for a certain level of professionalism. I just can't get out there and do that kind of experimentation at their expense. In order to do that kind of work, you need time.

Living with the music is the most important thing for me, more than thinking about what I should do. I don't consider myself an interpreter, but as more of a medium for the music. For me the score is the bible: I try to be as true to it as possible, but I cannot do that except on the surface if I only spend a short amount of time. It's the same thing for my colleagues: I must get to know them, I must trust them, I must have confidence in them so that I can throw myself into the void in front of them and know they'll catch me.

JODY: Where do you see yourself ten years from now?

BARBARA: That means that the kids will be out. I don't know, Tuscany. I've always loved it around Siena.

JODY: How about careerwise? What would you like to be doing?

BARBARA: Well, I certainly feel right now I am entering my best period, I've never sung better. I want to do certain things during this time. The only thing I could see that would be very different in terms of my career would be if what I'm doing in humanitarian action would lead me to, say, some position at the United Nations or some non-governmental organization. I don't know where that might lead, but it's certainly a possibility. I mean, I'm open to being Secretary General. Why not? When in doubt in a negotiation, I could always sing!

JODY: Do you like your life?

BARBARA: Oh, yeah. I think I did real well this time around.

Alice Walker

I love Alice Walker's work and had thought about interviewing her for a long time. But I felt timid about contacting her directly, so I wrote to Maxine Hong Kingston and asked if she would be willing to help. Maxine sent me the name and address of Alice's secretary and gave me encouragement. Without her intercession I undoubtedly would not have had the opportunity to do this interview, which I had long coveted.

Alice Walker lives in Northern California. We chose a specific date, but didn't decide whether we would meet at her home in San Francisco or in the countryside until a few days before the interview. It turned out to be the countryside, on one of those incomparable fall weekends when the landscape is beyond beautiful during the day, and at night the stars are as big as grapefruits. Alice Walker's home was warm, welcoming and personal, just like her. Our two hours passed quickly: I could easily have continued another two hours.

Alice Walker was born February 8, 1944, in Eatonton, Georgia. Her parents were sharecroppers and dirt farmers who supported the family on $300 a year plus the small salary her mother earned as a part-time maid. In 1952 one of Alice's brothers shot her with a BB-gun, resulting in permanent blindness in her right eye, temporary disfigurement and accompanying feelings of shame at how she looked, and withdrawal into introspection. She graduated as high school valedictorian and senior class queen and went to Spelman College on a scholarship. Her neighbors collected the $75 for the bus fare to college. Walker completed her sophomore year and transferred to Sarah Lawrence College in Bronxville, New York, a more progressive environment. In 1966 she was awarded a writing fellowship, went to Mississipi during the height of the civil rights movement and met Mel Leventhal, a civil rights attorney. They married in 1967 and divorced ten years later. Their daughter Rebecca was born November 17, 1969. Walker's first novel, *The Third Life of Grange Copeland,* was published in 1967; her second novel, *Meridian,* in 1967; short stories, *In Love and Trouble,* in 1973; more short stories, *You Can't Keep a Good Woman Down,* in 1981; and *The Color Purple,* for which she won a Pulitzer prize, in 1982; *In Search of Our Mothers' Gardens*, essays, published in 1983, was followed by *Living by the Word*, more essays, in 1988; then by *The Temple of My Familiar*, a novel, in 1989; *Possessing the Secret of Joy*, another novel, in 1992; and *Warrior Marks*, a non-fiction discussion of female genital mutation accompanying the film on the same topic made with Prathiba Parmar. In addition she has published books of poetry: *Once; Revolutionary Petunias*; *Good Night Willie Lee, I'll See You In The Morning*; *Horses Make a Landscape More Beautiful*; *Her Blue Body Everything We Know*; *Earthling Poems*; *To Hell With Dying.*

The Richness of
the Very Ordinary Stuff

An Interview with Alice Walker, Philo, California
Philo, California
October 1994

JODY: What was it like growing up the eighth of eight
children? How did being part of a large family affect you?
You write of the black southern writer's inheritance of a
sense of community: did the size of your family also play
a part in developing the passion for community and con-
nectedness in your work?

ALICE: Negatively, in a way. I was the last child and in
some ways a neglected child, although this was not something that was deliberate: my parents both worked, and
my mother and my father were very much partners in
what they did. I have five brothers and two sisters, and we
lived in very small, substandard houses from which we
were often driven after a year by the landlord, who
exploited the labor of the entire family. I was conscious of
crowdedness, and of not having enough of various things,
although we always had lots of food, and my mother was
a genius: she could create clothing out of all kinds of odds
and ends that people gave her.

I think the reason I love community and believe in it is
because the African saying that it takes a whole village to
raise a child is true—and part of the village certainly
helped my mother raise me. For instance, the first clothing
I received was not from my parents, but from the woman
who became my first-grade teacher. So I have a sense of the

ways in which people in the community can actually shape lives. What is very sad in this culture, and more and more all over the world, is that people are often afraid to be a community to children because there is so little respect for elders. And, generally, respect has declined.

JODY: Were you writing before you received formal training? Did your own method and style begin to evolve at that point, or did it come later? Where did it come from?

ALICE: My mother claims that I was writing with a twig into the margins of a Sears Roebuck catalogue when I was crawling, so sometimes I think it's a past-life activity. At other times I just think it was cheaper to write than to play the piano or paint, and that I was able to write about things that seemed far removed from my own misery but, in fact, reflected that misery. You develop what is called style by being as true as you can possibly be to the story you're telling and to give it all the time and space that it needs to be born whole. That's what style is, in a way; for me, that's what it has been.

JODY: How did you transform yourself from "someone nearly devastated by childhood suffering" into "someone who loves life and knows pleasure and joy in spite of it"?

ALICE: How did I do that? I think I did that by working very hard. But the foundation for that was my mother's connection to the earth and to wildness and to landscape and to natural beauty. Without that foundation in the natural world, I would have found it exceedingly difficult to survive.

JODY: You began *Warrior Marks* by talking about how important it is that we "adhere to our own particular way...in being true to our most individual soul." Was there a specific moment in your life when you became aware of the choice to be true to your own soul, that you started living out that choice consciously? If so, what has been the cost, and what have been the benefits?

ALICE: I don't know if I can actually pinpoint a moment;

in any life there would have to be many moments. For instance, when I was a student at Spelman, in Atlanta, I was there on scholarship and had struggled very hard to get there, yet I found it to be a fairly oppressive place. That made me terribly unhappy, and I had to make a decision to leave, even though I didn't know where I was going. Fortunately, one of my professors recommended Sarah Lawrence, which I had never heard of, as an alternative to Spelman. I made that choice without any assistance or guidance from my family because they also didn't know Sarah Lawrence—actually, they didn't know Spelman either.

I think that life is a series of choices like that, and they just come one after the other. It's about all kinds of things: where you will live, how you will live. When I went to Mississippi to live with my husband in an illegal marriage, it was necessary to decide consciously that this was where I would be and that if I couldn't be there, there was no point in trying to be anywhere else because, after all, this is one country. If there are places in it where you feel like you can't be—because of segregation, racism, bad laws—then it seems necessary to question one's citizenship. Mississippi's "anti-miscegenation" law said I was not a citizen. At the time this seemed to me really unacceptable.

JODY: Do you have any desire to return to the South, or are you settled in Northern California?

ALICE: I have some commitments there, but I have no desire to settle and live in the south. When I lived in Georgia during my formative years, and then when I lived in Mississippi, it was extremely violent, and for a long time that distracted me from the fact that the other part of it is often boring. It's enough to have lived there for all the years that I did. I don't really want to go back.

JODY: In *In Search of Our Mothers' Gardens* you said that like Rilke, you came to understand that "even loneliness has a use and that sadness is positively the wellspring of creativity." Could you expand on that? And how is that reflected in your own life?

ALICE: I think suffering has a use, although at the time you can't quite figure it out. I remember having a very difficult time about ten or fifteen years ago, and I was very aware that I was suffering. I was reading *The Gnostic Gospels*, Elaine Pagel's book, and there was a quote from Jesus in the Gospel that didn't make it into the Bible. (It seems to me that his best stuff was censored.) He said that if you learn to suffer, if you learn *how* to suffer, you will not suffer. It was such a mysterious thing to say, and yet I felt I understood it in the sense that suffering is inescapable, totally inescapable. So your task is to accept it as suffering and to get to know it and to learn it and to learn how to do it.

One of the ways you can learn how to do it is not to inflict it on other people, unless you just can't help it. You can try to know it so well that it doesn't really surprise you and leave you flabbergasted or enraged. To know it, to learn how to suffer, to learn what suffering is, what it feels like, not to deny it, not to deny that it's happening, not to deny that it's happening to you and to make of it a companion...it's right there. And true enough, when I learned how to suffer, which was mainly a matter of *accepting* that I was and that it was not to be escaped, I suffered much less! It was amazing; I felt an instant lightening of spirit.

There's another story in *The Gnostic Gospels* about how the Crucifixion is symbolic, that it's not the most important thing actually happening there. What actually happens is that the spirit of Jesus at this point rises above his own tortured body, laughing. It's not that he's not being killed, it's not that he's not being vilified and turned against. But he has managed to see crucifixion as part of what seriously out-of-balance people can do to you, and to see the humor of it and to understand that life is very long, time is very long, and you're pretty much very small, and even your suffering, whatever it is, can be seen in the context of what the whole world is going through.

JODY: Is it possible to separate Christianity from patriarchy? Must one give up Christianity in order to free oneself from patriarchy?

ALICE: I think we should just kidnap Christ and go off with him; he's the best of the whole bunch. I say that having struggled for many years trying to deny him, get rid of him or ignore him, because he is a captive of the church and they use him for absolutely everything. I feel myself to be a born-again pagan, and quite happy in nature. And I feel a great love for Jesus as a teacher and as a very feminine soul, especially during that time. His tenderness, his caring quality, always makes me think of someone who was raised by his mother. I mean, he's the son of a feminist. You can always tell the son of a feminist because generally speaking there is that ease that they have with women, and they seem to grip—*grip* is one of my daughter's words—things without having to have every little thing explained. You don't have to tell them that women don't like to be called "bitch" or "witch" or whatever in a negative way. They know this. It's a whole different sensibility from the sensibility of boys who are brought up with fathers in a patriarchal household. I love the sons of my feminist friends; they are very easy to be with, they're funny.

JODY: In her interview Marilyn French said that the true goal of feminism was to transform the world. In *Warrior Marks* your colleague Prathiba Parmar said: "We need to be willing to transcend all our differences without ignoring them, to build new communities that bring us nearer to our utopian ideals, to continue to redefine our ideas about womanhood and feminist politics, and to embrace concepts of justice and equality while at the same time recognizing the complexities of our diverse identities."

Is that possible? Are you optimistic about women's joining together to become a force for change? Do you agree with Marilyn French that we are living through the end of Western civilization as we know it?

ALICE: We're the only hope. Whether we can succeed is a question, but for sure we have to attempt it if we want to have any kind of world at all. The patriarchy has ruined the world; if it's not clear by now, I don't know what people need. And of course, yes, Western civilization, the world itself as we knew it, is no more.

When I was a child I assumed that the world was pretty much stable, that it was endless, that it was ever generative. I thought that it was clean, that the waters were pure, that the air was pure—and a lot of that was true. But even then they were felling the forests at an incredible rate so that now there are no big trees in Georgia except the ones that have been carefully preserved, like the giant oaks and the plantation tree boulevards.

I would only add that for me, the alliance is between women and children: it is us. I think that children should be permitted to vote, that they have to have much more of a say in running the world and that a twelve-year-old child, boy or girl, is often much more compassionate, astute, and open-hearted than the politicians who are regularly elected and who waste our money on extremely foolish things and who do damage every day. Children have been disenfranchised. They have been ignored, but they are natural allies of women and of men who understand that the whole thing has to change for any kind of high quality life to continue.

JODY: Was it difficult raising your own child and doing your writing?

ALICE: Actually, Rebecca was born three days after I finished my first novel, so she came at a natural break in the process of writing. I devoted myself to her for one full year, night and day, and then I enrolled her for half a day in the day care down the street. I could see the house from our yard, and I liked the woman who ran it. When we went to the Radcliffe Institute she went to the Radcliffe day care, and I wrote and I took care of her. It was diffi-cult—there were times when she was sick and it was very hard to get a doctor, and all those things—but I would have to say that I grew to understand the African woman who does her work with her child on her back, that this is all just part of life, this is part of what is. As long as you are not competing with some man who thinks that his balls are what can make you a writer, there's no problem. You just write as well as you can and you raise your child as well as you can.

Another way of thinking about it, which I really feel now, is that time is all there is, so there's no hurry either; there's no rush to do it. It's a very full life because a child connects you to the coming generations. Just from giving birth I felt a new understanding and respect for women. And then, because it is so miraculous, the whole process of conception and pregnancy and giving birth and watch-ing a child grow brought the miracle of life right up close where I could watch it every day.

When I look at my daughter I sometimes see the little child crawling, or the little girl in the yellow jumper who's rushing out to play with her friends, or the eleven year old who has a crush on somebody. To watch a tiny being grow up until, today, she is much taller than I am, she's so smart and caring and such a good person. It's just amazing.

JODY: You said some time ago, "I am preoccupied with the spiritual survival, the survival *whole* of my people. But beyond that, I am committed to exploring the oppres-sions, the insanities, the loyalties and the triumphs of black women." Would you add anything to that today?

ALICE: From *Living By the Word* to *The Temple of my Famil-iar*, I think in those books especially, I delved into my fascination with and interest in nature and my interest in tracing my own spiritual ancestry all the way back to 500,000 years of wherever. It became really crucial to me to reconnect with the prehistoric, because the historic—for women especially, and for people of color—is so negative and so one-sided. And it truly is *his*tory; it just leaves us out, or we are shown in such mutilated ways that the depictions of us are not helpful.

So I started dreaming my way back and through all of these lifetimes on this planet. Just in the natural course of existence my focus has moved to include more than people.

JODY: Do you have a familiar? And if so, what is it?

ALICE: What I was working on with *The Temple of My Familiar* was getting to the understanding for myself that your familiar is your own free spirit, and freedom is its temple. And that is what I have: that is my familiar. Frida* tries to be my familiar, but she just represents that part of myself that is the inner twin, the one who is free and is totally committed to being authentic, to being a free person. Your familiar is your own free spirit.

JODY: In one of the essays in *In Search of Our Mothers' Gardens* you talked about your aunts and your mother who worked on a farm and had strong muscles and would go out after working on the farm. "It is because of them that I know women can do anything, and that one's sexuality is not affected by one's work." If one's sexuality is not affected by one's work, what *does* affect one's sexuality?

ALICE: Well, one's passion, basically. I think it's not just in philosophy or even "life" that you follow your bliss, but you also follow your bliss sexually. I mean, that is what affects your sexuality—what you're attracted to and what you're drawn to and where your passion takes you. This doesn't always have anything to do with other people's notion of what *should* move you.

---

*the cat, named after painter Frida Kahlo.

I was writing in *Possessing the Secret of Joy* about a pan-sexual person, someone who is turned on by waterfalls and elephant rides and horseback riding and all of that. There was one reviewer who found this very funny, but actually there *are* women who are orgasmic riding horses and elephants and waterfalls.

I think of sexuality as something that, like spirit, has been colonized. It's the Bible again, that book that has done so much damage to women's self-image and their notion of what they're about. It says something like, "your desire will just be for your husband." In other words, if you're a woman, you're only supposed to be turned on to men. That's so limiting! It's hard to believe that people would limit themselves to men, or even to people. It's a world that is full of great sensuous experiences and it's like committing yourself to one religion or one way of thinking about things when in fact, the more we learn, the more mysterious the universe is. There is nothing that is solid, there is nothing that is hard, there *is* no hard copy. The universe is full of space and full of movement and full of flux and full of change. That's the nature of what reality there is.

JODY: I loved the section on Fanny and kissing in *Temple of My Familiar* and the wonderful descriptions of kissing. Kissing is fast becoming a lost art; one has only to look at American film and television actors, who are embarassingly terrible kissers. By resuscitating kissing in this country do you think we might succeed in bringing back intimacy?

ALICE: Oh, I think so! I am a great kisser myself. I love to kiss. Kissing is in many ways more a spiritual connection than making love because you exchange breath, and breath is the most ever present, everlasting thing that you will ever have as a living human being. It's very special. I just did a yoga retreat with a wonderful woman named Angela Farmer, and she was speaking of the breath as your most enduring lover. When you kiss, that is what you are offering, and that is what you are receiving. So it is a very high art, and it's a very high expression of soul.

JODY: You are one of the most respected writers in America today. Yet you have said, "To be an artist and a black woman, even today, lowers our status in many respects rather than raises it." What *does* it mean today to be a black woman and an artist?

ALICE: Well, in many quarters that's still true. Black women writers are constantly attacked, and, for instance, during *The Color Purple* film and book, these attacks were fast and furious, with people organizing to picket the film. Most of my life I have been called various things. I find it very difficult to talk about people's criticism and vilification. I accept it as something that they apparently need to do and will do, but I find no pleasure in it. With *Warrior Marks* there are many African women and American women, black and white, who take the position that genital mutilation is something that is not my business and not my place to write about, think about or campaign against.

When you say "respected," there are people who do respect what I do, and that's very good. But there are also people who hate what I do and who are very vociferous about it and have been from the very beginning of my career. I don't see that this is unexpected. I knew when I started writing that everything I wrote would be very hard, that it would be hard for people to accept, it would be hard for them to accept whatever life way I was indulging in, and that there would be criticism and that there would be hostility. At times this has been very painful; at other times it has been less so.

JODY: In an August '89 interview in *The Progressive* Claudia Dreifus asked you about the pain of getting mixed reviews, primarily from male critics, and said they can hurt. You replied, "They can try. But what can I do about it? I can only persist in being myself." Who are you these days? And where do you find the strength and courage to be yourself?

ALICE: I don't see that I have an alternative. I'm very happy to exist in this one lifetime that I have for sure as me. It seems ridiculous to try to live your life at any time as anybody else or as anybody else's version of how you should be. It's a waste of time, really, and as I said, time is all you have, so why waste it? I find it amazing that people do, that there are people who care more about what other people think of them than they care about what they think of themselves. It's almost something that I can't grasp because the pleasure of being who you are is very great, there's nothing like it.

One of the things that I've been attacked for is my insistence on affirming my mother's Cherokee grandmother and the Scottish-Irish whoever-he-was rapist who was my father's grandfather. Their take on this is that somehow it's a way of trying to get away from being a black person, which I think is incredibly backward. What people fail to understand is that the real pleasure of life is in what is unique. The world has such incredible variety: why not join it, be that different thing, that other expression—since that is what you are anyway—and love it?

It is such an affirming pleasure to rummage through your soul and to find the lost Scottish-Irish whoever-he-was and take him to task, and to rummage through your soul and find this great-great-grandmother, who apparently was very mean, and who had a story of her own that we may never know. How did she get into the family? And why is it that so many of us in my family either look very much like her or we have characteristics that are very much hers?

And then the African. I go to Africa every once in a while and I feel so tender, I have a tenderness for that strain of who I am, it just overwhelms me. It's almost like a puzzle, to trace one's emotional attachment to one's ancestry. Like why, why do you have these loves and these uneasinesses?

JODY: It's as if you belong to the whole world.

ALICE: Of course I do, and so do you, and so does everyone. So why sit in a corner somewhere and try to be just one thing when you are all of it? I'm listening to a wonderful tape on Ayurvedic Medicine and the Science of Life. Their way of looking at reality is that we are all made up of five elements—earth, water, fire, air and ether—and that, literally, you have attributes that correspond to these factors. Even without having known their way of thinking about it, that is the way I feel.

I feel like that same microscope that looks at a leaf and eventually finds nothing but emptiness and some tiny little thing in there at the end of the magnifying process— some tiny, tiny, tiny little thing that you can't even tell is there except by its shadow—that's exactly what's happening in me, that's what's happening everywhere, and that is *matter*, that is what is here on this planet. It really helps to put things in perspective.

JODY: Where do your characters come from? From what elements are *they* made?

ALICE: Imagination, and tiny bits or large bits of reality, love for certain people, and commitment to telling a story which, unless I told it, wouldn't make it. In the tape I made together with Isabel Allende and Jean Shinoda Bolen, I talk about my first novel and how, when I was thirteen, I saw this woman who had been murdered. Her husband had shot her, she was really poor, she had this one shoe left on and it was stuffed with newspaper, she had all these children, and her last name was Walker, although she wasn't related to us, to my knowledge. Domestic violence is something that today we have a handle on, although it's even worse than we thought. But back then there was really no one to analyze this and put it somewhere where it could be useful. What it needed was a story to contain it and to make it possible to share it without bludgeoning the reader or the hearer. Over time I had to go to school and learn how to do it, but I finally did write this story. And so she's remembered.

JODY: At one point you commented that your characters come through you, that they speak to you. I remember you said that when you were writing *The Color Purple*, your characters told you to sell the house in New York and move to Northern California.

ALICE: Oh well, they just said they didn't like New York, and of course, they're me, you know. I love that Harriet Tubman and Sojourner Truth had this way of always saying, "Well, God told me that I had to pack up and cross the river, and that if I would just take these slaves ten miles he would take them the rest of the way." Every time I read those women I just love them more. It also is sad, though, because you realize that the spiritual colonization of people is so intense that most people cannot take responsibility for their own desires and their own will. So it was impossible for either Sojourner Truth or Harriet Tubman to say, "I just decided that I'd had it, and I was going to go and I was going to take all these people." In the same way you have a dialogue with the imaginary, and that's what happens. It's all you, and you don't really forget that, but there's that wonderful, playful quality of knowing that you have dreamed up people who are walking around and who have opinions.

That's what happens too when you have long bouts of silence: it becomes such an echo chamber: you're dreaming people, you're creating people, they do surprising things, but it's only because you have given them that freedom in creating them. So it *feels* that way. I explain it as well as I can because many people think I'm talking about channeling, and I'm not talking about that at all. This is all hard work: it takes solitude, it takes money so you can do it for a year or so, it takes time and sweat—and sometimes wonderful swims in the river—but it's work. You open yourself to creativity really just by being receptive to it.

JODY: When you write, how do you start? Does a book start with a character? Does it start with an idea, does it start with a story?

ALICE: It can start with any of that, there's no special way.

JODY: And where do your images come from? There is one in *Meridian* that I still remember: "He cried as he broke into her body, as she was to cry later when their children broke out of it."

ALICE: By then I had had a baby and I had some sense of that breakage. I think that for many women the first sexual act, and sometimes later acts, are really break-ins; they're not something that the woman is particularly ready for or caring about. And I think some men, and maybe this is what's happening with this man in *Meridian*, some men are sensitive enough to realize that penetration is a kind of violation, it's an entering into a sacred space, and you are really blessed to have been invited.

JODY: Celie, Shug and Olivia from *The Color Purple* show up in later books. Was it your intention to create a kind of saga, a larger family, a community? Why did you do that?

ALICE: Let's see. I wanted to show what Shug and Celie were like later on in life. I felt like they founded a kind of womanist household, and they were a foundation for these children, Benny and Fanny, so this is a whole new beginning with this matriarchy. I also wanted to discuss ways in which they did have strife with each other. But with Tashi, I never forgot that she was a character who had endured something very strange, painful, destructive, and that I kind of left her there, mainly because the book was going somewhere else. I struggle with characters only because they are still with me, not because I'm trying to impose something on the work. I mean, if they don't come back to haunt me, I don't bother. There are people in those books—who knows—but I don't think they will ever show up again.

JODY: What is the role of forgiveness in your work?

ALICE: Forgiveness is absolutely crucial to any kind of going forward, even though, as you know, it's extremely difficult because by now you think there are so many things that are totally unforgivable. But, in fact, they are so horrible that it becomes clearer than ever that you can only move beyond them by forgiving them. It's the stuff of which the soul is made; it is such hard work that to get there changes you completely.

JODY: In *The Temple of my Familiar* the story of Zede and Zede the Elder has a happy ending, if I may call it that: the story of Suwelo and Carlotta has a happy ending, the story of Ayurveda and Fanny has a happy ending, the story of Lissie and Hal has a happy ending. There is all this tragedy in the book, yet there are also all of these happy endings. Your works are generally upbeat despite the dreadful things that happen to your characters over the course of their lives. One is almost always left with a sense of triumph at the end, including in *Possessing the Secret of Joy*. Do you do this because unmitigated suffering is too depressing or because you are by nature an optimist?

ALICE: I do it because they're not happy endings, they're *plateaus*. I think everybody has a plateau and then they start all over again. That seems to be the nature of the thing to me. You know, suffering is totally with us. It is completely a part of what is life, and yet, right along side it, there is so much beauty and joy and happiness and understanding and peace and good will and good cooking and beauty, that it is again a waste of time just to focus entirely on how, when you are suffering, you may not ever get anywhere but there. Also, in my own life I feel that I so often get to the other side, and I get to the other side with the gift of whatever the suffering was, so I can't even regret it. Given that it has happened and there's no changing it, I have to say, "What is the gift of this? Whatever it is, what did I learn from this?"

If I had the power to design life on earth, maybe I would just make everybody happy all the time; but maybe I wouldn't, because sometimes people who are happy all the time and who don't go through these crucibles are really shallow, and you don't want to be with them for very long.

I am optimistic because that's my spirit, and again, I trace it to my mother, who was a warrior and very at home on earth. You know, many people are really not at home on earth. I wish they would just leave right now and stop using up our tax money to do it...get on a ship or space craft and move on out to wherever it is they want to go. Because there are earthlings who *feel* like earthlings and have no desire to go anywhere but to just be here and to really love and worship what is here.

JODY: How do you sustain yourself within a specific work and for so long a period of time? What happens to your personal life over the time that you are involved in writing a book?

ALICE: I live in a world that I am creating, and I am usually very happy there, no matter what the story is. It could be a very sad tale, but I am very happy because I have survived to tell it. My partner has to understand that I need long periods of silence, so that he or she, depending on whom I am relating to, will have to be fairly quiet on long drives, for instance, or be very conscious that I am creating something. And while I am doing that, then they are free to be creating something, too. I give myself over entirely to this process: I try to find a year or two to really look at whatever it is I'm interested in and to really tell the story the way it should be told. I love this: it is not at all a hardship. It used to be, but now it's a relief to say no to practically everything that anyone proposes... not to see people, and to just be very quiet and intent on what I'm doing.

JODY: Have you always kept a journal? If so, what is the relationship between your journal and your published writing?

ALICE: I have kept a journal for maybe twenty-five years or more. It's a companion and a place to watch yourself grow and hopefully develop. It's very much like meditation: when your teacher is teaching you how to meditate, there's always a moment when they say, "There will be days when nothing much will happen and you will find yourself making your grocery list, or thinking about laundry." And sure enough, there are those days when you sit there, and you try to meditate, and you can't stop thinking about what you're going to make for dinner... just trivia.

A journal is kind of like that: there are times when you just have that shopping list feeling, and you're kind of jotting down everything. But then there are times when you make a breakthrough, and the breakthrough of course is what you've got to wait for, although you're not supposed to wait for anything, you're supposed to just be. That moment sometimes comes when you back up in your journal, and then you have the breakthrough. There you sit—I usually write my journal in bed—and you flip back to, say, the first of the year—you're now in September or October—and low and behold, you start to see the pattern of whatever it is that is a subconscious snarl. Then you see what you need to do to change it. I think that people who keep journals are a lot more lucid and a lot more clear about who they are and what is the essential *me.* That's what I think is really revealed in a diary or a journal.

JODY: I read recently Toni Morrison's *Playing in the Dark:*

Whiteness and the Literary Imagination. In her preface she said: "For reasons that should not need explanaton here, until very recently, regardless of the race of the author, the readers of virtually all of American fiction have been positioned as white. I am interested to know what that assumption has meant to the literary imagination." What do *you* believe that assumption has meant to the literary imagination in general, and yours in particular?

ALICE: It's meant a lot more hard work for those of us who are not white because you have to feel the story, whatever the story is, identify with characters who are usually very much on the surface not like you; you have to go for the heart and the soul. But again, it's one of those funny things: it really enlarges your ability to be empathic.

It's so curious about things that are obstacles…how they are so often things that cause you to grow in ways that you would not otherwise. Because of course, Toni Morrison and all of us writers and readers—black people, Native American people, Chinese people—we have been reading all of these books. I loved *Jane Eyre*—that was my favorite book. Now on the surface, especially in the South, if Jane Eyre had come out of the nineteenth century and stopped at our house it would have been extremely shocking. The white people would have had a fit—they would have come and snatched her away—because it just wasn't done. This was classic segregation, so I was supposed to think that there was no connection. But there was every connection in the world because it was about the soul, it was about the heart, it was about courage, it was about being a real person.

I think all of us had that experience of being able to identify with what was really important. That means that if you turn it around, white people—you can see this with white women—in the last ten or twenty years have started to be able to do that with work which is not about white people, where they say, "Ah, this is the heart: my

heart sees that heart, my soul sees that soul. That is why
your friends and you read my work and you don't feel like
it is written by someone who is so out there that you can't
relate, or that I would think or feel that you were somewhere out there that was impossible to reach. So, that
assumption which was meant to limit has in many ways
enlarged capacity to feel for people at a soul level.

JODY: The enlarged capacity to feel brings to mind one of
my favorite writers, Albert Camus.

ALICE: Mine too.

JODY: I felt that kinship very strongly in your work. Someone once asked him what his ten favorite, in the sense of
most meaningful, words were. So many of those words are
central to your work as well—compassion, justice, love.
Were I to ask you that same question, what would your
ten most important words be?

ALICE: I think love, freedom…I love this tape on
Ayurvedic Science that I am listening to because they are
the first people I have ever heard who said that love and
freedom are the same. There's usually that question, "If
you could choose love or freedom, which would you
choose?" And I would always choose freedom! But they
say that they are the same, and I think that's brilliant.

Anyway: love, freedom, justice, compassion, hope, joy,
struggle. That's what comes to mind now.

JODY: How does it feel to have achieved recognition as one
of the most important American writers of the twentieth
century and a Pulitzer prize-winning novelist?

ALICE: I'm pleased. I was in Aotearoa, New Zealand, a couple of years ago with the Maori. They took me to one of
their meeting houses, and immediately, just across from
me, was one of their seers, and she started to weep the
minute I set foot inside the door. Of course I wanted to
know why. Had I stepped on something, or whatever? It
turned out that there was a message she wanted me to
take to the Cherokee, my ancestral people. (I can't tell you

about that until I actually get around to taking it.) But the other thing she said was, "So many people came through the door with you, you're just surrounded." That's why I'm pleased: when I walk through the door I'm surrounded by so many people that I bring in with me, and that feels very good.

JODY: Are you fearless? What frightens you?

ALICE: I think the thing that frightens me most is that I won't follow through on something that I believe in.

JODY: What have you not yet accomplished that you would like to do?

ALICE: I am dyslexic with manuals, I can't operate things. When I look at your recording machine, I know I want one just like it because I see how you operate it and I figure I can do that by watching, and if you point out a few things to me. I have a jacuzzi and I'm trying to clean it out for the first time myself. I've been on the phone with my friend Deborah down in the city; she had to tell me how to do it because I had looked at the manual and it gave me such a headache. I want to clean out this jacuzzi, and I want to do it right. I want to get it really clean, and I want to put that polish on it that she says I should put on it, and I want to put the right amount of bromide in it so that I don't kill my guests who get in, and then I want to get it running again. I have no idea if I'll actually be able to pull it off, but that's the kind of challenge that is intriguing to me now.

I have Oprah Winfrey's cook's cookbook and they have a recipe in there for crab cakes. I've been dragging this cookbook back and forth between the city and the country, picking up ingredients as I go because I don't have everything—I didn't have any baking soda, I didn't have any baking powder—but I'm going to get those crab cakes. I want to make that dish. I want to learn how to make really good pasta. I want to be able to give dinner parties for my friends without feeling so nervous that the food won't taste like anything, or that I will not have enough, or something.

I want to do things like that that seem to me to be about creating a space where people can kick back, eat, laugh, tell stories, be comfortable, and by extension send that vibration across the world. Because, really, what's important is not so much the frenzied activity that we all have been in—if we're not still in it—but the slowness of the daily, and the richness of the very ordinary stuff.

This first edition of
The Power to Dream
is published by
Global City Press
New York.

It is designed by
Charles Nix.

The typeface is
Garamond Three.

Production management is by
Burton Shulman.

The printing is by
Offset Paperback Mfrs., Inc.
Dallas, Pennsylvania.

n